INVISIBLE CHAINS

Shawn Hornbeck and the Kidnapping Case that Shook the Nation

KRISTINA SAUERWEIN

THE LYONS PRESS
Guilford, Connecticut

An imprint of The Globe Pequot Press

The Lyons Press is an imprint of The Globe Pequot Press.

Designed by Sheryl P. Kober

Library of Congress Cataloging-in-Publication Data is available on file.

ISBN 978-1-59921-344-6

Printed in the United States of America

10 9 8 7 6 5 4 3 2 1

For my family: Tom, Zoe, and my babies;
you are always loved.

CONTENTS

Contents

PROLOGUE

Two Missouri families prayed for a miracle on January 12, 2007.

One family had started praying four and a half days earlier, when their thirteen-year-old son disappeared after a school bus dropped him off in front of their home in Beaufort.

The other family's prayers had begun 1,558 days earlier, when their then-eleven-year-old boy vanished on a sunny Sunday afternoon while riding a bicycle less than a mile from their house in Richwoods. Every day, for four years, the boy's parents appealed to a higher power to bring home their son.

On that bleak, icy day in January, the families' prayers were answered.

The miracle had occurred.

CHAPTER 1

Shrouded in Secrecy

Richwoods, Missouri, is the perfect place to get lost.

The area is shrouded in lush layers of trees: red oaks, white oaks, pines, hickory, ash, cherry, walnut, and other native eastern hardwoods in forests so dense, there are parts where the sun struggles to shine through and temperatures drop slightly. The thick trees offer obscurity, as do rocky ridges of limestone snaking across the bramble. It's a topographical topsy-turvy, where sinkholes and cave pits depress into the countryside, rolling hills meander across the landscape, and cascading creeks canter every which way. Inexperienced trekkers, beware: Abandoned mine shafts and tailing ponds threaten to swallow. Old rusted farming equipment, shabby sheds, and mangy mobile homes litter the hollows.

In these woods, it is easy for a person to disappear—by choice, or by accident.

CHAPTER 2
A Mother's Intuition

October 6 had all the makings of a memorable day.

The frothy forests surrounding the small town of Richwoods still resembled summer on that Sunday afternoon in 2002. Big, green leaves draped the rising red oaks. The townsfolk still favored cotton shirts, drove with the windows down, and relished ice-cold cans of Pepsi-Cola and Milwaukee's Best beer. Daytime temperatures with highs in the sixties had replaced the scorching heat and suffocating humidity that mark summers in Eastern Missouri. Lower temperatures seemed to have buzzed away the pesky mosquitoes that thrive in the old tailing ponds left over from the town's mining days.

Not too hot. Not too cold. Just perfect. Even the children seemed to know that they had to seize the day and play outside, realizing that soon they would be confined inside, cooped up. Bone-chilling temperatures were only weeks away, or possibly days away, given the area's unpredictable weather patterns. It seemed as if all the boys and girls of Richwoods spent that Sunday outside, jumping on trampolines, tossing balls and Frisbees on green grassy lawns, and riding their bikes along Highway A, a windy, two-lane road that cuts through the town's center.

Shawn Damian Hornbeck had awakened to a day that seemed to promise the carefree spontaneity that eleven-year-olds like him reveled in and that overworked, over-scheduled adults envied. His stepfather, for one, probably would have appreciated such a luxury. That morning, Craig Akers had skipped his Sunday ritual of cooking a hearty breakfast of sausage and eggs, according to the *St. Louis Post-Dispatch*; instead, he opted to sleep late, exhausted from all of the overtime he was working at his job as vice president of technology at Fastrans Logistics, located about an hour's drive away in north St. Louis County. That morning, with his parents and two teenage sisters all doing their own things, Shawn basked in his freedom to spend his time as he pleased, the newspaper reported: he fueled up with a Pop-Tart, the sugary sweetness most likely a treat in itself, and set out for a day of fun in his hometown.

Settled by the French in the 1770s, Richwoods is a former mining community that sits roughly sixty miles southwest of Greater St. Louis, the largest metropolitan area in Missouri. Many of the townsfolk root for the city's professional sports teams: Major League Baseball's St. Louis Cardinals, the National Football League's St. Louis Rams, and the National Hockey League's St. Louis Blues. And with employment opportunities limited in Richwoods, some of the people commute to and from metro St. Louis for work. But that is where the common bonds end between Richwoods, a town of approximately 1,300, and the St. Louis area—with nearly 2.8 million people, it's the eighteenth-largest metro area in the United States.

Richwoods is an economically sluggish, nearly all-Caucasian community with winding two-lane roads and occasional one-lane bridges. Old farmhouses and mobile homes scatter across the town. No big-box stores or chain restaurants call the area home. It is one of eleven townships in Washington County, which has a population of approximately twenty-four thousand people who live in a swath of the state known as the Missouri Ozarks. Parts of the county contain a portion of the Mark Twain National Forest, a haven for hunters, fishers, and outdoor enthusiasts as well as 530 native wildlife species such as aquatic three-toed salamanders and sorrowful-sounding mourning doves. The county seat, Potosi, a city of nearly 2,700 people approximately twenty miles to the south of Richwoods, is home to the century-old county courthouse, a Wal-Mart Supercenter, and the Potosi Correctional Center, a maximum-security, state-operated facility housing eight hundred high-risk male inmates including those on Missouri's death row.

In the county in which Richwoods sits, just over half of the residents have obtained a high school degree or higher. Unemployment rates consistently hover above state and national averages, some years more than doubling it. Median household and per-capita incomes sink below state and national figures as well, mostly due to Washington County's limited job opportunities, which are mainly confined to local educational and health care agencies, retailers, and a dwindling number of manufacturing companies. To find work, about half of the residents—such as Shawn's stepfather—have to travel outside of the county.

It used to be that people flocked to Washington County to mine the land rich in lead, iron ore, and barite. But three centuries of mining have contaminated soil and water, bequeathing health problems to hundreds of current county residents, including children poisoned by lead. In May 2007, the *Post-Dispatch* reported that the U.S. Environmental Protection Agency had slated $8.5 million for waste cleanup of old mining operations in Washington County, where there are 1,431 documented sites, a significant number of them in Richwoods. Many households must drink bottled water because of high traces of lead and other contaminants in the well water systems.

None of the problems plaguing the Richwoods area seemed to bother Shawn or most other residents on October 6, a Sunday with such pleasant weather it invited folks to forget worries and savor the moment.

For Shawn, that meant hanging out at home, meeting friends, and riding his bike. Later, his parents, Pam and Craig Akers, would recall to the media how Shawn had started his Sunday morning nestled in a recliner, relaxed and focused on a PlayStation high-speed-racing video game that blared across his family's big-screen television. They would remember Shawn's love of electronics and engines: He was a video game fanatic. He liked monster trucks and motocross racing. When Shawn grew up, he wanted to become a computer programmer like his stepfather, partly because the boy loved machines and partly because he loved Craig, really the only dad he had ever known. When Shawn was a baby, Craig stepped into the role of father, just like that. It was as if the two had always shared the same bloodline. Just three years earlier, Shawn had walked his mother down the aisle and given her away when she married Craig. In fact, the Akerses were in the midst of completing paperwork that would have allowed Craig to legally adopt Shawn. His parents recalled all of that to the media, as well as how Shawn was a happy boy, intelligent and affectionate. He had a lot of friends. He liked eating junk food, playing with dogs, and watching cartoons such as *SpongeBob SquarePants.*

More significantly, he was a boy who feared the dark.

It was the dark that made Pam's stomach sink that Sunday in October. Shawn had not come home. And it was dark out. Like a lot of kids his age, he sometimes had trouble coming home on time. But not when it was dark outside. He always made it home before the sun set—darkness frightened him that much. So when Shawn left to go outside that afternoon, around one o'clock, and promised he would be home by 5 p.m., Pam thought nothing of it. Kids in Richwoods played outside by themselves all of the time.

Of course Shawn would be home in time for dinner.

He left his house to meet his friends, riding his lime-green mountain bike. Shawn had received the twenty-one-inch NEXT-brand "Shockzone" boy's bicycle for his eleventh birthday about three months earlier, on July 17. To celebrate, his parents had taken the family to Swing-A-Round Fun Town, approximately an hour's drive away in Fenton, a growing St. Louis suburb of newly built homes, industrial and tree-lined parks, and chain-store strip malls. A popular birthday party venue among the preteen set, Fun Town is filled with attractions such as bumper boats, batting cages, mini-golf courses, "kiddie karts," and a twelve-thousand-square-foot indoor arcade with more than eighty games, a pizza and ice cream parlor, and, according to the company's website, "the newest, fastest go-karts and the longest track in the St. Louis area." It was the perfect spot for a spunky boy who loved racing, loud engines, video games, and junk food.

That Sunday, several townsfolk had spotted Shawn riding his birthday bike, ambling about on his afternoon adventures. He was hard to miss on his lime-green bike, with a shock of dark hair and dressed in a pair of blue jeans and a bright-orange

T-shirt bearing the name of the DeSoto Astros, the Little League team he belonged to—Shawn played second base and outfield for the team in a larger town approximately fifteen miles to the east. Just about all of Richwoods' residents knew Shawn, as is likely to happen in a small town where watching people come and go is often a favorite recreational activity.

Sometime that afternoon, Ron and Shirley Cobb, owners of the only food store in town, Cobbs Grocery, greeted Shawn when he walked into the shop, which seems almost cave-like with its dropped acoustic ceiling and all of the items dangling from it: spider ferns, plastic machine guns, St. Louis Rams championship pennants, plastic American flags, Marlboro cigarette advertisement signs, and dozens of bejeweled purses featuring Betty Boop, Elvis, Marilyn Monroe, and Princess Di. The floor is a patchwork of plywood, linoleum, matted shag carpet, and unfinished wood, winding through narrow aisles and past shelves stocked with everything from Betty Crocker cake mixes and Spam to cans of baked beans and Sloppy Joe sauce to off-brand diaper creams, disposable douches, and other toiletries.

In the back of the store, an old refrigeration system has been turned into a display case, a museum of sorts, featuring Ron's collection of World War II memorabilia and Native American artifacts, much of which he accumulated more than thirty years ago when he visited Wounded Knee, South Dakota, site of an Indian massacre. Behind the glass, behind the thick chain lock, behind the sign reading ITEMS IN CASE ARE NOT FOR SALE, are rows of primitive arrows from the Sioux, Navajo, and Cherokee tribes, an Arapahoe tomahawk with blue beading, shotgun shells, and an 1885 Winchester rifle with a letter of authenticity. Although the makeshift museum is a local attraction, most of the townsfolk come into the store for soda, beer, and cigarettes. "Marlboro is the most popular brand," Ron said.

On that October afternoon, the Cobbs recalled greeting Shawn but not what he purchased. Probably if he bought anything, it was candy, because that's usually what the town's kids shopped for. Ron and Shirley had seen him dozens of times before. He did not strike up a conversation or go out of his way to be polite. But he did not talk loudly, nor did he loiter out front on the store's wooden porch or act boastful like some of the other young people. The older couple thought of Shawn as a normal boy who preferred to keep to himself when in the presence of grown-ups. Nothing unusual at all. Just a typical kid.

Other townsfolk remembered seeing Shawn at various points along Highway A. There he was hanging out by the basketball court at the Richwoods Lions Club, the town's gathering and entertaining hall chartered in 1975. There he was riding his bike past his school, Richwoods Elementary, a two-story building with a mostly stone facade and a gravel parking lot. There, Shawn was one of seventeen students in Donna Miley's fifth-grade classroom. Some time after 4 p.m., one person sighted him riding his bike near an auto salvage yard near the highway crossroads. Around the same time, an alarm sounded, but law enforcement officials reported finding nothing out of the ordinary.

The last Shawn sighting occurred around 4:30 p.m. He was seen riding his bike westbound on Highway A from the intersection of Highway A and Highway 47, near his elementary school. He appeared to be headed toward home. He was about a half a mile from his front door, where inside Pam Akers probably was preparing for dinner, expecting her only son to walk into the house at any moment.

Certainly, Shawn would be home by 5 p.m. before it got too dark.

Pam started feeling nervous after the clock ticked five o'clock, then 5:30, 5:45 p.m., and Shawn had not yet walked through the front door. She reminded herself that sometimes her son was late.

But she had a bad feeling deep in her gut. A mother's intuition. Pam turned to her husband: something is wrong with Shawn.

At six o'clock, Pam started contacting his friends. One of them was Patrick Reeves, who was eleven years old and played with Shawn on the same Little League team. Patrick's dad knew Shawn fairly well, too. He coached the DeSoto Astros. Since the second grade, Patrick and Shawn had been best friends, according to media reports; and on that evening when

Shawn went missing, Patrick told his friend's parents that he and Shawn had not hung out together that Sunday afternoon and he did not know if Shawn had any secret hiding places. Patrick held out hope that his best friend would return home at any moment.

By eight o'clock, Shawn was three hours late.

And it was just too dark.

Pam called the police.

Her boy had vanished.

It was a day she would never forget.

CHAPTER 3
The Monster Man Strikes

Secrets as dark as that Sunday night in October linger more than four years after Shawn Hornbeck disappeared on his mountain bike near the intersection of Highways A and 47. The nitty-gritty details of the abduction may never be known to anyone other than Shawn and the monster man who lurked late that afternoon in the wooded town of Richwoods.

Most likely Shawn is haunted by the secrets, seared into his soul at the tender age of eleven, squashing the boy's innocence and potentially changing him forever as a person. And it is true: Without the proper psychological help, said Dr. Lenore Terr, a world-renowned child psychiatrist who specializes in trauma, as adults, child victims can encounter horrific memories "that have been locked up for a long, long time, that can come back and start bothering them at 3 a.m., and they feel like they're going crazy."

After the monster man was caught and caged, and after months of gathering criminal evidence, law enforcement officials in 2007 released to the public a basic sketch of how Shawn vanished: A hulking savage named Michael John Devlin had driven approximately sixty miles southwest from his home in suburban St. Louis, trolling rural Washington County for his prey.

He had a penchant for boys. He had hate in his heart. He had a gun.

Devlin zeroed in on a brown-haired, brown-eyed boy riding a lime-green bike headed toward the main drag in Richwoods. He probably considered Shawn an easy target. At the time, Shawn stood four feet, eight inches tall and weighed ninety pounds; by contrast, the predator stood at six feet, four inches and topped the scales at around three hundred pounds. In addition to size, Devlin had more than two decades on Shawn's young age. And being only eleven years old, Shawn was likely to be impressionable, as trusting as a puppy dog, as are most children that age. Based on the typical development of children his age, child psychologists and educators note that it would have been perfectly normal for Shawn to be unaware of his surroundings, focused on the self-important details of his own little world.

At first, Shawn may not have noticed Devlin driving along his hometown's rural roads. Even if he did, the boy may not have thought twice about it. Why should he? People drove by all the time. Plus, horrible, headline-grabbing events such as a stranger kidnapping did not happen in his small hometown. Not under the hawk eyes of the townsfolk. Anyone with the audacity to roam Richwoods uninvited may as well parade down the dusty, narrow roads naked—that's how obvious interlopers are in these parts. Even people who live there acknowledged that it takes time to wear down the walls of distrust, to fit in well enough to be ignored. Longtime residents remember how difficult it was to blend in when they first moved to the town.

"It was hard at first," recalled Shirley Cobb, who moved from the St. Louis area to Richwoods with her husband, Ron, in 1981. "It takes a while for people to get to know you. It's a quiet little place. Now we like it OK."

"At first, I thought we made a huge mistake moving here," said Kim Evans, who moved to the country town after spending most of her life in middle-class and upscale St. Louis suburbs such as Ladue, Kirkwood, and Ballwin. She and her husband moved because rents in metro St. Louis were too high and they had two kids. In the wooded outpost, the couple paid cash for a starter house on three acres. "I hated it at first. Everybody knows everybody here. Nobody trusted us because we were new. It took a while for people to warm up to us. It's hard for a city person to adjust. But now I like it."

Of course, the suspicion Richwoods residents have toward newcomers is not uncommon in rural settings. People move to remote locales to get away from city hassles—and, often, to distance themselves from other people. Newcomer sightings were rarer before Shawn went missing. Many city and suburban dwellers from St. Louis had never heard of Richwoods, only an hour's drive away. Even those with weekend homes in Washington County bypassed Richwoods, for the isolated town is not the type of country that uppity yuppies favor.

Richwoods does not offer the quaint Kountry Kottage type of stores that sell just-add-water scone mixes in eye-pleasing bags tied with raffia bows, or mass-produced patchwork quilts, or faux antique furnishings in which the paint coat is professionally crackled for an "heirloom-quality" shabby chic flavor. The town does not boast an outdoor farmers' market selling a rainbow array of fresh flowers, beeswax candles, and homemade lavender-scented soaps. Nor does it have overpriced bistros, diners promising down-home cooking, or charming bed-and-breakfast accommodations. If an outsider wants to spend the night in Richwoods, he better have a sturdy sleeping bag and a can of super-strength bug spray, because there are no hotels. The town does not even come close to offering the same urban-country appeal as a Nantucket or a Napa Valley; or the Missouri equivalent of a downtown St. Charles or Ste. Genevieve.

Richwoods is unabashed country. The real thing.

After the boy disappeared, quiet Richwoods became the center of attention, a town besieged by an onslaught of strangers, and not necessarily the friendly kind: Law enforcement officials combed every inch of the area, searching rickety trailers, abandoned sheds, and forest hideaways, thereby riling the meth-heads who used those places to get high. And while townsfolk initially embraced members of the media because the news-gatherers had the power to publicize the missing-child case, most easily outwore their welcome once they began asking one too many questions in that inane, arrogant, self-serving manner that journalists are prone to. Then there were the gawking lookie-loos, a version of a tornado chaser, but who, instead of getting their jollies following the path of a destructive twister, engaged in the freakish follies of becoming a part of—however vicariously and insignificantly—the latest human tragedy making the news.

To be fair, the people of Richwoods have had every right and reason to distrust newcomers since that October Sunday in 2002. One of their own—an innocent child, no less—was snatched from their midst during daylight hours.

To the monster man, Richwoods's remoteness, its unguarded innocence, and its lack of potential witnesses seemed to make it a good place to pilfer a child. Devlin was familiar with the area's back roads and pockets of people.

At the time, he co-owned a vacant parcel of lush land in a development called Woodland Lake Estates in northwestern Washington County, approximately twenty-five miles from Shawn's hometown. There, he camped and kept his twelve-foot fishing boat for use on the area's thirteen lakes. He was headed toward his property on that beautiful Sunday afternoon.

According to law enforcement officials, media accounts, and FBI reports, the abduction—which Devlin said was a random act—unfolded as follows:

Devlin spotted the boy riding his bike on a gravel road next to a church. He passed Shawn and stopped his truck to watch the eleven-year-old's every movement. He trailed Shawn along the road. "Shawn was riding on the passenger side of the truck and Devlin tapped him with his truck just to startle Shawn," an FBI report stated. "Devlin stopped and got out of the truck and acted like he was making sure that Shawn was OK. When Devlin got to the passenger-side door of the truck, he opened the door and pushed Shawn into the truck."

He threatened the boy with a gun.

Devlin taped together the boy's hands, the *St. Louis Post-Dispatch* reported, and informed Shawn that he "was in the wrong place at the wrong time."

He drove the boy to suburban St. Louis. At one point during the ride, he placed his hand on Shawn's groin. Back at his apartment, Devlin sexually assaulted him numerous times. That night, Devlin "tied a rope around Shawn's waist and tied it around his own hand or waist before going to sleep," the newspaper reported.

The next morning, before he left for his go-nowhere job at a nearby pizzeria, Devlin "tied Shawn to a futon and put duct tape over his mouth," according to a report released by the Washington County Sheriff's Office and cited by the *Post-Dispatch*. "He repeated the practice for about the first month of the boy's captivity."

During his work breaks, Devlin came home to give Shawn food and allow him to use the bathroom. "Devlin told his co-workers that his cat had mites and that he had to go home each day for lunch to give his cat medicine," an FBI report said. "Devlin would go home to feed Shawn and then return to work."

But not before binding and gagging the boy.

For four years and three months, the monster man succeeded in his heinous heist. He stuck it to law enforcement officials, delivering a silent but sounding "screw you," leaving them with what authorities publicly called a nightmare investigation. He left no clues as to Shawn's whereabouts; not even a tire mark in the dirt. He left no evidence; not even the lime-green bike could be located during the intensive search for Shawn that left no leaf in the dense forest unexamined, no rocks in the karstic landscape unturned.

To each other and to the media, the townsfolk would shake their heads in disbelief, shrug their shoulders, and reiterate: It was as if Shawn had vaporized into thin air.

CHAPTER 4
Searching for Shawn

The morning after Shawn Hornbeck disappeared, not all of the people in Richwoods had heard that one of their town's children was lost. By the time Shawn was reported missing to the authorities Sunday, many people had already settled in for the night, watching their favorite television shows, tucking their kids into bed, and, in some cases, turning in early in preparation for the busy upcoming week, although no one at the time could have fathomed the frantic nature of the days that loomed ahead.

The morning after, temperatures were mild, promising yet another pleasant autumn afternoon. Pleased, Kim Evans was driving her kids along Highway A, as she did every weekday, heading toward St. Rose of Lima, a private Catholic school in the nearby town of DeSoto. Evans had not driven far when she noticed a swarm of about ten to fifteen police cars, pickup trucks, vans, and all-terrain vehicles gathered around the Book of Acts Methodist Church near the crossroads of Highways A and 47. Helicopters hovered above. A flurry of activity swirled around the men and women in uniforms.

Uh-oh, Evans thought: Must have been one big drug bust.

Clusters of ATVs, pickups, and police cars were not an everyday occurrence in Richwoods, but they were not unheard-of. While many of the townsfolk are decent, hard-working people who savor the area's forests and faraway feel, Richwoods does have its share of drug users, specifically abusers of meth-amphetamine.

The region's compounding problems and limited resources have helped to fuel a meth problem in Richwoods and Washington County in general. Highly toxic, makeshift meth labs mar the landscape, where the lush remoteness offers meth users privacy for "cooking" the drug and getting jacked up on the highly addictive stimulant made from over-the-counter cold products, lithium batteries, rubbing alcohol, starter fluids, drain cleaners, and other products commonly found around the home. Meth is so prevalent that even the mayor of one of the county's towns was charged with possession of the drug that law enforcement authorities link to crime, and health care officials deplore as a strain on an already stressed medical system.

So when helicopters buzzed overhead that morning and the police vehicles, pickups, and ATVs descended on the town, it was quite understandable that some of the townsfolk thought that there had been a big meth bust.

If only that morning's adrenaline-packed activities were police catching a bunch of loser meth-heads.

Evans's husband, Wayne, a truck driver, also had noticed the vehicle swarm on Highway A. He had heard a grumbling helicopter. He did not have to wonder long what all the commotion was about: the radio informed him that Shawn Hornbeck of Richwoods was missing. A search was currently under way.

The Evanses knew the eleven-year-old boy. Shawn had played at their house with their kids, jumping on the trampoline in the family's front yard, laughing like he had no cares in the world.

"My God," Wayne's wife recalled him saying to her, "if this were my child, I would want all of the help I could get."

Wayne unloaded his truck right then and there and joined in the search for Shawn. He vowed to put his life on hold to help find the missing child. He would do whatever he could. He would spend days combing the surrounding woods, looking for the boy, for evidence, for clues to his whereabouts. Looking for anything. His wife, Kim, encouraged his commitment to the search, telling him to do whatever it took. The petite brunette also volunteered, putting in long hours manning phone lines at the makeshift command center along Highway A. At the moment, all that seemed to matter to them was helping to find Shawn and bringing him home to his family.

At Cobbs Grocery, Ron and Shirley Cobb had heard the news, too. As the search for Shawn began mounting early that morning, the gray-haired couple decided to donate supplies to the rapidly growing number of locals who had joined law enforcement in the search for Shawn. As the owners of the only grocery store in town—whose customers had included Shawn less than twenty-four hours earlier—they felt they had an obligation to help. They donated packs of batteries for flashlights. They gave more than one hundred bags of ice. Ron even drove about fifteen miles to a Sam's Club, a discount warehouse store owned by Wal-Mart, for cartons of bottled water.

By noon, it seemed as if everyone in town knew of Shawn's disappearance. And like the Evanses and the Cobbs, everyone—young and old—seemed to want to help in the search, officially being conducted by the Washington County Sheriff's Department and the Richwoods Fire Department. At the time, authorities were hopeful that Shawn's being gone was an accident; perhaps the boy had just lost his way and was waiting to be found. Shawn running away was unlikely, and the possibility of abduction is always there, but more likely, everyone thought, the boy was alone, scared, and ready to be rescued.

The number of volunteers reached more than one hundred people, an effort coordinated in part by an organization of off-road enthusiasts belonging to the Midwest Trail Riders Association Motorized Search and Rescue Team. The group provides invaluable help in these types of situations because its members are experienced navigators of difficult terrain and smart about safety; for instance, during the search for Shawn, they prodded volunteers to sign in before trekking into the thick forest as a way to ensure that no one else got lost.

By foot, by ATVs, and by horseback, volunteers and their scent-detecting dogs assisted law enforcement in searching the roads and wooded areas near Shawn's hometown. Since many of the volunteers came from Richwoods, nearby towns, and the surrounding rural areas of Jefferson and Franklin Counties, most were prepared to tackle the rough terrain characterized by dense forests, sinkholes, caves, farm fields, bramble, dilapidated outposts, discarded junk, hills with sharp turns, limestone ridges with steep drop-offs, and narrow mine shafts abandoned decades ago.

Although the locals knew the area, the backwoods proved more frustrating than expected. Jerry Sessums, who drove to Richwoods from neighboring Jefferson County to help search for Shawn, recalled his shock at the brush. He had never seen anything like it. Grass so tall and shaggy, Sessums had to crawl to get through some parts. He'd blink his eyes and think: Which way did I come from? Which way am I going? All around him, the woods looked the same, a dizzying, maddening kaleidoscope of greenery.

"You would go through an area that could be looked at ten times and not know for sure if you have already examined it," Sessums told his family and friends in the days after the search, shaking his head in amazement. "Never seen anything like it."

Despite the intimidating countryside, Sessums pushed aside any fears and kept looking for Shawn. He volunteered to join the search immediately after he heard the news. A retired assembly-line worker and repairman for the DaimlerChrysler plant in suburban south St. Louis County, Sessums is friends with Shawn's maternal grandmother, Doris Duff. He is also the father of three grown children and the grandfather of two girls, ages two and seven at the time. "As a parent, I felt real bad for the family," said Sessums, who was on the brink of turning sixty in 2002 and, astounded by the rugged terrain, was physically exhausted after trekking through the woods. But he did it for Shawn and the boy's family. "I can't imagine anything worse than losing a child."

Even members of the media, generally recalcitrant by nature, had converged upon the area, eager to get out the word about a missing local boy. At the time, no AMBER Alert system was in place in Shawn's hometown; however, that did not stop local journalists from broadcasting and publishing Shawn's photograph. With sensitivity and urgency, they chronicled the volunteer search mission, which included Shawn's stepfather, Craig Akers, who tearfully scoured the backwoods on his ATV, tired and dusty but undaunted in his determination to locate his son and grateful to the volunteers, some of whom he had never met, who displayed amazing dedication in their quest to find Shawn. He was photographed in a local newspaper wearing a T-shirt Shawn had painted by hand and given him for Christmas. In the accompanying article, he vowed to wash the shirt every night and wear the shirt every day until his son came home.

While her husband searched the woods, Pam Akers stayed at home, near the phone in case someone called with news, near the front door in case her son walked through it. Weary and worried, she logged on to her computer and created fliers featuring Shawn's photograph. She held on to hope that her son would come home safe and sound.

By Tuesday morning, a day and a half after Shawn vanished, volunteers were baffled. They had begun their search the day before optimistic that they would find the boy disoriented in the forest, possibly injured but not mortally. Kids got lost wandering the woods all the time out here. Even adults, experienced woodsmen, could lose their way in these parts.

It was easy to speculate on the different scenarios. Maybe Shawn had decided to take his mountain bike into the forest and got turned around. Maybe he rode his bike too fast and tumbled into the trees. Maybe he fell into an old mine shaft.

Maybe, maybe, maybe.

These thoughts made the volunteers feel hopeful, and hope propelled them further along in their search. They examined every tree, often walking through the woods shoulder to shoulder to mark grid patterns and to ensure that they would not miss any possible clues. They peered over every ridge, they searched lakes, and they shone flashlights into dank mine shafts, shabby outposts, and abandoned objects ranging from an old refrigerator to a junked car to a ramshackle mobile home.

"We looked in places where even the rabbits would not go," one searcher said.

But they held on to hope. With so many people looking for Shawn, surely they would discover the boy, a clue, anything. And yet, no one found him, a piece of evidence, anything.

Despite the frustration and the perplexing circumstances, on Tuesday the volunteers remained hopeful that this would be the day that they would find their boy, for Shawn had become everyone's child in a sense, representing an innocence so pure just about everyone, even the most hardened of souls, felt compelled to protect it. To mothers and fathers everywhere, the missing fifth-grade boy triggered one of the darkest fears parents could have: losing their child, snatched away by an evil force inflicting harm on the boy or girl who will always be their baby. The insidious truth of the matter—a child disappeared and is nowhere to be found—gnawed at the heartstrings.

To forge ahead, volunteers needed to focus on the positives, however few. In their corner in the fight to find Shawn, to save Shawn, were several positive factors: The often temperamental weather patterns of Eastern Missouri had, so far, remained calm since the boy disappeared, with pleasant temperatures and clear skies. Another asset to the search team was the increasing number of volunteers, which had doubled to two hundred with people trickling in from all over the St. Louis metropolitan area, including from across the Mississippi River in Illinois. Not only were there more volunteers, but the quality and integrity of the searchers were unrivaled. The people who had come to find Shawn displayed genuine empathy for the family, a primal sense of concern for the child, and hard-core dedication—they camped out on benches and in church pews or slept in their cars, staying for days on end despite their own families and jobs.

Volunteer central was inside Richwoods's firehouse, where cigarette smoke choked the air as workers paced, raced to answer ringing phones, and downed caffeinated soda and coffee. They analyzed aerial maps as well as maps of Washington County that were organized into grids in which up to ten searchers were assigned to a section.

Rose Hoffman directed volunteer crews as chief of the Richwoods Fire Department. "We're leaving no stone unturned," she told the *St. Louis Post-Dispatch*. To the searchers she said, "I want you to count every blade of grass."

Law enforcement agencies, too, appeared committed to Shawn's case. The Missouri State Highway Patrol, for instance, had entered the search, providing a body heat–detecting helicopter equipped with infrared and night vision technology.

Surely, this would be the day that Shawn would be found. That he would come home to his family.

Nightfall came Tuesday, and still no signs of Shawn.

The next day, the hunt for the boy continued. Wednesday proved to be a day of ups and downs, of promising leads and dashed hopes, of renewed commitments and heartbreaking resignation. At one point during the day, law enforcement officials had a lead: Trained search-and-rescue dogs appeared to have detected Shawn's scent near a former strip mine. But that scenario evaporated after a detailed investigation.

Authorities had another lead that day, too: a Washington County woman with a banged-up car was under suspicion for hitting Shawn while the boy was on his mountain bike near the highway intersection. After questioning by police, however, it was determined that the woman had not struck Shawn that Sunday evening but rather an animal, perhaps a dog. The woman had a bad day—although she was no longer a suspect in Shawn's case, law enforcement officials still arrested her because she had warrants from another county. Authorities also impounded her car, which lacked the proper registration.

By Wednesday evening, the exhaustion intensified as did the emotional havoc stirred by continuous hours of futile searching that uncovered no signs of Shawn, just dead ends and a growing feeling of despair. No one liked to say it out loud but the nagging thought taunted: the odds of finding the boy alive were decreasing by the minute.

That night, the Richwoods Fire Department halted the volunteer search operation, claiming that they had conducted a thorough search that, sadly, had come up empty. The local fire officials explained that they had done all that they could. Their decision to stop looking for the fifth-grader initially infuriated Shawn's stepfather, Craig Akers, and the dozens of people who had devoted their time and attention to finding the boy.

Authorities also announced that same night that they would switch their focus from a search-and-rescue mission to a criminal investigation of a possible abduction. "We've searched for three days and checked everything at least three times. We've covered every piece of ground within a twenty-mile radius, and we've found absolutely nothing. No sign, no anything," Washington County Sheriff's Deputy Jim Nichols told the media. "Even if he has been abducted, we're hoping he's still alive. We're going to say that he is until we find reason to believe that he's not."

Although the shift in focus was disheartening to Shawn's parents, to say the least, they later acknowledged to the media that their local fire department's decision to suspend the search and turn it over to larger law enforcement agencies was actually positive in that it would accelerate the investigation and provide authorities with more resources. His parents also vowed to continue doing all that they could to bring home their boy, including organizing their own volunteer search mission, a move endorsed by law enforcement agencies working on the case.

That day, the family also launched an Internet site, www. shawnhornbeck.com, with the help of Fastrans Logistics in north St. Louis County, where Shawn's stepfather worked. The website was designed to be proactive, with printable "missing" posters featuring Shawn's photograph, a detailed physical description of the boy, and law enforcement contact information. Another sobering element was a to-the-second update of how long it had been since Shawn disappeared. By midnight Wednesday, Shawn had been missing approximately seventy-nine and a half hours— or 4,770 minutes.

As clouds darkened the sky Thursday, the gloom mirroring the community's growing sense of doom, two new command posts were established. The first was a high-tech outfit located outside of the Richwoods fire station and run by the FBI and the Missouri State Highway Patrol Division of Drug and Crime Patrol. The Washington County Sheriff's Department continued to assist in the investigation as well.

The second command post was set up at the Book of Acts Methodist Church by Shawn's parents, who organized a volunteer search group that would later become the Shawn Hornbeck Search and Rescue Team, a nonprofit of trained volunteers who are called out at any time of day to look for missing people in seven states, including Missouri.

But on that desperate day in October, the volunteer search effort was focused on finding Shawn. On television, on the radio, on the Internet, and in newspapers, the boy's parents pleaded for volunteers to help in the search. "It's a race against the clock at this point," Shawn's stepfather told the Associated Press. "We've got to cover areas that need to be covered before the rain sets in."

On that drizzly Thursday, one media outlet reported that the number of volunteers had dropped from two hundred to thirty.

And as the prospect of discovering Shawn—especially finding him alive—dimmed by the minute, hope continued to fortify the boy's family and friends with the emotional and physical strength needed to continue searching. "I won't allow myself to think bad things," Shawn's mother confided to the Associated Press. "He's either gotten hurt and can't come out, or someone has him. The emotions of not knowing anything is hard. I want to know everything is OK. Sometimes I feel it's not OK, but some other times I tell myself it is."

At that night's National League play-off game between the St. Louis Cardinals and the visiting San Francisco Giants, volunteers distributed "missing" fliers of Shawn to fans, placing them on parked car windows near Busch Stadium in downtown St. Louis.

Later on Thursday, a psychic notified Shawn's family that the boy's body was buried by a motorist who had struck Shawn. The psychic advised authorities to investigate a wooded ravine along Highway 47, approximately one mile from where Shawn was last spotted.

Finally. A clue. Even if the news was bad, at least family and friends would have some answers, some closure.

KSDK News Channel 5, the NBC affiliate in St. Louis, reported that, based on the psychic's tip, police had found vehicle skid marks near the site as well as bike parts. But like all the other leads in this case, the psychic's theory fizzled. A motorist did lose control of a car near that area Sunday night, but after a thorough investigation, law enforcement concluded that the event was not linked to Shawn's disappearance.

It still seemed as if Shawn had evaporated into thin air.

The frantic but futile search for Shawn registered as a big story in Eastern Missouri, but to the frustration of the boy's family and friends, the national media had for the most part paid scant attention to the missing child story—or "overlooked [it] after a summer filled with heartbreaking stories around the country," according to a broadcast by Katie Couric, then the popular coanchor of NBC's top-rated morning show *Today*.

At the time, Couric—or simply Katie, as she was known to her legions of fans—was a network darling, dubbed by TV critics as the queen of morning television and America's sweetheart. Landing an interview with her, as Shawn's parents had, was a coup, and the visibility of appearing on the country's most-watched morning news show would publicize Shawn's picture to millions of households nationwide.

Just one pair of eagle eyes might break the case and find Shawn.

Encouraged, Pam and Craig Akers reportedly made the approximately 120-mile round-trip car ride early Friday morning for the *Today* show interview at NBC's studios in downtown St. Louis. The couple appeared articulate, determined, and focused on finding Shawn while Couric expressed hope that the broadcast would help in the investigation.

> **Katie Couric:** Can you tell us a little bit more? Perhaps it will be helpful for people watching, about your son, Mrs. Akers, about what kind of young man he is? Also, perhaps, about what he was wearing when he disappeared?
>
> **Pam Akers:** Shawn is a very bright, happy boy. He never met a stranger. The shirt that he was wearing is the shirt that you can see here on his baseball team from the last year. That is the exact shirt that he had on when he left home.
>
> **Couric:** Do you think that there's a chance . . .
>
> **Craig Akers:** He was also . . .
>
> **Couric:** Go ahead, I'm sorry.
>
> **Craig Akers:** He was also wearing blue jeans, white Nike sneakers with the blue Nike emblem on the sides.
>
> **Couric:** Do you think he could have run away, Mrs. Akers?
>
> **Pam Akers:** That's not a possibility at all.
>
> **Couric:** What would you like to say to the individual or individuals who might be involved in his disappearance?
>
> **Pam Akers:** If there has been an accident and you're scared, just please call the authorities. If you have him, just release him. Let him call home. Let him come home. And if there's just anything at all that

you can provide the authorities to find my son, I
would just greatly appreciate it.

The *Today* show interview seemed to have buoyed the community. On Friday, the number of searchers increased, with
various media outlets counting between seventy and one hundred volunteers in donated orange safety vests braving the
rough terrain. In the woods, they discovered old car parts
and even an empty casket but nothing that directed them to
Shawn. Meanwhile, law enforcement officials investigated
other leads locally and out of state. One involved a Richwoods man's suicide, but like all of the ones before it, the lead
proved meaningless.

The family's search efforts also got a boost Friday from
Bob Walcutt, executive director of the Laura Recovery Center,
a nonprofit in Friendswood, Texas, approximately twenty-five
miles south of Houston. Named after Laura Kate Smither,
who was twelve years old and jogging when she was abducted
and murdered near her home during spring 1997, the group
helps families across the United States in their search for missing children. The organization assists families and law enforcement agencies for free, paying all of its own travel expenses
thanks to generous donors.

Two days earlier, on the Wednesday when the local fire
department suspended search operations, Shawn's parents had
called the Laura Recovery Center seeking guidance on how to

better coordinate the volunteer rescue efforts. Overall, Walcutt was impressed; however, he immediately noticed a glaring problem. In the control room, a map that tracked the search teams was hanging on the wall, exposed to the public. A TV crew or newspaper could publicize the information, which should have been classified. He explained to Shawn's parents that advertising—however unwittingly—search-operation strategies potentially put their son at risk because the abductor could wander into the command post, study the sensitive information, and gain valuable insight that would allow him to succeed in his sinister act.

Walcutt also assisted in administering forms identifying each searcher as well as advising the family, primarily for safety and liability reasons, to discontinue allowing Shawn's schoolmates to participate in the search, particularly given the dangerous terrain. Plus, if searchers found Shawn's dead body, as many expected they would, it would be too traumatic for a minor to witness.

"Seeing the body is a shattering experience for an adult," Walcutt said. "For a child, it just would be too much."

As he boarded the plane back home to Texas, Walcutt thought about Shawn, as he would in the years to come.

"I will not forget this child," he said, making a vow to himself, the same promise he has made—and kept—about dozens of missing kids nationwide. "I will always remember Shawn."

That Friday, five and a half days since Shawn disappeared,

ended with hope. The TV show *America's Most Wanted* posted Shawn's photograph and pertinent information on its website. Maybe this would produce a tip that would break the case. If that didn't help, maybe money would. A $10,000 reward was available to anyone with information leading to Shawn's return. That amount was doubled by week's end.

Law enforcement officials forged ahead with the investigation. That weekend, they studied tickets and citations they had issued on the day Shawn went missing. They examined the list of visitors on October 6 to the Missouri prison in Potosi, roughly twenty miles away. They stopped motorists near the intersection where Shawn was last spotted and peppered them with questions: Had they been driving here last weekend? Had they noticed anything unusual? Had they seen an eleven-year-old boy with dark hair and an orange shirt riding a lime-green mountain bike?

Volunteers, too, continued their search, still determined to find Shawn but less likely to get excited about new leads. All the other ones folded into dead ends. Rather than burn out, for many, it was easier on the emotions to remain guarded and cautious. They lived in what is nicknamed the Show-Me State, so why not take the Missouri approach to situations: Show me Shawn's Shockzone mountain bike, and I'll believe we have a solid lead. Show me where Shawn is, and I'll believe he has been found. Just show me. Show me anything. Anything at all.

By the one-week anniversary of Shawn's disappearance, it was getting harder for volunteers to have hope. They were tired, with visible circles under their eyes. They were drained, with many in need of a hot shower to soothe sore muscles and wash away the red-clay mud that stuck to their skin and, it seemed, everything else. They felt heartbroken, with Shawn still missing and nothing to show for their efforts. However reluctantly, many volunteers, such as Kim and Wayne Evans, would need to return to their lives, their jobs, and, most importantly, their children, whom they hugged just a little bit tighter at night.

One could only imagine how Shawn's family felt. Bob Smither knows firsthand the gut-wrenching grief that consumes you in the wake of a child's disappearance, the brain-wracking confusion about how it could have happened. Everyone handles such a crisis differently, but the insurmountable pain is a constant. "Your whole world changes," said Smither, the father of Laura, namesake of the organization in Texas that he and his wife founded to help recover missing children. "You are never the same."

And it is true: no one but Shawn's family members know what went through their minds during those dark hours when fear silences hope, when grief masks optimism, when sheer terror reigns. Those moments of waking up sweaty and screaming at two o'clock in the morning, your heart pounding by the second, panicked because someone you love is gone and you ache for the person so bad, you collapse on the inside, shake on the outside, and sob a primordial howl that sends shivers up the spine.

To the public, however, Shawn's family represented rock-solid strength in their conviction that their boy was still alive out there—somewhere—ready to be found, ready to come home. Their unfettered hope inspired volunteers to continue trudging through the knee-deep grass, the thorny brush, the densely disorienting forests punctured by dangerous mine shafts. When their son vanished, Pam and Craig Akers made a promise to do everything in their power to save him. And the commitment they made to their son is what they held on to—Craig in his hand-painted T-shirt that Shawn had given him, Pam with dark circles under her eyes, her already-small self vanishing into bones.

"Shawn will come home," Pam told the *Post-Dispatch*, she told herself, she told anyone who would listen. "There's something out there. . . . People don't just disappear."

In her gut, she knew Shawn would come home.

CHAPTER 5

The Search Continues

Things did not look good in the weeks after Shawn vanished.

Bone-tired and bewildered after unsuccessful searches, volunteers devoted to finding the boy began to head home, their numbers dwindling by the day. But some still came. A week after the fifth-grader went missing, thirty or so volunteers combed the banks of the nearby Big River, a slow-flowing tributary of the Meramec River. The Meramec is one of the longest waterways in Missouri, home to poisonous cottonmouth water moccasins and fish such as sturgeon and sunfish, which, at various points in time, state and federal health officials have warned against eating due to contamination from lead and other minerals once mined in the area.

Law enforcement authorities appeared to have resigned themselves to the fact that Shawn's case might not be solved anytime soon. Sometimes they seemed to act short and standoffish to the hungry media; but in actuality, it probably was that they had nothing new to report: still no clues offering insight into Shawn's disappearance. No signs of the boy, the bike, anything. Just a bunch of leads—more than two hundred—that warranted investigation but eventually self-aborted. The latest involved a tip that prompted authorities to dredge a lake and a farm pond. It turned out to be nothing, just like all of the other leads. Eight days after Shawn disappeared, FBI agent Mike McComas, who was working on the case, canceled a press conference because there was no news to report.

Three days later, on October 17, law enforcement officials disbanded their command center in Richwoods. With no active leads, police explained, they would continue their investigation in the regional offices. They promised that pulling out of their post in Washington County by no means indicated that they were giving up looking for Shawn. Since no evidence of foul play had been discovered, he could be found alive.

But still. The situation looked grim. The first three hours of a child's disappearance are the most critical because if an abductor plans to murder, it generally occurs within this time frame, according to an often-cited study by the Washington State Attorney General's Office, which was originally released in 1997 and updated in 2006 and is considered groundbreaking because it offers the most detailed analysis of child-abduction murders to date. What's more, incidents involving stranger kidnappings represent both the most dangerous and rarest types of abduction, as most children are taken by family and adults whom they know, according to the National Center for Missing and Exploited Children (NCMEC) in Alexandria, Virginia.

Of the children abducted by strangers, the NCMEC reports, about 40 percent of them also are murdered.

As frightening as the situation is to imagine, Shawn's parents took that statistic and flipped it: More than half of kids kidnapped by strangers are *not* killed, so if Shawn was abducted, as police suspected, there was still a good chance that their boy was alive.

Pam and Craig Akers had to be positive. Hope sustained them. Law enforcement's pullout from the area disappointed them, but it had no bearing on their course of action. On what they needed to do. Had to do. And that was to continue searching for Shawn and to continue imploring kindhearted folks to volunteer in the effort to bring home their boy, whether that meant scouring the dangerous terrain, manning phones, distributing "missing" fliers of Shawn, or donating search supplies or money to help pay for materials.

The Akerses had not forgotten the promise they made to Shawn after he went missing: They would do whatever it took to find him.

True to their word, they organized a search during that second weekend after Shawn went outside to ride his bike and never came home. About seventy volunteers arrived, including fifty police cadets from the St. Louis area, to investigate an expanded area that encompassed a twenty-five-mile radius from the intersection where Shawn was last spotted. The weekend ended with the familiar but formidable scenario: no Shawn, no clues, no evidence. Nothing but questions. The same unanswered questions that, for weeks now, had plagued Shawn's family, law enforcement, and all of the people who cared about the boy and his plight: How could an eleven-year-old disappear without a trace?

By late October, the volunteer searchers continued looking in forests blazing with red, orange, and yellow autumnal hues, a stark contrast to three weeks earlier when green canopies billowed in the trees on the Sunday afternoon that Shawn disappeared. The warm, end-of-summer temperatures were a distant memory, too. A chill nipped at the searchers, whose numbers by now had fallen to ten.

In the days leading up to Halloween, a hypothesis began to emerge about how the eleven-year-old vanished. The supposition renewed vigor in the case because the premise seemed plausible and could explain the intrinsic bizarreness surrounding Shawn's disappearance. The theory being investigated by Washington County Prosecutor John Rupp involved meth-heads, and folks in these parts knew that addicts high on methamphetamine would do crazy things for the drug. Meth's possible entanglement in the case made sense.

Although the theory took on several variations, for the most part, the story buzzing about Richwoods and surrounding towns went like this: While playing outdoors that Sunday afternoon, Shawn accidentally discovered operators of a backwoods lab where meth abusers cooked the stimulant in a toxic stew brewed from ordinary household items. Hotheaded and high on meth, the druggies killed Shawn and discarded his body in a wooded area rife with natural hiding places such as caves and sinkholes as well as strip mines and other man-made spaces that would serve as an ideal disposal site for human remains.

The county prosecutor's confirmation that authorities were investigating a meth connection in Shawn's case generated a flurry of media activity. "Yes, Washington County has a meth problem, and Richwoods has a meth problem," Rupp told the Associated Press. "There is a theory, and it cannot be overlooked, that meth might have had something to do with Shawn's disappearance. But that is one of many theories, and it's absolutely a theory not supported by any facts or solid evidence."

That the meth connection was unsubstantiated did not matter to followers of the case. Already, there had been television-broadcast reports that meth-heads—some angry after having their labs uncovered by searchers, some nervous about the possibility of being discovered, and others ticked off because the search for Shawn was hurting their illegal business—had threatened several volunteers whom the druggies perceived as invading their privacy in these remote woods. Sometimes, tall tales about encounters between the meth-heads and the searchers morphed into harrowing, life-or-death situations.

Even tamer versions of the story were dismissed by authorities as hearsay.

Some followers of the case also subscribed to another popular theory, influenced no doubt by a highly publicized lead police investigated and dismissed three days after Shawn disappeared: on that October day, a motorist struck the fifth-grader with a vehicle and the distraught driver buried the boy's body. Another scenario had a group of people high on meth hitting Shawn with a vehicle, shooting the eleven-year-old, and jamming his body down a well. The meth hypothesis persisted, developing into a ruralized urban legend, with different versions becoming the hot topic in towns across Eastern Missouri as well as favored fodder in Internet chat rooms and on blogs and websites created by amateur crime sleuths, newshounds, and local folks.

The speculation frustrated the county prosecutor. "It has gotten a little too far out of hand," Rupp said in an interview with the Associated Press regarding the theory that Shawn had accidentally wandered into a meth lab. "We take every threat seriously, even if it's from some nut case with no intention of carrying out the threat. But we don't have any direct threat. If someone makes a threat, we've got to take it seriously, whether it's credible or not. But is the family in danger? I don't think so. Are the searchers in danger? I don't think so. We won't tolerate this type of nonsense that diverts us from the real purpose of finding Shawn."

Rupp's verbose rant to the media seemed to indicate that his level of frustration was high. Generally, law enforcement officials working on an active case are concise and calculated in their statements to the media. Failing to be brief puts authorities at risk for creating a media frenzy and a public relations headache, caused by a reporter who runs with a sensational-sounding quote while ignoring other important parts of an interview that would have given a story proper context.

Years after Shawn disappeared, Rupp acknowledged to *St. Louis Magazine* that he regretted a conversation he once had with a reporter who was covering the search for Shawn. He recalled describing Richwoods as a "suspect-rich environment" because a "lot of people are there because it's a great place to disappear." He told the magazine that making such a public observation "only perpetuated the rural legend that druggies did in Shawn."

It is true that the rumors became fact to many people. At post offices and in general stores in Richwoods and surrounding rural towns, folks in the weeks, even years, to come continued to trade stories about the druggies who killed Shawn, shaking their heads with regret and shrugging their shoulders in defeat.

Unsubstantiated theories served as a distraction to Shawn's parents, who tried to remain focused on the facts. It was sometimes hard to do when people, often anonymously, called the command post with time-wasting tips, fabricated leads, nonsensical rants, and outlandish theories. As if Pam and Craig Akers did not have enough to deal with.

To stay focused, they thought of their brown-eyed boy who loved video games, riding his mountain bike, and revving up anything with a motor. Shawn's fresh-faced smile greeted passersby in Richwoods and surrounding towns from a spattering of mini-shrines created in his honor. Vehicles zoomed by with the boy's picture plastered on the windows as well as messages such as "We will never give up" and "Come home Shawn."

The media chronicled the tributes showing images of balloons, streamers, and stuffed animals clustered around Shawn's photograph. In an article published on October 28, 2002—twenty-two days after Shawn vanished—the *St. Louis Post-Dispatch*, for instance, deftly described the scenes, ranging from the yellow ribbons and handwritten notes from classmates—one simply declares in silver glitter paint, "Shawn Hornbeck is my friend"—adorning Shawn's school desk at the 175-student Richwoods Elementary to the homage in front of the house where Shawn and his family lived:

> *A photograph of Shawn is staked near the road in Pam and Craig Akers' front yard. His smiling face greets visitors beneath a single word: Missing.*
>
> *In the weeks since Shawn disappeared, the sign has become a sort of shrine. There's a toy truck beneath the sign, beside some flowers and a red teddy bear.*

The picture on the flier, identical to hundreds of others that have been taped to store counters and placed beneath the wiper blades on car windshields as far north as Busch Stadium, has already begun to fade.

Throughout Eastern Missouri, Shawn's photograph loomed, serving as a minute-by-minute reminder of what had happened to him, his family, and his hometown. Surely, the boy's playful grin juxtaposed next to the bolded, all-caps word "missing" gave passersby pause. At least it did in the beginning. But in a twenty-four-hour, media-heavy, technology-driven culture that inundates and saturates the masses with tales of terror, it is likely—and in a way, understandable—that folks eventually numb themselves to the sadness.

It is like when a person you love dies—your spouse or partner, your mother or father, your sibling, your close friend, or, God forbid, your child—and in the days immediately following, you are supported by well-wishers and other caring people who hold your hand when you cry, send you flowers, and cook up large pans of lasagna that you can stick in the freezer and microwave at will. Then a week, then two, then months pass since your loved one died, and those well-wishers have gone back to their own lives, but your grief is as raw as ever, even more so without all the pomp and ceremony of laying your loved one in a final resting place. And all that is left is the cold, dark descent into despair.

The media portray the tragedy, the agony, as they did after the September 11 terrorist attacks on the World Trade Center and Pentagon, as they did after the massacre at Virginia Tech, as they did in the days after Shawn disappeared. The public feels terrible and then moves on, "busy with their own lives, busy with their own problems," said Dr. Kathryn Kuhn, an associate professor of sociology and criminal justice at Saint Louis University. "Subconsciously, we let the media dictate what we should be concerned about. Once the media moves on to another story, so do we. In a way we have to. Social life cannot continue if we are stuck on a tragedy for too long. Even after 9/11, the people in New York moved on."

And that is what happened. All around Pam and Craig Akers, life was going on normally. As it did every day. As it did before, when Shawn was at home, and as it did after, since he had been gone.

Shawn's classmates rode their bikes along the streets, tossed balls in backyards, and ran around the playground at Richwoods Elementary, just as the children had done before. Neighbors drove to work, decorated their homes for Halloween, and exchanged pleasantries at Cobbs Grocery, just as they had done before. People laughed and joked. The sun rose and set. The seasons were changing. The holidays were fast approaching, with or without their son. Even Shawn's two teenage sisters had returned to their classes at Potosi High School.

It is a jarring experience when a loved one is gone but the mundane and magical moments of life march forward, as if nothing had happened, as if the person had never existed. Because when a loved one is gone, life often stops for those left behind. And it seems audacious for the sun to rise, disrespectful for the holidays to arrive, and uncouth to laugh. Make a joke? Never. And yet life moves on, nudging—sometimes shoving—those left behind into the minutiae of everyday life with seeming disregard for their pain. The incongruity of it all can startle and sting.

Not knowing what happened to a missing loved one compounds the difficulty, the desire to, as they say, get on with life. Was Shawn alive? Was he dead? With each day that passed, the likelihood of Shawn being alive decreased. It is true that many of the volunteer searchers and even law enforcement officials were certain that if Shawn had been discovered at this point, they would not have found a vibrant eleven-year-old but rather his cold, dead body.

Still they pressed forward and looked for the boy, innately knowing that if Shawn was dead his family deserved, as mental health professionals would say, "emotional closure," which could be achieved in part by burying the boy's body. By saying their final good-byes.

Like the families of September 11 victims, of mortally wounded soldiers in Iraq, of casualties of a natural disaster, like the loved ones of anyone who is missing and presumed dead, locating the remains—as gut-wrenching and heartbreaking as the discovery will be—allows people psychologically to move forward with the grieving process, with their lives.

"Human beings do not deal with uncertainty that well," said Dr. C. Robert Cloninger, an internationally noted psychologist, psychiatrist, and geneticist at Washington University in St. Louis. "And so, if you are dealing with something that is emotionally important to you, and you are not 100 percent sure of the facts, then it just makes it harder for you to deal with the situation realistically. Often, it is healing to just have to face the truth and whatever that truth is rather than living with the unknown, or a fantasy. It helps people to move on with their lives."

Dr. Cloninger added: "What would Shawn's mother think if she had given up and then later her son is found? Then she might say, 'What if I looked harder? Maybe he could have been found sooner.' But clearly Shawn's parents did everything that they could to facilitate finding their son."

One month to the day after Shawn vanished, it looked as if family and friends finally would receive some answers. A woman came forward with what appeared to be credible information: A motorist had hit Shawn near Highway H, approximately a quarter of a mile from where Shawn disappeared. The motorist then tried to dispose of Shawn's remains—the evidence—in the grassy area near the highway.

The tip sent Shawn's stepfather and ten volunteers to the

site, where the crew did a hands-and-knees search in which they examined every blade of grass until they came across a bloody, clumpy mass of . . . what was it? No, it couldn't be. They looked closer. It was: intestines!

Along with the blood and guts, volunteers also discovered two pairs of brown gloves and a one-gallon plastic container of milk, which the tipster said was used to wash away the blood. The woman also told searchers that Shawn's mountain bike had been incinerated in a brush pile near Big River.

"We don't want to know that this is going to come to an unhappy conclusion," Shawn's stepfather told the media after the gruesome discovery. "But, at this point, any conclusion at all would be welcome."

The FBI collected the evidence for laboratory testing. The almost-immediate results determined that the guts were unrelated to Shawn's disappearance.

Alas, the blood and bowels had come from a pig. A homeowner had slaughtered the swine on his property.

Another lead imploded. Hopes dashed again.

Based on more information from tipsters, volunteers drained another lake, to no avail. They then began focusing even more intensively on the area's abandoned mine shafts, cisterns, and antiquated wells, studying old maps and talking with longtime residents in Washington County to identify and compile lists of previously unknown locations. Once again, it was all for naught.

By mid-November, six weeks after Shawn vanished, Pam and Craig Akers became angry at their county's law enforcement department. Previously, they had publicly stated that they were pleased with the help that they were receiving from the Washington County Sheriff's Department. But on that autumn day, November 12, Shawn's parents, along with about fifty of their friends and family members, picketed the office of then-Sheriff Gary Yount and demanded that he call in the St. Louis Major Case Squad to help look for their son.

The Major Case Squad of Greater St. Louis, as it is officially called, is a multi-jurisdictional police agency serving more than 2.5 million people who live in six counties in Missouri and four counties in Southern Illinois, which sits just across the Mississippi River and is included as part of the St. Louis metropolitan area by the U.S. Census Bureau. Highly trained law enforcement authorities belong to the Major Case Squad and pool their skills and resources to solve big crimes in the area.

However, it was a source of anger for Shawn's parents that the squad was not called to investigate their son's case. And despite the desperate parents' plea, the squad would not be deployed to Richwoods for two reasons: Washington County is not one of the Missouri counties served by the Major Case Squad; and rules generally require that the squad be called in within four hours after a crime has been reported.

Of course the Akerses' aggravation and anger was understandable: six weeks had passed and still no sign of their son.

Circumstances were not improving, either. In an unexpected turn of events, the Washington County sheriff, without explanation, removed the lead detective in Shawn's case and replaced him with a part-time deputy and investigator from the county prosecutor's office. The move increased the couple's frustrations since they liked the way the detective had kept the family updated with information.

Dimming the situation even more was the start of deer hunting season, a much-anticipated event in Richwoods and surrounding rural counties. Shawn's parents scaled back the search effort for fear of injury to the volunteers. For their part, the hunters assured the Akerses that they would be on the lookout for Shawn.

Another ominous factor was the weather. Mid-November weather in Eastern Missouri can chill the bones. Snow is imminent if it has not already made its first-of-season debut. If by chance Shawn was alive and still lost in the woods, it certainly did not look good.

Despite the grimness, Pam Akers continued to have hope. In her heart, she believed her child was alive. Most likely, he had been abducted, since searchers would have found him by now, but in any case, she believed Shawn was alive. She told the *Post-Dispatch*: "Some people say I'm in denial but, as a mother, I don't have a bad feeling yet. I guess it's probably because, as a mother, I'm so hopeful that we're going to find him and bring him home. In my heart and in my gut, I know somebody out there knows something, and eventually, they're going to have to say something. If they've got any heart or conscience at all, they're going to have to say something."

If that somebody has a conscience. If that somebody has a heart.

CHAPTER 6

A Perfect Suburb

About sixty miles to the northeast of Richwoods, a two-story run-down apartment complex sits in an industrial patch of an upscale St. Louis suburb, the transient unit sandwiched in between two bustling train tracks. It is situated near boxy warehouses and distribution centers as well as busy on- and off-ramps to Interstate 44, which runs west from St. Louis metro through rural Missouri, Oklahoma, and Texas, its endpoint.

Built during the mid-twentieth century, the apartment complex in the 400 block of South Holmes Avenue in Kirkwood resembles hundreds of other tiny redbrick boxes dusting the Midwestern landscape. At this particular location, six rectangular buildings sit perpendicular to the busy street, low-slung into the sloping ground and facing another redbrick apartment box and a large parking lot for two telecommunications firms and a manufacturer of screws, nuts, and flanges.

The one- and two-bedroom units offer just the basics in terms of amenities: a weedy patch of dying grass for the shared courtyard, uncovered parking spaces, and cheap rents that average between $400 and $600 a month. Living conditions are cramped, with clusters of families squeezed into small spaces, on top of each other, mashed beside one another, separated only by paper-thin walls. If someone turns up the volume on a stereo system or television set, or speaks too loudly, or thrashes about, neighbors can hear.

For most residents, the apartment complex is a pit stop, a place to crash for a few months, maybe even a year or two, so they can regroup, get their lives in order, maybe save a little money for a nicer place to live. It is a place where folks generally act civil to one another but, for the most part, keep to themselves, often preoccupied with their own problems, working in low-paying jobs and living paycheck to paycheck.

Besides, there is no need to form deep attachments to neighbors who may or may not be here tomorrow. No need to make the apartment units feel like a home when a renter may or may not be here tomorrow. The transience is apparent in the appearance of the units: Bedsheets and cardboard boxes often serve as window dressings. Furnishings are sparse—one family set up lawn chairs in their stark white living room. Trash and other unwanted items such as discarded sneakers, broken toddler toys, empty beer bottles, and cigarette butts blight the property on any given day.

The apartment complex sits in an industrial section on the outskirts of Kirkwood that many of the city's nearly twenty-eight thousand residents either ignore or remain oblivious to, simply because it does not fit the community's white-picket-fence image as the quintessential American suburb.

Kirkwood is better represented about half a mile to the northwest of the apartment building, where expensive homes—some worth more than a million dollars—idle on large grassy lots shaded by mature pin oaks, Bradford pears, maples, and sweet gum trees. This particular neighborhood around Holmes, Monroe, Argonne, and Woodlawn Avenues is one of Kirkwood's priciest, with new construction of McMansions mingling with Civil War–era and turn-of-the-century houses that boast wraparound porches, cupolas, gingerbread trim, and, in some cases, an official landmark designation by various historic preservation groups. In this neighborhood, streets yawn past manicured lawns and professionally landscaped yards; past driveways full of high-end SUVs, minivans, and sports cars; past big backyards with deluxe doghouses and $1,000-plus playsets with swings, slides, and rock-climbing walls.

Established in 1853 as the first planned suburb west of the Mississippi River, Kirkwood is a mostly middle- and upper-income, mostly Caucasian community in west St. Louis County. The city has high property values and taxes, low crime rates, academically superior public and private schools, and more than three hundred acres of parkland. The largest area,

Kirkwood Park, features an ice-skating rink, an aquatic center, outdoor amphitheater, ball fields, tennis and racquetball courts, picnic tables, jungle-gym play areas, and a fishing lake complete with a bridge leading to a tiny island with flocks of ducks as well as bronze turtle sculptures that children love climbing.

Its historic downtown, known as Kirkwood Junction, features vintage buildings that house upscale boutiques and eateries and a large outdoor farmers' market with live bands on summer weekends, outdoor dining, and seasonal attractions such as a pumpkin patch and Christmas-tree lot. The focal point of the city's downtown is the railroad station, a shingled limestone depot built in an architectural style known as Richardsonian Romanesque. The city is, in fact, named after James Pugh Kirkwood, the engineer in charge of building the Pacific Railroad through the community. Today, the train station serves as a main freight line for Union Pacific and Burlington Northern Santa Fe railways as well as Amtrak, which has operated continuous passenger service through Kirkwood since the mid-1800s.

Long dubbed "the queen of the St. Louis suburbs," Kirkwood's small-town charm, high quality of life, and its fourteen-mile proximity to downtown St. Louis attracts doctors, lawyers, investment bankers, and business executives to settle in the area with their children.

It is not the type of place where a monster man would hold hostage and torture small boys.

CHAPTER 7

Nice Enough, Sometimes Odd, and Kind of a Loner

Unbeknownst to everyone, the monster man lived with his prey in the run-down redbrick apartment complex at 491 South Holmes Avenue in Kirkwood. Inside Unit D, Michael Devlin suddenly acquired a brown-eyed boy with dark hair who weighed less than one hundred pounds and appeared to be eleven or twelve years old. His name was Shawn.

Not that anyone cared much—at least not in the beginning.

Nobody cared much about Devlin, either. Despite his looming stature and three-hundred-pound girth, he was the type of guy who blended into the background like boring beige paint. He was nice enough, sometimes odd, and kind of a loner. Most of the time, his demeanor was polite—he'd greet you with a casual hello, possibly a handshake. He appeared laid-back and friendly, especially when you got him talking about something of interest—then watch out, his mouth ran nonstop. He had no criminal record other than a few traffic violations, and he had no apparent addictions—in fact, he shunned beer, even when his boss bought employees a round after a work shift. His obvious vices included smoking menthol cigarettes and chugging Mountain Dew like water.

By his own admission, Devlin was lazy. His brown hair often looked unkempt, his beard scraggly, and he usually wore wire-rimmed glasses and wrinkled shirts that needed washing. In 2002, he was in his mid-thirties and still working for Imo's, a Midwestern pizza-parlor chain based in metro St. Louis. Most of his friends had moved on to higher-paying, more prestigious jobs. Some were married and having children. Sometimes, he felt left behind and lonely, but he did not appear to do much to change his life. Devlin had worked for Imo's since high school, when he started as a delivery boy. With benefits, Devlin earned slightly more than $20,000 a year working as a manager at the pizzeria in historic downtown Kirkwood, about a mile from his apartment.

Devlin had all the makings of an ideal employee: Never late. Never asked for a raise. Rarely missed a day of work. Reliable enough to have a set of keys to open or close the restaurant as needed. Trustworthy enough to count his boss's money at the end of a long shift. Mostly, he practiced good customer service, going out of his way to deliver food to people waiting outside of the restaurant or in their cars, just to be nice. He was conscientious, so much so that during his decades of employment at Imo's he never once took home a free sixteen-inch pizza for dinner, even though his boss would not have minded if he had. He was such a good employee that his boss was happy to act as a reference when Devlin applied for a moonlighting position at Bopp Chapel Funeral Directors in Kirkwood, one of the oldest funeral homes in metro St. Louis. He got the job, answering phones during the overnight shift on Sundays and Tuesdays. He was a good worker there, too, noted for being prompt, proficient, and polite.

At Imo's, Devlin earned high marks as an efficient cleaner and a meticulous timekeeper. He is also known for making a good pizza pie, in the St. Louis style that Imo's is famous for: a thin cracker-like crust cut into squares and covered with a sugary-sweet tomato sauce, a blend of spices that seems heavy on the oregano, and, instead of traditional mozzarella, Provel cheese, a local specialty, a combination of cheddar, Swiss, and provolone that melts into a gooey white mass. The taste and texture evoke a passion in even the most mild-mannered of folks—you either love Provel cheese or you hate it (most St. Louisans love it).

Everyone at the pizza parlor called Devlin by the nickname Devo. His mostly male coworkers generally liked him, despite his sporadic bouts of grumpiness. They traded politically incorrect jokes, talked about fantasy football, and playfully insulted each other like typical guy friends. Devo would engage in a competitive chess game with other employees until the boss, owner Mike Prosperi, broke up the match, cajoling them back to work. Occasionally, Devo played poker or video games with some of the guys after their shifts ended. He also sometimes joined coworkers on fishing trips; his friends always thought he was eager to go because he waited to be picked up on the sidewalk near his apartment with his duffel bag, boots, and gear ready to go. He rarely invited anyone to come inside his home.

Before he started having bad foot pains in 2002, Devo sometimes spent his days off work rollerblading in the nearby Target parking lot. During the fall, he often drove into the Missouri backwoods an hour or so away to go deer hunting with Prosperi and a couple of other guys. Devo's hunting style—or lack thereof—provided joke fodder, ammunition so to speak, for the guys to tease him, to break his balls in the way that guys are prone to do when a bunch of them get together and hang out with a few beers, although Devo never joined in the drinking. "He liked the idea of deer hunting more than actually hunting deer," Prosperi recalled with a chuckle. "Devo would get all geared up and then spend his whole time sitting in a cabin and watching TV."

Devo's real passion was playing computer video games. He was a bit obsessed with role-playing fantasy games such as Final Fantasy XI. He liked chatting online with other players and, for his game tag, used his last name spelled backwards, NILVED. He told people video games were his main source of entertainment, and he talked about them in great detail all of the time, although, truth be told, Devo could converse about almost anything as long as it did not pertain to his personal life. He appeared well read and was a know-it-all. Politics, religion, sports, current events—he knew the latest and did not hesitate to expound upon any topic with Imo's regular customers, which included law enforcement authorities from the Kirkwood Police Station, approximately a half a block north of the pizzeria.

He was known for butting in on conversations. Prosperi would be sitting at one of the pizzeria's wood tables talking to an important person, perhaps a sales representative, and, before he knew it, Devo had come out from behind the counter, pulled up a chair, and chimed in to share his opinions, which usually were pessimistic and went something like this: He hated the Catholic Church. He hated President Bush. He hated the crap played on radio stations nowadays, which, in turn, launched him into a tribute extolling the musical and lyrical brilliance of 1970s rock bands such as Steely Dan, Marshall Tucker, Charlie Daniels, and the Allman Brothers.

Despite Devo's sometimes-annoying, sometimes-amusing know-it-all personality trait, coworkers and customers, for the most part, liked him well enough. They all said he was just a normal everyday nice guy. People might have wondered whether Devo dated, but they did not ask because he never brought up that kind of stuff. He was too private. It was as if he had no romantic interest in women or men. In fact, interacting with women generally resulted in him rolling his eyes, grunting, or calling them stupid behind their backs; as for men, he was always up for cracking a derogatory joke about homosexuals.

Folks figured he was asexual—or maybe he was just self-conscious about dating. Those who knew him described his appearance as "dorky." He had a bumbling way about him, as if he was uncomfortable in his own skin. Plus he was about one hundred pounds overweight. Maybe, they thought, he never put himself out in the dating arena because he feared rejection. Most anyone who has ever experienced that awkward phase as a teenager could relate: best not to badger the poor guy about his personal relationships; besides it was nobody's business but his own.

His coworkers and customers, however, could not help but notice that Devo was intelligent, hardworking, and fastidious in some regards. They could not help but notice that Devo probably could make something more out of his life beyond managing a pizza parlor.

Even his boss, Prosperi, recognized this fact, periodically asking one of his star employees: "Devo, what are you doing still working here?"

Devo's reply was always the same: "I'm basically a lazy guy."

Prosperi hired Devo when he was a sixteen-year-old fat kid from a leafy, well-to-do St. Louis County suburb. For more than half of Devo's life, Prosperi had been there, acting not only as a boss but as a mentor and a friend. He treated Devo, as he does his other eighteen or so employees, like extended family, always inquiring about their well-being, asking how he could help them better their lives, serving as a role model, instilling a good work ethic so they will succeed in future jobs. Prosperi is not an absent boss but rather a restaurant owner who, side by side with his staff, makes pizza sauce from scratch, cleans out the deep fryers, and wipes down the counters.

To his staff at Imo's, Prosperi is a surrogate father in many ways. "If an employee needs extra money, he comes to me," the boss said with a grin, "just like a dad." Clean-shaven with neatly-trimmed gray speckled hair and animated bluish eyes, he often dresses casually in wrinkle-free polo-style shirts and jeans, as if he were on his way to a family-style Sunday dinner or a back-to-school night.

Now and then, Prosperi would become concerned because Devo seemed more tired than usual, even exasperated.

"Are you getting burnt out as manager?" Prosperi would ask. "Do you want to focus on making pizzas for a while, instead of managing people? Do you need some time off?"

"No, thanks," Devo would reply, as he mopped the floors, wiped down the tables, and continued with his job at the popular pizzeria in a slate-blue clapboard building at 215 South Kirkwood Road.

Prosperi thought it was curious that Devo did not aspire

to achieve more with his life professionally. But so be it. "Some people just like to skate through life," Prosperi would tell himself with a shrug. "That's their prerogative."

Devo seemed to feel the most comfortable on life's sidelines. He was the sort of guy who could leave a room and no one would notice. That is, unless it was a hot day. For the only thing that really stood out about Devo was his body odor. He reeked. Sometimes people literally recoiled when they caught a whiff of Devo. Especially during the hot, humid summer months after he worked in the steaming restaurant kitchen, an inferno with two stainless-steel chef ovens that baked pizza dough and cooked sandwiches and pasta dishes, and two commercial-grade deep fryers that sizzled chicken wings and breaded meat raviolis. (The latter is another St. Louis delicacy called toasted ravioli, an appetizer of fried breaded ravioli squares dipped in marinara sauce and sprinkled with parmesan cheese.)

Devo often appeared unkempt, wearing the same stinky shirt day after day and sometimes coming to work with hair that looked like it needed a good shampoo. But he was a stickler for employee hand-washing and disapproved of the unshaven teenage boys who were hired helpers but lacked the professional acumen to cut their hair. He hated it, too, when the young workers arrived late to shifts. He would complain about the irresponsible-kid behavior to Prosperi, who would laugh and remind Devo, "That's how you used to be. Don't you remember?"

His employee would shrug, either forgetting or feigning ignorance about his early days working for Prosperi at an Imo's in the nearby suburb of Webster Groves, where Devo grew up. When he was sixteen, maybe seventeen, he would sometimes fail to show up for his work shift. Prosperi would go to the Devlin family home, where his young employee lived with his parents, and knock on Devo's bedroom window. Devo often was sound asleep, and waking him up was not easy. He seemed to be able to snooze through anything. Prosperi recalled once when Devo slumbered as professional painters worked on the house, scraping the walls next to his bedroom window. Eventually, Devo would wake up and drag his sullen self into work late.

Only a few other things aggravated Devo enough to cause a spike in his temperament. Those hot days working in the kitchen could get to him; but to be fair, the heat at one time or another could get a rise out of most of the workers. During the summer, temperatures behind the pizzeria counter sizzle to one hundred degrees, with ovens belching cooking fumes and exhaust fans sucking in the air-conditioning that cooled the public part of the restaurant. Add to the heat toiling at a customer service–based job—in which some patrons complain, act rude, and make big messes—and the potential for employee temper tantrums is high.

"Go inside the refrigerator and scream," Prosperi would tell Devo and other employees when they became too hot and too agitated. The commercial-quality refrigerator is roughly 150 square feet and forty degrees.

"Go in there and cool down," Prosperi urged. "Scream as loud as you want. No one can hear you."

Another irritant for Devo was the teenage boys who came to the pizzeria for an after-school snack and social time. Students from nearby St. Peter Catholic School, Nipher Middle School, and Kirkwood High School would come into Imo's with their backpacks and big attitudes. They spoke loudly, spilled soda on the floor, dripped tomato sauce on the tables, and sometimes acted rude toward workers behind the counters. Not all of them were good about cleaning up their messes or leaving tips.

Generally, they were good kids. They were just acting like typical teenagers unwinding after school. But their hyper habits and high-pitched voices sometimes drove Devo behind the counter and back into the kitchen, where he would shake his head and fume.

"I don't want to wait on those kids," he would say to Prosperi.

"You have to, Devo, you're the manager."

And back into the dining area Devo would go, reluctantly serving the teenage boys soda, sandwiches, and pizza—and then cleaning up their messes.

"The kids always annoyed him," Prosperi recalled. "Or at least that is how he acted."

As a student in middle school during the early 1990s, Dan Schwabe and his friends used to grab a bite to eat at

Imo's—and apparently, they irked Devo just as the other kids did. Although Schwabe eventually took a job at Imo's in 1995, he recalled to the *Riverfront Times,* an alternative newspaper in metro St. Louis, how he and the other kids disliked Devo: "He was a complete dick. . . . All the other guys who worked there were cool with us except for Devo. Me and a couple of my friends just steered clear of him."

It is true: Everyone just assumed that Devo was not into kids. That he had lived by himself too long, he was too set in his ways, he was too much of a loner. Not that there was anything wrong with that. Not everyone has the patience for the under-eighteen crowd.

Even so, Prosperi once in a while would spot Devo driving around town with a dark-haired boy in a white Nissan pickup truck. Prosperi thought nothing of it. Devo came from a big family. The boy must be a nephew.

At times, Devo even showed polite interest in and genuine concern for Prosperi's family. The pizza-parlor owner is married with four daughters and one son. One day just before Christmas in 2006, Prosperi, who wanted to buy his teenage son a computer as a gift, asked Devo for his advice about different models, since Devo used computers all the time and seemed to know everything about them.

Devo offered his boss some unsolicited advice: "Whatever you do, Mike, don't let your son go online to chat rooms. There are a lot of weird people out there. I just came across some weirdo in Minnesota. Whatever you do, don't let him go to chat rooms."

Prosperi respected Devo's advice. He has known Devo's family for nearly three decades, employing not only Devo but two of his brothers, both of whom moved up the career ladder while their brother clung to the bottom rung. "The Devlins are a wonderful family," Prosperi said. "They are the nicest people you could meet."

Devo grew up in Webster Groves, which, like nearby Kirkwood, is one of the St. Louis metropolitan area's oldest and most respected neighborhoods. Like Kirkwood, Webster Groves also has been dubbed by city enthusiasts as the "queen of the St. Louis suburbs," offering charming old houses on streets dotted with mature oak and elm trees. Webster Groves boasts excellent public schools and parks as well as upscale eateries and boutiques in a small-town setting approximately ten miles southwest of downtown St. Louis.

And like Kirkwood, railroads run deep in the history of Webster Groves, with its location on the Pacific Railroad line spurring the city's development during the late nineteenth century. In fact, Webster Groves and Kirkwood residents have a longstanding, albeit friendly, rivalry as to which community is more perfect. The annual Thanksgiving Day football game between the Webster Groves High School Statesmen and Kirkwood High School Pioneers is the oldest high school football rivalry west of the Mississippi River. The tradition began in 1907, and the winning team's trophy is the Frisco Bell, which a railroad company donated in 1951 and which receives prominent display for a year at the winning school.

Home to a private university, a Christian theological seminary, and a prestigious all-girls Catholic high school, Webster Groves is a mostly middle- and upper-class neighborhood that has been the subject of national media stories seeking to spotlight a Mayberry-like suburb in America's heartland. In 1966, the CBS television network produced and Charles Kuralt narrated the award-winning documentary *16 in Webster Groves*, which examined the life experiences of the community's teenagers and, to the outrage of residents, concluded that the town was superficial, status-oriented, cliquish, and prejudiced. In 1999, *Time* magazine featured a cover story on Webster Groves High School students to gauge the mood on campus after the deadly shootings at Columbine High School in Littleton, Colorado. Again, Webster Groves was chosen as a place to spotlight, according to the article, "for the same reason marketing experts and sociologists like to wander this way when they are looking to take the country's temperature: the state of Missouri, especially the regions around St. Louis, are bellwether communities, not cutting edge, not lagging indicators, but the middle of the country, middle of the road, middle of the sky."

For the first half of his life, Devo called idyllic Webster Groves home. Born November 19, 1965, he was adopted as a baby by James and Joyce Devlin, East Coast transplants who moved to the St. Louis area in 1955 after James, an insurance executive, received a job offer. The couple had two baby girls, born in 1955 and 1956; during the 1960s, settled into a house in Webster Groves, the Devlins became foster parents and adopted four boys—Jamie, Patrick, Brian, and Michael.

Michael never knew his birth parents. His childhood, however, appeared to have had all the makings of an ideal one—solid, pleasant, and full of promise, according to media accounts in the *St. Louis Post-Dispatch* and *New York Post*, and by the Associated Press: Nicknamed Chicken Little by James Devlin, Michael spent his days climbing trees, devouring his dad's barbecue, and playing with G.I. Joe figurines in the basement. His adoptive parents, the only mother and father he has ever known, dressed him and his brothers in suits to attend Sunday mass at Holy Redeemer Catholic Church, where some of the Devlin sons were altar boys. During the summers, the family drove in a station wagon to vacation at a cottage along Lake Michigan. They also took road trips to Yellowstone National Park and New York City.

Michael stumbled through private Catholic and public schools, graduating from Webster Groves High in 1984. For whatever reasons, his senior photograph was not included in the school yearbook; however, in 1983, his junior class photo depicts a fat-faced kid with a slip of a smile and a pouf coiffure that looked like it could be lifted on and off his head like a helmet.

Former classmates and neighbors—at least those who remembered him, as he did not have many friends or stand out in any way—described Michael as friendly, quiet, and smart, although his mind did not impress in academic circles nor did it motivate him to accomplish any big feats. Michael was neither brain nor brawn. Nor was he a big man on campus, unless you went by his physical size alone. Kids taunted him for being overweight. He was unathletic and carried himself in a clumsy manner. His dork quotient was high. He was teased for being reserved, for being a loner. It is unclear, however, whether Michael retreated into himself because he was picked on by peers or because it was part of his natural disposition. Maybe it was a bit of both.

Susan Dames, who grew up near the Devlin house on Oakland Avenue, postulated to the *Post-Dispatch*: "[Michael] was teased, and it made him a loner."

Michael's classmate Karen Waller, who also graduated in 1984, told the newspaper: "The guy was just a nice guy, like a big teddy bear."

A neighbor described Michael to *Time* magazine as "a big, friendly marshmallow."

People seem to agree that everyone and everything in the Devlin family exuded normalcy. Even after Michael Devlin became public enemy number one, after his secret life as a mastermind child kidnapper and sexual pervert was revealed to the world, folks who knew the family had nothing but nice things to say, a rarity in the modern-day celebrity-crazy culture in which a nobody like Kato Kaelin can become a household name, in which people seeking their fifteen minutes of fame slither out of the cracks to bad-mouth a person at the center of a high-profile media maelstrom.

But there was not one negative word about James or Joyce Devlin.

"They were the nicest people you'd ever want to meet," the couple's former neighbor Jack Seibert told the Associated Press; as did another previous neighbor, Antonietta Corno: "A lovely family. The kids all seemed to be nice."

It is true that nobody knows what happens behind closed doors, in the privacy of one's own home or buried in the deep recesses of one's psyche. But if anyone had a motive to point fingers at James and Joyce Devlin, to blame them for raising a monster man like Michael Devlin, it was Brian Devlin, the couple's estranged adopted son. Two years older than Michael, Brian has acknowledged that he was the family "black sheep," a drug and alcohol addict who once stole a car, has numerous charges for driving while intoxicated, and has a prison record, his sordid story the subject of a prominently played article in the *Post-Dispatch*. "I was a nightmare to the Devlins," Brian told the newspaper. "I think I was the only one who gave them hell."

Since he was seventeen years old, Brian has had little contact with his adoptive parents, who turned him away after he tried to come home as a teenager, and he has not seen his brother Michael in more than two decades, the *Post-Dispatch* reported: "All of the other kids were good kids, even Michael," said Brian, who lives in a timeworn trailer in rural Missouri, about an hour's drive from where he grew up. "It was a loving family. Anything that happened to Michael, that had nothing to do with his upbringing. Whatever happened with Michael, it just happened for God knows what reasons. . . . [James and Joyce Devlin] did everything in the world for me."

On February 13, 2004, the day before Valentine's Day, the local weekly paper, the *Webster-Kirkwood Times,* along with its sister paper, the *South County Times,* ran a column by publisher Dwight Bitikofer celebrating the Devlins' marriage and their commitment to their children. Headlined "Grounded in Matrimony," the tender tribute tearfully moved some readers of the papers, which have a combined circulation of slightly more than seventy-six thousand:

> *One January Friday evening about a month ago, I observed my neighbors from across the street getting into a vintage, white Rolls Royce limousine. Must be a special occasion, I mused.*
>
> *The next day my daughter and I visited their house on Emma's quest to break her old record in Girl Scout cookie sales. We learned that the Rolls I had seen was a 1954 model, the exact same age as the marriage anniversary Jim and Joyce Devlin were celebrating. Mr. Devlin was evidently pretty happy. He ordered 20 boxes of cookies.*

Jim and Joyce grew up during the war years along "the main line" that served as the artery for Philadelphia's western suburbs. But they didn't meet until October 1952, when both were living in Boston's Beacon Hill neighborhood. Joyce was a flight attendant for United Airlines. Jim lived with a roommate in a basement apartment while working his first insurance sales job.

Joyce learned a boy from Philadelphia lived nearby. She caught a glimpse and she wanted an introduction. He invited her out "for a few dime beers."

Joyce remembers the conversation that night included characteristics of potential spouses. Neither fit each other's image of that person. But there were commonalities in family background. For instance, each had a father who was gardener of a large estate. Joyce's parents were second generation Irish-English; Jim's were second generation Irish. And Joyce was attracted to Jim and Jim to Joyce.

Joyce remembers her excitement at finding the perfect wedding dress at Filene's Basement, a popular discount store in Boston. She paid only $14. They were married on Jan. 16, 1954.

There was a sacrifice in getting married. United Airlines insisted its stewardesses must be single. A Boston Globe photo from their wedding was captioned, Grounded In Matrimony. Joyce went to work at Harvard Law School.

The Devlin's first daughter, Beth, was born a year later. At the same time, Jim was asked to take over his company's St. Louis office. They moved with a one-month-old baby to a faraway place where neither knew a soul.

Their first home was in a University City apartment complex where many young families lived. They quickly made friends from all walks of life. Jewish friends helped trim the Christmas tree. The Devlins learned about Chanukah. Women from the South introduced Joyce to coffee klatsches. A second daughter, Kaki, was born in 1956.

Around 1960, the Devlins bought the first of five Webster Groves homes. They took in foster children. Three sons, Jamie, Michael and Patrick, were added to the family. [Brian Devlin was not mentioned in the column.] *Joyce immersed herself in 10 years of Girl Scouting and church work. She said her troop was the first integrated troop in Webster Groves. Joyce's Girl Scouts started a recycling project. They collected glass, and smashed it to bits in the family garage. Jim remembers the recycling project as a time when he had dozens of flat tires.*

"If a marriage stays together through all of that, it doesn't have much chance to fail," Jim mused.

In the late 1960s, Joyce returned to school and emerged a teacher. In 1997, she retired after 25 years at The College School in Webster Groves. She has since gone back to work there part-time.

The 50 years together have included some big challenges. The Devlins credit their abilities to be supportive of one another's activities, the inclusion of many friends in their family circle and holiday traditions—and humor— for making it work.

"He always knew how to make me laugh," said Joyce. "And I have always believed in him."

The Devlin love story is a sweet one, the type of tale that marketers, sociologists, and journalists at *Time* magazine would expect to find in the middle of the heartland, in the middle of a sweet suburb that embodies apple pie, baseball, and white picket fences, all the clichés of Americana at its best, all of the things in life that people work so hard—and hope so hard—to achieve.

James and Joyce Devlin personified the American dream and provided it to their children.

And yet it was not enough to stop their son the monster man.

CHAPTER 8

The Mean Guy in Unit D

At the run-down redbrick apartment complex, nobody called Michael Devlin by his nickname, or engaged him in discussions about religion or politics, or even really said hello. The nice guy whom people knew at Imo's morphed into the mean guy in Unit D.

Residents steered clear of Devlin, whom they viewed as a bad-tempered boor, a hothead who hated people and preferred holing up in his one-bedroom, ground-floor apartment with an undressed window in the back room. His neighbors seemed to move in and out of the complex all of the time, but no matter who they were or where they came from, they all seemed to draw the same conclusions: that Devlin was an irascible loner, gruff and always in a huff, ready to unleash the beast at a moment's discontent.

Take, for example, the parking-spot incident. Near the rows of overflowing dumpsters in the small lot for the tenants, a white sign clearly states: Reserved Parking for Residents of 491 S. Holmes.

Devlin took the sign's proclamation very seriously. A rule is a rule. And it is one that makes sense. Non-tenants should not be afforded the luxury of a spot when they do not pay rent entitling them to the parking privilege, one of the few amenities the complex has to offer. Fair enough: An interloper who parks in a resident-only slot probably would irk most tenants who might brood on the injustice. Or quietly curse the transgressor. Or roll their eyes and heave a loud sigh. The more brazen folks might even politely ask the offender to move his vehicle. For most people, at that point, the drama over a parking peccadillo would be over. No sense in letting an annoyance fester into anger.

But again, Devlin took the parking rules very seriously.

So when he pulled into the asphalt lot one autumn evening in his white Nissan pickup and saw a strange car parked in a spot that was designated for tenants, a spot he had every right to use, he became livid. Devlin demanded that the violator, Rob Bushelle, move his car to an unassigned parking area.

Bushelle refused, explaining that he had dropped by to visit his friend, Mario Rodriguez, who lived in the brick-box building facing Devlin's apartment, across the courtyard overgrown with grass.

Devlin reiterated to Bushelle, a landscaper: move the car. His face turned red. He shouted obscenities. He pounded on the white parking sign for added emphasis.

Once more, Bushelle refused. He figured he was seconds away from getting into a fistfight.

Go call the police, he told Devlin.

Without hesitation, Devlin called the Kirkwood Police Department. Within minutes, the city's officers arrived and spoke with Devlin. As authorities were settling the matter, Rodriguez glimpsed a brown-eyed teenage boy with dark hair rolling out of the pickup truck and walking into Devlin's apartment.

There goes the guy's son, Rodriguez noted, not giving the kid another thought.

Rodriguez, who has children himself, had seen the boy around the apartment buildings before, riding his bike and skateboard, hanging out with other kids in the complex, coming and going with Devlin, who was probably his dad, a single father—such a common scenario nowadays that nobody paid much attention to the pair.

The boy, however, was not around when Devlin moved into the apartment complex in mid-2001. It is not as if other tenants would have noticed or remembered. Most were living elsewhere back then. Unlike many of his neighbors, Devlin was a fixture on South Holmes Avenue, a longtime renter in good standing with his landlord, who appreciated his tenant's timely payments.

In 2001, Devlin's only purported roommate was a cat he brought with him when he moved into Unit D. The eleven-year-old boy with the brown hair settled into Devlin's 450-square-foot apartment more than a year later, on the night of October 6, 2002, the day he disappeared while riding his lime-green bike in the rural Washington County town of Richwoods, roughly an hour's drive from the Kirkwood residential complex.

Nobody but Devlin, Shawn, and law enforcement authorities know the true extent of the sexual, physical, and psychological torture that occurred inside Unit D's drab walls. This is true even now, after Devlin pleaded guilty in October 2007 to eighty-six charges of kidnapping, sexual abuse, attempted murder, making child pornography, and transporting a minor across state lines for sex. The pleas, made in three Missouri county courtrooms as well as in federal court, unveiled heartwrenching tidbits of the torture inflicted upon Shawn. St. Louis County Prosecuting Attorney Robert McCulloch told the *St. Louis Post-Dispatch* that the revelations were only "a very small taste" of all that happened.

What is known is sickening enough. It shocked the public and misted eyes in even the most hardened law enforcement officials and police-beat reporters who attended Devlin's court proceedings. The hearings uncovered that Shawn's torture began immediately, starting with Devlin brandishing a gun when he kidnapped him. Devlin tied the boy to a futon in the tiny apartment during the first few weeks after his abduction. Sexual abuse was constant, and is reported to have occurred just about every day during Shawn's captivity.

Almost a month after the kidnapping, Devlin tried to kill Shawn. "I took him from my apartment and drove to a gravel road in Washington County and took him out of the truck," Devlin told the judge during his plea and sentencing in Washington County, according to the *Post-Dispatch*. "I put my hands on his throat and attempted to kill Shawn. He stopped me and talked me out of it."

Devlin then sexually assaulted Shawn.

An FBI report documented the attempted murder in more detail:

During the first few weeks of captivity, Devlin assured Shawn that he would return the eleven-year-old boy home to his family in Richwoods. Around Halloween, approximately three and a half weeks after the abduction, Devlin told Shawn that he was taking him home. He put the fifth-grader in his truck and headed southwest from the Kirkwood apartment toward Washington County.

But Devlin bypassed the roads to Richwoods. Instead, he headed onto a gravel logging road near the camping property he co-owned at Woodland Lake Estates.

Devlin told Shawn that he intended to kill him.

His preferred method was strangulation. A gun, he later explained to the FBI, "was too messy and left too much evidence."

Devlin bound Shawn's arms. He covered the boy's mouth with duct tape. He placed his hands around the eleven-year-old's throat.

Crying, Shawn begged for his life.

Devlin tried to choke the boy but stopped. He just couldn't do it.

Shawn was crying. Devlin was crying.

Devlin explained his dilemma to Shawn: he couldn't keep leaving work at lunch to take care of him.

Shawn offered a solution: He'd forget about Devlin trying to murder him. He wouldn't try to escape. He would do whatever it took. He was satisfied with just being alive.

And so a deal was made.

A deal with the devil.

A deal that saved Shawn's life.

It lasted for 1,558 days. No one who knew Devlin suspected his sinister secret life. Not even his boss at Imo's restaurant, whom he saw five days a week. "He never gave any indication that he had done anything wrong," Mike Prosperi said. "He acted like he always did. There were no clues."

In fact, whenever the restaurant's TV broadcast stories about child abuse or kidnapping, Devlin would sneer and "make comments like abusers were 'scum of the earth,'" the *Post-Dispatch* reported.

After Devlin's arrest in January 2007, Prosperi reviewed payroll documents from 2002 and 2003 and determined that his star employee did not miss any days of work around the time that Shawn disappeared. However, Prosperi's records showed that Devlin took off from January to March 2003 to recover from surgery. Devlin told his boss that since he could not drive after the operation he would convalesce not at his apartment in Kirkwood but rather at his parents' house in nearby Webster Groves. Prosperi remembered calling James and Joyce Devlin's residence to see how his employee was doing and when he planned to return to work. On several occasions, he spoke with Michael Devlin and his mother. No one mentioned a boy named Shawn.

Presumably, no one knew about Shawn. While he recuperated at his parents' house, Devlin called Shawn at the apartment, the *Post-Dispatch* reported, based on documents it obtained from the Kirkwood Police Department. He had left the boy money to order pizza (probably not Imo's). Later, Devlin "occasionally stopped by the apartment to make sure Shawn was still there and had enough money," according to the newspaper.

To Prosperi and workers at the pizza parlor, Devlin's health situation marked a change in his demeanor. In 2002, Devlin began bellyaching about a pain in his foot. He started limping. He complained to anyone who would listen, and even to those who would not. Prosperi recalled Devlin telling him about a family Christmas party that year, when Devlin's brother-in-law noticed his relative's rotting toes, including the big one, on his right foot. The brother-in-law ordered Devlin to go to the hospital, where Devlin was later diagnosed with Type II diabetes and underwent amputation of two discolored, foul-smelling toes that were decaying from gangrene.

A few weeks later, Devlin told Prosperi that he would need to have another surgery—this one more serious, involving a stent and an incision beginning in the groin area and extending down his leg to the ankle bone. The procedure stimulated blood flow back into Devlin's lower extremities. All told, Devlin missed approximately three months of work, which caused a major upheaval in scheduling at Imo's, but Prosperi considered it a minor hassle. He was more concerned about his employee's health and well-being.

Around the time of Devlin's diagnosis and surgeries, some people started to notice a shift in Devlin's laid-back, nice-guy persona. At times, he became cantankerous, short-tempered, and less likely to engage in a friendly conversation. Other times he reverted back to his talkative, know-it-all self. His erratic personality startled those who knew him. They speculated that maybe Devlin's moodiness was caused by medical problems that required him to give up smoking, rollerblading, and Mountain Dew, his high-sugar, high-caffeine drink of choice. Devlin, after all, had complained about not being able to hunt and fish because of his foot. Perhaps, his friends and coworkers figured, Devlin's diagnosis and amputation had frightened him, made him a bit depressed. Maybe the diabetes caused erratic spikes in his blood sugar level, affecting his disposition.

Devlin's dual personalities, which alternated between good-natured guy and grump, persisted at varying levels in the years following his surgery. Former Imo's coworker Gus Nanos noted Devlin's personality change to the *Post-Dispatch:* "He went from being such a teaser to a much quieter person. I felt like he had been humbled by his health problems. . . . Years of downing Mountain Dew and smoking menthol cigarettes probably caught up with him." At times, Nanos told the newspaper, Devlin was "an incredibly nice and thoughtful person."

Another Imo's coworker, Kimberly Lawyer, recounted a story to the newspaper about how, in 2005, she was the target of Devlin's wrath because he disliked the way she did her job: "He was really angry, like red in the face," Lawyer said in an article. "I just remember him hitting the wall or hitting refrigeration equipment."

Back at the apartment complex, neighbors on occasion would hear Devlin yelling behind closed doors, with "fuck" being one of the few discernible words amid all the thrashing noises. Sometimes, they heard the boy whine like a kicked puppy. Harry Reichard lived in an apartment on the floor above Devlin's place. "He says he often heard 'weird sounds,' like whimpering, screaming and pleading," according to a *Newsweek* cover story. "'Once,' says Reichard, 'it was like Shawn was trying to get [Devlin] to stop doing something.' At another time, Reichard says, he heard Devlin yell, 'What the f— did you do that for, you f—ing idiot?' The shouting was followed by what sounded like a blow. There was often loud banging and blaring music, including 'horrorcore' bands like Insane Clown Posse and Twiztid. 'It was like a maniacal workshop,' says Reichard, who thought Devlin and Shawn were having father-and-son disagreements."

A person's knee-jerk reaction to Reichard, or to any other neighbor who heard the loud, violent noises, is generally accusatory, one of blame, as in: Why didn't you call the police?

The answer, however, is anything but simple. The inaction of Devlin's neighbors on South Holmes Avenue falls into a social phenomenon that psychologists and sociologists call a "diffusion of responsibility," in which a group of people allow an event to continue, either by their actions or inactions, which ordinarily they would not permit to go on if alone. "Everyone assumes that someone else is calling the police," explained Dr. Kathryn Kuhn, an associate professor of sociology and criminal justice at Saint Louis University. "They don't want to call and be singled out as the snitch, they don't want to be called to testify, and they don't want to get involved in general. In our society, we value privacy, and if people are fighting in public, one way to give them a sense of privacy is to ignore it."

Diffusion of responsibility can range from the mundane— everyone thinks someone else will weed the communal garden, pick up litter in a suburban subdivision, or wash out the coffee pot in an office kitchen, for instance—to the more egregious, a classic example of which was the 1964 murder of Catherine

"Kitty" Genovese, a young New York City woman who was stabbed to death and sexually assaulted near her apartment in Queens. An investigation into the Genovese case by law enforcement officials later revealed that about a dozen people had heard or witnessed parts of the attack but did not call the police because they did not realize the gravity of the situation, because they thought someone else would call, because they thought the loud noises were, perhaps, nothing more than two lovers arguing or two drunks being obnoxious. One neighbor even reportedly turned up his radio to drown out the screams for help. The terms "bystander effect" and "Genovese Syndrome" emerged from the case.

A norm of noninvolvement exists in other cultures but thrives in an American culture that prizes individualism, Dr. Kuhn explained, in which every person has the freedom to be him- or herself, which in turn piggybacks on a desire for privacy, particularly when it comes to one's home, often viewed as a castle or sanctuary regardless of whether home means a nice house or a crappy apartment like the ones on South Holmes Avenue, where neighbors who heard loud noises coming from Unit D shrugged it off as a father-son disagreement.

Besides, Devlin was not the only loud person at the apartment complex. Other residents fought, too. It is a common occurrence, neighbors said, because people there have a lot of struggles and stress, with problems often revolving around a lack of money. With units so close together, all loud disagreements are broadcast to the entire complex. The Kirkwood Police Department investigates incidents at the complex about two to three times a month, said Officer Tom Ballman, who serves as a spokesman for the agency. "Usually, it's for loud parties, stolen bikes, a mother and a child not getting along, fighting, that kind of stuff," Ballman said. Before two kidnapped boys were discovered in his apartment, he added, "Devlin did not appear to be any worse than some of the others there."

In fact, he was known to call the cops on other residents, as demonstrated by the parking-lot incident. Mario Rodriguez, whose friend angered Devlin by taking a tenant-only parking spot, feared Devlin would dial 911 at a moment's provocation. The best defense was to avoid the man. "We stayed out of his business," Rodriguez said, "and we hoped he would stay out of our business."

Indeed, the residents of the South Holmes Avenue complex saw no need to report Devlin to police. Sure, his moods alternated between aloof and angry, but so what? A lot of people acted the same way. It was not as if Devlin was obviously sinister, as if he caused other neighbors to fear for their lives or for the safety of their children. He came off more as "an everyday asshole," as one neighbor put it. "His bark was worse than his bite." He was a harmless jerk. Not a monster man.

Besides, for the most part, the dark-haired boy acted normal, fine even, certainly not like a tortured victim of a heinous crime. He told people that his name was Shawn Devlin. His mother was dead. She had passed away in a drunken driving wreck.

He told one teenage girl from Kentucky, whom he chatted with on the Internet, that he was a preschooler when his mother was killed, according to the *Post-Dispatch,* where the girl described Shawn's story: "A drunk driver hit his mother's car head-on when she went out to buy him food, and he still feels guilty about it. A therapist had told him it was all his fault. That made him angry, he confided to her. 'Some days he'd be fine,' she said. 'And then some days he'd be—not mad at one thing—but just mad in general.'"

He told people he lived with his dad—other times, Devlin was his godfather. He said he attended a private school—other times, the story was that he was homeschooled. Occasionally, Shawn appeared dour, but didn't all teenagers pout their way through a sullen stage?

Those who knew the boy as Shawn Devlin even thought he had it pretty good. Yes, he lived in a dilapidated apartment complex, but his dad bought him expensive gadgets and video games, cool stuff that most any kid would envy. Shawn had an Xbox 360, an iPod, a cell phone, a computer, and a dad who seemed to like playing with all of those electronic toys as much as any teenager. Shawn had a skateboard and a 2003 Diamondback Joker BMX—and seemed to be allowed to ride them around the apartments and adjacent parking lot whenever he pleased.

Shawn's dad also gave him freedoms other kids would have envied. He let the boy drive his white Nissan pickup. He gave the boy a library card and city passes to Kirkwood's water-park pool area. He allowed the boy to hang out at home by himself and blast the music of the shock-rock group Insane Clown Posse, the thrashing, thumping, bumping beats banging against the walls, often disturbing the naps of the small child who lived in the unit next door. He seemed to have no problems with Shawn hanging out with other kids in the apartment complex, no qualms whatsoever about Shawn spending the night at his buddy's house or going with his friend's family to the St. Louis Zoo in Forest Park in the city, approximately a fifteen-minute drive from Shawn's apartment complex.

The 1,293-acre Forest Park is one of the nation's largest urban parks and site of the 1904 World's Fair—it is also home to an annual hot-air balloon race, which Shawn attended with his friend's family in 2003. A relative of Shawn's friend told KTVI Channel 2, the Fox affiliate in St. Louis: "He even went up to the Energizer balloon. They gave out free markers and crayons. He's a normal kid, sitting there coloring right on the ground in front of everybody, never giving any indication that he was kidnapped and longing for his family."

The balloon race attracts coverage from just about all St. Louis media outlets, which can reach Shawn's hometown of Richwoods. Local TV stations could have easily aired pictures of Shawn hanging out by the bright-pink balloon of the drum-beating Energizer bunny mascot. The "hot hare balloon," as it is known locally, always gets tons of media attention, since it is the world's largest hot air balloon. Also, the battery company's corporate headquarters is in suburban St. Louis, and Missourians take pride in the famed advertising slogan: "It keeps going and going." Anyone who wanted to hide from the public would never go near the Energizer balloon.

But Devlin did not seem worried.

Shawn even spent major holidays with his friend's relatives, generally a special time when most parents would insist that their child stay home and celebrate. The family of Tony Douglas—who lived in the same apartment complex as Shawn—welcomed Shawn at holiday gatherings but did think it was strange that the boy's father would leave his son to visit relatives whom Shawn told them he disliked, according to *Newsweek*. "[W]e learned early on that he [Shawn] was not comfortable talking about his family," one of Tony Douglas's relatives told the magazine.

For his part, Tony Douglas described to *Newsweek* that Shawn was "like a brother to me," his best friend of three years. Shawn was his buddy who hung out at the mall with him, with whom he rode bikes to a nearby Wal-Mart and played video games such as Dragon Ball Z, Phantasy Star, and Gears of War. Tony's mother, Rita Lederle, is quoted in the magazine as calling Shawn "real nice, real polite, a very sweet boy."

According to *Newsweek*: "Tony began spending nights over at Shawn's, a messy one-bedroom apartment where Shawn slept on a futon in the living room. Dirty dishes were often piled high in the sink, and trash lay around the floor. Devlin seemed quiet, almost monosyllabic to Tony. He liked Final Fantasy, a role-playing video game. Devlin was never affectionate with Shawn, Tony later recalled to *Newsweek*, though he remembered they would sometimes play-fight, punching each other jokingly. From time to time, Devlin blew up at Shawn, one time for somehow messing up his Final Fantasy game."

At times, Shawn and his friends would be watching television when the local news would broadcast a story about Shawn Hornbeck, the missing boy who disappeared from some country town an hour away. The station would show an image-progression photograph of how an older Shawn would look.

His friends laughed. "You look just like him," they'd say.

Shawn shrugged like it was no big deal, like they were stupid.

His response was a brush-off. "Shut up," he'd say. "Whatever."

Shawn gave no indication that he was the missing boy.

The boy most people thought was dead.

CHAPTER 9

A Miracle by Most Accounts

As years passed with no signs of Shawn Hornbeck, with nothing but cold leads and collapsed hope, it is understandable that many people, including the prosecuting attorney overseeing the case, presumed the missing boy was dead.

Statistically, however, it is not a miracle that Shawn came home, as most stolen children are returned to their families, including those who are the victims of the rarest and most dangerous type of abduction known as stereotypical kidnappings. This category refers to a "nonfamily abduction perpetrated by a slight acquaintance or stranger in which a child is detained overnight, transported at least 50 miles, held for ransom or abducted with intent to keep the child permanently, or killed," according to the U.S. Department of Justice's National Incidence Studies of Missing, Abducted, Runaway and Thrownaway Children, which was released in 2002 and is widely cited today by experts in the field as well as organizations such as the National Center for Missing and Exploited Children.

The study derives its statistics from data collected between 1997 and 1999, when 1.3 million children went missing. According to the findings:

- About half of the 1.3 million were runaways or children ordered out of their house by an adult.
- Approximately 200,000 were minors taken by a family member, often as part of a custody dispute.
- Roughly 58,200 children were victims of nonfamily abductions, perpetrated by family friends, long-term acquaintances, neighbors, and caretakers, among others.
- Of the 58,200 incidents, 115 represented cases of stereotypical kidnappings.

Michael Devlin's abductions of Shawn and of Ben Ownby, kidnapped in 2007, fall into the stereotypical kidnapping category, cases of which generally make the national news because they are so terrifying, shocking, and representative of a parent's worst nightmare. Although endangered by all accounts, the majority of these children come home. Of the 115 cases in the study:

- 57 percent of the children were found alive
- 32 percent were injured
- 40 percent were murdered
- 4 percent were never recovered

So rare are child abduction murders that they represent less than one half of one percent of homicides committed each year in the United States, according to a report commissioned by the attorney general for Washington State and the U.S. Department of Justice that was originally released in 1997 and updated in 2006. Of the children who are kidnapped and then murdered, 74 percent die within the first three hours of the abduction.

Experts who study this subject and work in the field acknowledged that the longer a child is missing, the worse the prognosis for finding the child alive.

And four years and three months is a long time to be missing *and* alive.

Statistically, Shawn may not be a miracle. But by all other accounts he is.

CHAPTER 10

A Criminal Curiosity

As a criminal, Michael Devlin is a statistical curiosity.

To people who specialize in deviant human behavior, his mind is like a new species, with unknown characteristics and unexpected quirks. He represents a fascinating case study, a wicked wonder who, in many ways, defies psychological profiling. He is the sickest of the sick.

Proof is in the eighty-six charges of kidnapping, sexual assault, and attempted murder, among others, that Devlin pleaded guilty to in October 2007—and the resulting life sentences, more than seventy, all but guaranteeing Devlin will die alone in a jail cell.

Devlin's successful kidnapping of Shawn Hornbeck also speaks to his criminal skills. For more than four years, he kept the boy in an apartment an hour's drive from Shawn's hometown. The abduction left no clues, confounding law enforcement and volunteer searchers. He allowed Shawn to roam freely, for all to see. He spoke with police on numerous occasions, as if he were so confident no one would ever suspect he was a mastermind child torturer. And the truth is no one did.

"I think at some point, Devlin made a game out of it," Washington County Prosecuting Attorney John Rupp told the Associated Press. "Let's hide you [Shawn] in plain sight and let's see how dumb everyone is."

Indeed. Four years after Shawn's kidnapping, in January 2007, Devlin swiped another boy, thirteen-year-old Ben Ownby, from a rural area about an hour's drive from his apartment. Devlin probably thought he could get away with it, too, and maybe he would have if he hadn't been careless by leaving a clue.

During the kidnapper's guilty pleas in multiple courts, Devlin never publicly apologized to Shawn, Ben, or their families. He never looked at the boys' parents in the courtrooms (Shawn and Ben were not present). He was clean-shaven, matter-of-fact, and soft-spoken. He expressed as much emotion as a stone. "Evidence at the hearings painted Devlin as a calculating predator with a seemingly bottomless appetite for inflicting pain on young boys," the AP reported, "and an uncanny ability to manipulate the circuits of a child's mind."

For that reason and others, a multi-jurisdictional task force is investigating links between Devlin and other missing children from the Midwest, with some cases dating back to the late 1980s. One involves an eleven-year-old named Charles "Arlin" Henderson, a slight, brown-haired boy, who disappeared in

1991 while riding a bike in a rural area roughly an hour's drive outside of metro St. Louis. Another case centers on Steven Kraft, another slight, brown-haired boy who was twelve when he vanished while walking his dogs in rural Benton Township, Michigan, on February 15, 2001. Devlin used to vacation near the area with his family.

Through his lawyers, Devlin has denied kidnapping or abusing any other children besides Shawn and Ben.

Devlin's claim isn't stopping law enforcement from its investigation. "People that commit these types of crimes don't just wake up one morning and say, 'Gee, I'm going to start to be a sex offender,'" Franklin County Sheriff Gary Toelke told the media in early 2007, after Shawn and Ben were discovered in Devlin's apartment in Kirkwood.

On the day of his arrest, Devlin acknowledged to the FBI that "he has had thoughts of having sex with boys all of his life but that he did not act on it until he was 36 years old and when he took Shawn," a report stated. "When he was younger, around 14 or 15, Devlin used to babysit to make money. Devlin stated that he had those kinds of thoughts then so he quit babysitting and went to work at Imo's."

Shawn told police he "never saw any evidence in the apartment that other boys had been kidnapped before him," according to the *St. Louis Post-Dispatch*.

With Shawn and Ben, Devlin committed the rare crime of stranger abduction. In nearly half of all nonfamily child kidnappings, the victim was sexually assaulted, according to the 2002 U.S. Department of Justice study on missing kids. In roughly a third of these cases, the abductor physically assaulted the child; and in 40 percent of the cases, he used a weapon. "He" is used because the overwhelming majority of perpetrators of both stranger kidnapping and sexual assault cases are male.

Devlin did all of those things. From there, however, his modus operandi often veers from established criminal behavioral profiles, according to interviews with more than a dozen of the nation's top authorities on child abduction and sexual assault who were not involved with the case but are familiar with it. Child sexual predators, for instance, loosely fall into three simplified categories:

The Generalist: That's "general" as in most common. Nearly 70 percent of sexual abusers molest children in their immediate and extended families, according to the 2001 Abel and Harlow Child Molestation Prevention Study, conducted by the Atlanta-based husband-and-wife team of Dr. Gene G. Abel, an award-winning physician and psychiatrist, and Nora Harlow, founder of a day care center. These types of offenders are fathers, grandfathers, uncles, and other relatives who can appear as everyday Joes, even upstanding community members. Law enforcement and other authorities who study these cases say the molesters often coerce children with pressure— for instance, "You know how much I like this" or "If you love me, you'll touch me here." And they rely on the blood bonds that tie families—even a horrible parent is often loved by a child. Also at play is the child's dependence on the molester for basics such as food, clothing, and shelter.

The Groomer: These are the Little League coaches and Boy Scout leaders, the teachers, ministers, and priests, the almost cliché examples of men who gain access to a child's world and befriend the girl or boy. Many times, they zero in on children who are emotionally vulnerable—perhaps they come from abusive homes or were abandoned by their fathers. The molester establishes trust and showers the child with affection, compliments, and gifts. The sexual abuse is often ongoing.

The Grabber: These are strangers and slight acquaintances who tend to resort to violence—for instance, ambushing a child behind a building or luring the boy or girl into a car and forcing the child to perform sexual acts. A weapon may be involved. It is the stuff of Hollywood movies, but, in reality, stranger sexual assaults comprise only about 10 percent of all child molestation cases, according to the Abel and Harlow study. Experts say the sexual abuse generally lasts for a short period—for example, ten to thirty minutes—and then the victim is released or, in a few rare cases, killed. Some kids are returned in such a short period of time that no one knew of or reported their abduction. If the perpetrator strikes again, it is usually with another victim.

Sexual offenders can overlap groups in terms of their control techniques. For instance, the Little League coach may resort to violence while an uncle molesting his niece may also pressure his niece's best friend to have sex. And most experts on human behavior, particularly those studying criminals, will acknowledge that categorizing anyone is difficult. Nothing is absolute. The human psyche is just too nuanced—and a criminal, deviant by nature, is even more complex. Still, analyzing common characteristics can help define and understand patterns of behavior.

Devlin's devilish deeds, however, seem to resist classification. He is, by all accounts, a criminal curiosity. That his offenses have nothing to do with his family already makes him a statistical minority among child kidnappers and sexual offenders. That his victims were male—as females are more likely to become victims of sexual assault and stranger abductions—also sets him apart. But based on court evidence, law enforcement reports, and media accounts, Devlin continues to deviate, for he is not a generalist, a groomer, or a grabber; but rather, a grabber-turned-groomer-turned-generalist.

Armed with a gun, he grabbed Shawn out of his rural hometown, repeatedly sexually assaulted the eleven-year-old, and, for the first month, tied him up on a futon. He even attempted to kill Shawn. Eventually, he gave the boy freedom to venture outside, for only a few moments at first. Devlin then evolved into a groomer, showering Shawn with expensive gifts such as an iPod, an Xbox 360, a cell phone, a bike, and a skateboard. Shawn was told he didn't have to go to school. At some point, Devlin became a father-like figure to Shawn. Not a good parent, as Devlin's abuse of the boy was ongoing. But for more than four years, Devlin fed the boy, clothed him, and provided him shelter. The two were seen hanging out together, pitching a tent on the grass, doing laundry, and playing video games. Devlin even taught Shawn how to drive. He told authorities he "loved" Shawn like a son.

"Michael Devlin fits no mold," said Stephen Thompson, an associate professor at Central Michigan University in Mount Pleasant who teaches courses on sexual assault and has published books and academic articles on the behavioral profiles of sexual aggressors and violent offenders, which are based on thousands of interviews he conducted with victims and criminals.

"Michael Devlin is unique," Thompson said, "and as a professional, this case is very interesting."

Stunning, in fact. Thompson travels frequently to Missouri to train law enforcement officials on sexual assault and other violent crimes, so he had been familiar with Shawn's case since the beginning, in 2002. He wholeheartedly believed that Shawn was dead. But on that January day in 2007, the boy's very-much-alive face dominated the TV screen in his family room in Michigan.

"Holy cow," Thompson thought. "Shawn's alive."

And then: "This Devlin guy is weird."

Even among child kidnapping cases, Devlin's crimes swerve into the bizarre. Few cases can compare to this one. There's Elizabeth Smart, who was fourteen years old in 2002 when she was reportedly stolen from her bedroom in Salt Lake City, Utah, and allegedly kept captive by a husband and wife who took her out in broad daylight before Smart was found nine months later. There's Natascha Kampusch, an Austrian girl who was abducted in 1998 at age ten and initially kept in a dungeon; later, she was given freedom and, at age eighteen, escaped her captor. And then there's the case of Steven Stayner, abducted in 1972 at age seven in Northern California and living near his home in plain sight; Steven hitchhiked to a police station eight years later.

These stories make headlines because they defy conventional profiling. Most stranger kidnappers, for instance, have no use for their victims once their desire for control and sexual gratification is satisfied. But Devlin appeared to need Shawn. He bought the boy presents and acted like a father—not to reel in Shawn but to keep him put. Apparently, Devlin wanted the companionship. He was forlorn. His friends from Imo's pizza parlor were now married with children. They had no time to play with Devlin: video games, Texas hold 'em or craps on Missouri's gambling riverboats, all the stuff he used to do with his buddies. He bemoaned all of that and more to the *New York Post*. During his four-plus years with Shawn, he told the newspaper, "I guess I was relatively happy."

Although he befriended Shawn, Devlin appeared to hate other kids. Most child sexual predators make it their business to know what kids like. They watch *Sesame Street* or Hilary Duff flicks for pleasure. They hang out where the kids do, at parks, malls, and after-school pizza joints like Imo's. At his job, Devlin would have had the perfect venue for grooming his prey. Only Devlin loathed the young people, especially the boys, populating his place of employment. He ranted and raved and sometimes stormed into the back kitchen just to avoid them.

Perhaps Devlin reacted this way because he needed to fight piercing pedophilic urges, which he must have known were socially unacceptable, since he has been described as a well-read, somewhat intelligent guy. Like a cocktail tantalizing an alcoholic, a cigarette tempting a smoker, or a buffet causing an overeater to salivate, the kids at Imo's might have triggered Devlin's darkest drives.

Pedophilia is a sexual attraction to prepubescent children, a mental disorder classified by the *Diagnostic and Statistical Manual of Mental Disorders,* a widely used reference book published by the American Psychiatric Association. The affliction affects approximately 4 percent of the population, mostly men, and can be further broken down into more specific definitions: ephebophilia, for instance, means an inordinately heightened sexual attraction to older adolescents; while pederasty refers to erotic practices between adults and adolescent males. But for discussion purposes, pedophilia can be used as an umbrella term, "a shorthand way of talking about the nature of a person's sexual makeup," said Dr. Fred Berlin, one of the nation's leading authorities on the topic. He is an associate professor in psychiatry and behavioral sciences at the Johns Hopkins University School of Medicine in Baltimore, Maryland, an attending physician at the school's hospital, and founder and director of its National Institute for the Study, Prevention and Treatment of Sexual Trauma, one of the few clinics of its kind in the nation.

According to Dr. Berlin and other experts, pedophilia is an involuntary condition that generally emerges during puberty. Causes can be diverse, unknown, and biologically based, from chromosomal abnormalities to rare instances of traumatic brain injury altering a person's sexual makeup. Psychologically, past incidences of sexual abuse among boys can arrest their psychosexual development and predispose them to the condition. Although past sexual abuse often seems like a given answer for explaining the origins of one's sexual deviance, in the case of pedophilia, it is a factor in roughly a third of all cases.

"Why are most of us attracted to adults of the opposite gender? Why are some of us attracted to persons of the same gender? Why are some people not attracted to adults and their current needs run toward children in a sexual way?" asked Dr. Berlin, often cited for his published research on pedophilia, including a 1991 study in the *American Journal of Forensic Psychiatry* that found low recidivism rates among people with pedophilia who complied with treatment. "My point is: None of us as children ask ourselves the question, Who do I want to be attracted to when I grow up? A man, woman, boy or girl? We discover growing up who we are attracted to."

That being said, Dr. Berlin emphasized, "It's not a person's fault they have pedophilia, but it is a person's responsibility not to act on it, to do something about it. But doing something about it may mean getting access to proper treatment and, unfortunately, in our society, because of the horrible stigma that has become attached to it, the last thing, in my judgment, that a young boy growing up and discovering that he may have pedophilia is likely to do is raise his hand. He's going to keep it a carefully guarded secret."

But a secret can fester and often reveals itself. Those who knew Devlin say he was private about his sex life, never mentioning romantic interests or reacting to a person's good looks. He appeared asexual, which makes sense since his sexual appetite leaned toward prepubescent boys. In spring 2007, the task force investigating possible connections between Devlin and other missing children eliminated him as a suspect in two cases involving missing girls. Missouri State Highway Patrol Sergeant Al Nothum, head of the task force, told the *Post-Dispatch* that Devlin "knows what he is interested in, and it wasn't females."

Devlin's situation underscores the intricacies of the disorder. Some pedophiles have an interest in both adults and children, while others are attracted to children exclusively, which, in disguising their taboo secret, is why they may appear outwardly asexual. Devlin told the FBI he has never had an adult male lover. After his arrest, however, "a St. Louis man says he was Devlin's boyfriend for a period in 2000," the *Post-Dispatch* reported. "The man also tells police Devlin bragged of a sexual encounter with a 14-year-old boy in Michigan that same year. . . . But investigators found no outside evidence to support the claims."

If Devlin gravitates toward boys exclusively, then he would not be classified as a homosexual, since he has no interest in adult males; rather he would be a homosexual pedophile. A man who is attracted to adult women and boys, for example, is not considered gay. "One of the problems with the Catholic Church scandal is that it was assumed that a number of the priests who had been involved sexually with children were gay," said Dr. Berlin, who has treated priests for pedophilia. "Many of these men had an opportunity to be involved with men their own age, they just had no interest."

Another important distinction to make is that not all pedophiles are criminals, and even among those who are, Devlin's deeds diverge into the category of extremely rare. "It's a very, very tiny percentage of people with pedophilia who would actually kidnap a child, just as it is an extremely tiny percentage of heterosexual men who would actually kidnap and rape a woman," Dr. Berlin said. "There is no character profile of a person with pedophilia, just as there is not one for a heterosexual or homosexual person. If you have pedophilia with antisocial character traits, that can be a problem. One begins to wonder what else is going on if an individual kidnaps a child because that's outside of the range of what ordinarily would be expected simply based on pedophilia."

Nobody but Devlin knows what lurks deep in his mind. But based on what is known about the case, a personality disorder appears likely, although labeling a specific type would be difficult to say without psychiatric evaluation. In his big, book-laden office in St. Louis at Washington University's School of Medicine, ranked as one of the nation's top medical schools and medical research centers, Dr. C. Robert Cloninger has not examined Devlin, but as a psychiatrist specializing in personality disorders, he has pondered the criminal's mind.

"I find it interesting that he offered the explanation that his friends were getting married and having children and that he was happy while he was taking care of a child [Shawn]. There is a lot of perversion and pathology in that explanation," said Dr. Cloninger, a professor of psychiatry, psychology, and genetics at Washington University who is acclaimed for his research in the genetics, neurobiology, development, psychology, brain imaging, and psychometric assessment of the human personality and its disorders, as well as in the diagnosis and treatment of psychopathology.

"Michael Devlin is clearly acting in a very immature way, and this does suggest the likelihood that he has a personality disorder, which means he's very low in self-directedness, that he doesn't accept responsibility and tends to blame and rationalize things," said Dr. Cloninger, the author of eight books and more than three hundred articles. "He isn't someone who has a real sense of meaning and strong purpose in life, so there's an emptiness that he's trying to fill, even if it's taking advantage of someone else to fill the void. We often see that people can live fairly structured lives and do things in a routine way, such as working at a job, but they don't feel fulfilled, they don't have a lot of self-confidence. There's a lot of emptiness in them."

Dr. Cloninger continued: "The other aspect of a personality disorder that is very prominent is not to be very good at forming attachments with people that are mature, generous and giving. Someone who has a personality disorder is more likely to have poor quality relationships with other people. I get the feeling that Michael Devlin was rather isolated socially and he just created this small world for himself without a lot of adult friends. That would also be suggestive of someone who has a personality disorder in that he has low cooperativeness. Is he truly someone people like to be around because he's generous and kind, or is he someone who has a chip on his shoulder, feels alienated, rejected or inadequate in some way?"

For Devlin, the answer appears to be both. At his job, people generally liked him, particularly before the amputation of two of his toes which, the *New York Post* reported, forced him to relinquish his "passion" for hunting and fishing: "I used to be an outdoorsman," Devlin said, "but not anymore." At his home, however, residents at the Kirkwood apartment complex claimed he was angry and antisocial, not someone they necessarily feared but more an arrogant ass to avoid.

Devlin hid his secrets well by balancing his demented inner self with his outward persona. "Most individuals who commit these really weird, sensational crimes have fairly good social skills even if they don't care for people in reality," said Dr. N. G. Berrill, a licensed psychologist and executive director of The New York Center for Neuropsychology and Forensic Behavioral Science, a diagnostic, consulting, and treatment center in Brooklyn and on Long Island. "They don't really have a true or empathetic attachment to other human beings. They act as though they're normal or reasonably so. If they were stark raving lunatics, they would be picked up by police or ambulances would come."

In fact, in his sadistically skewed mind, Devlin probably thought nothing wrong of his apparent collection of boys, to shower them with gifts, to tend to them sexually, to own them. Often in cases of serial kidnappers, Dr. Berrill said, "there are fantasies of being a parent, so that they morph into a parent almost. The identity and reality of the relationship probably becomes very diffused, very confused on the part of the offender, as in 'I did something good,' 'I took them from a bad situation,' and 'Look at what I'm offering them, this wonderful life.' And they believe it because there is a rupture in reality testing. There's more than just a character disturbance. They're a little crazy for sure. They think this is perfectly acceptable—that if you become a mentor, a parent, a lover or whatever, then what's so bad about that? Otherwise, without the fantasy, these boys would have been discarded."

Devlin told Shawn that he eventually planned to take Ben's life and that he "had no intention of taking the risk to create another 'son' as he had with Shawn," according to an account in the Associated Press based on an interview with Washington County Prosecuting Attorney John Rupp. "He told Shawn that was his plan—he was going to keep Ben for a while and then kill him," Rupp said in the AP story.

A defense attorney for Devlin, Ethan Corlija, told the AP he was unable to comment specifically about Rupp's assertion but acknowledged that the "feelings that Devlin had for [Shawn] Hornbeck ran much deeper than they did for Ben Ownby. He wasn't as attached to Ben Ownby."

But Devlin told authorities he kidnapped Ben because he sexually desired a younger boy. Experts in pedophilia and deviant behavior note that most offenders have a preferential age range for their victims—and once their targets get older, they are often replaced. Devlin appears to be attracted to boys in the preteen and early teenage years, and he contemplated abducting a younger boy for three months before he stole Ben, according to an FBI report. At age fifteen, "Shawn was getting too old" for Devlin, the report stated, "and he wanted a younger boy."

Of course this begs the question: What would have happened to Shawn had he not been discovered four and a half days after Ben's abduction?

After all, Devlin had tried to kill Shawn once.

"Seems to me that if you have a kid that's running around the neighborhood unaccompanied, you either have to be sure that he has been so psychologically well trained and indoctrinated," Dr. Berrill said, "or you're going to have to kill him because you're facing obvious detection."

Ever the master manipulator, Devlin unleashed another psychological ploy on Shawn by forcing the teenager to accompany him on the day he kidnapped Ben and threatened him with a gun in January 2007. Shawn had known for months of Devlin's desire to abduct and abuse another boy, and the teenager vehemently opposed his abductor's plan. "Shawn just went ballistic on Devlin, telling him: 'There's no way another boy should have to go through what I went through,'" Rupp told the Associated Press.

The AP article continued: "But Shawn's resistance to Devlin had grown so intense by late 2006 that Devlin realized his normal threats of murder or sexual violence wouldn't control the boy, said Scott Sherman, an attorney representing [Shawn] Hornbeck and his family. . . . 'When none of those threats can work, and Shawn was going nuts, then the only thing that was left was that Shawn had to be in as much trouble' as Devlin was, Sherman said."

Clearly, Devlin was desperate. Allowing Shawn to live could have been too risky, experts say, because if he had been abandoned to the streets, chances are high that law enforcement authorities eventually would unravel the crime. Even if a victim being phased out was so psychologically brainwashed, bringing another victim into the situation can be the criminal's undoing. That is what happened in one of the few comparable cases.

In December 1972, seven-year-old Steven Stayner was abducted near his Northern California hometown of Merced by a convicted pedophile and an accomplice who lured the boy into their car under the ruse that they were going to drive to the second-grader's house and ask his mother for a church donation. From there, according to a 1984 *Newsweek* article, Kenneth Parnell, the forty-eight-year-old pedophile, "became both his [Steven's] daytime father and his nighttime sexual abuser. Parnell sodomized him on their first day together, threatened him with beatings, convinced him he wasn't wanted at home and gradually demoralized him into half-willing captivity."

Parnell even told Steven that he had legal papers to change the boy's name from Steven to Dennis. He asked the child to call him "Dad." He sent him to schools where missing posters of Steven once hung, but no one recognized the boy.

"Despite the constant fear and sexual abuse, Steven settled into a semblance of family life as Parnell's son," the *Newsweek* article stated. "He created a fictional family history to answer ordinary questions school chums asked about his life. He got Christmas presents and birthday gifts, made friends and went to school—though he was repeatedly in trouble for setting fires and fighting."

Around age nine, Steven began doubting his abductor's lies, but fear kept him shackled, unable to escape. All that changed on Valentine's Day 1980, when Parnell came home with five-year-old Timmy White, who cried and pleaded to go home. Upset at Timmy's anguish and ridiculed by Parnell for being too old, Steven fled with Timmy sixteen days later to a police station in Ukiah, California.

The boys were reunited with their families. Parnell served five years in prison; in 2004, he returned to a penitentiary where he is currently serving twenty-five years to life for trying to procure a boy for $500. The accomplice in Steven's kidnapping served two years in prison.

Steven told *Newsweek* that he empathized with the five-year-old: "I couldn't see Timmy suffer. It was my do-or-die chance."

Like ice water to the face, witnessing Timmy's distress allowed Steven to see himself in the painful context of victim, to see past the lies and evil ways of his abuser. "It unlocked the situation so he could move away from it," said Dr. Lenore Terr, a clinical psychiatry professor at the University of California, San Francisco School of Medicine who had no professional involvement in the Stayner case but followed it closely as one of the world's foremost experts on childhood trauma.

Besides compassion, experts in pedophilia, childhood abuse, and human behavior say other factors likely compelled Stayner to save Timmy, reasons rooted in the insidious nature of sexual abuse. Reasons that make most people cringe, squirm, and change the subject, because topics that mingle children and sexuality are bound to stir discomfort. But the truth about sexual abuse, experts say, is that many children, at the time it is happening, feel ambivalent about the acts—or even enjoy them.

The subject is so taboo and misunderstood, that such admissions can rile and cause people to blame and shame victims, as if they, too, are as perverse and promiscuous as their perpetrators. This is not the case, experts say, because they were just boys and girls when the abuse occurred, and children lack the emotional maturity, mental awareness, and psychological development to engage in sexual intimacy. For adults, sex can be powerful and primitive, a tangled and emotionally charged act with the potential to either uplift or crush our spirits. For children, it is too much to handle, and the burden of engaging in sexual acts can lead to future problems, particularly in self-image and self-esteem. And for all of these reasons and more, sex with a minor is abusive, immoral, and criminal.

But the fact remains that at the time, it can feel good.

This is biologically based. Just as a touch to an ice cube is cold and a touch to a flame is hot, a touch to the genitals generally is pleasurable. This is a response from the body—not the mind, not the soul, not the heart. And therein lays the knotted nature of the abuse, because victims know—either intuitively or later, as they mature—that what happened is bad, but that it felt good physically. Maybe they go along with it, and maybe the perpetrator praises or validates them for doing it. But they know it is not right and begin to believe that they are the bad ones instead of the person who took advantage of their innocence, trust, and vulnerabilities.

"You can make a sex slave out of a child," said Dr. Terr, who has treated dozens of abused children during her forty years or so as a child psychiatrist. "You can introduce certain sexual practices that a child would have never thought of but become needed. A child can become very dependent on it, and it's a new kind of food that the child needs that he never would have thought of before." Creating such dependence is a way to control the child, coerce a child into submission, and paralyze a child from leaving the situation and getting help from another adult. It is one of the psychological tools likely used by Kenneth Parnell to indoctrinate little Steven Stayner into his sick world of lies, to prevent the boy from going to the police earlier. Whether perpetrators in these types of situations are acting subconsciously or by conscious calculation, "most of these guys are good at what they do," said Dr. Berrill, an adjunct professor at the City University of New York's John Jay College of Criminal Justice. "They have some well-developed hunting skills."

And all seems to go according to plan until the abuser introduces another victim into the mix, often sparking jealousy in the victim remaining. It is a dynamic often seen in what some law enforcement officials call acquaintance molestation cases—roughly the groomer profile. "Now the first victim becomes angry because he is no longer the special interest, he has lost his sexual appeal," explained Kenneth V. Lanning, a retired FBI special agent who specializes in behavioral analysis of sex crimes and child victims and serves on the research advisory board of the agency's prestigious National Center for the Analysis of Violent Crime. "So in many of these types of cases, the victim will try to get attention in some other way, by making himself useful, maybe by acting as an accomplice in a crime, anything to get the abuser to recognize his worth. Then after a few days, a week, a month, the victim thinks, 'I can't do this any more.' And maybe he runs away or maybe he is kicked out."

Or, in rare instances, maybe he is killed.

Devlin attempted to kill Shawn, and threatened to do so numerous times. However, no evidence revealed, thus far, indicates that he is a murderer. But no doubt law enforcement authorities are looking into it, especially as they investigate Devlin's possible links to other missing children. A 2006 study by the attorney general of Washington State and the U.S. Department of Justice that analyzed approximately eight hundred child abduction murders provides a general profile of child abduction murderers. They tend to be:

- males between the ages of eighteen and forty years old with a mean age of 27.8
- predominantly Caucasian
- "social marginals" who are mostly single and "had no intimate attachments or bonds with another person at the time of the abduction and subsequent murder"
- living with someone else, whether a roommate, romantic partner, or, in the majority of the cases, with their parents
- unemployed in almost half of the cases; if they have a job it tends to be in low-skilled occupations such as in construction or in the food industry
- described as "strange" by people who know them in one-third of the cases
- on probation or parole at the time they committed the child abduction murder in approximately 20 percent of the cases
- abusing alcohol or drugs in nearly a quarter of the cases
- experiencing "more serious personal behavioral problems than the typical killer," with more than three-

fourths of them exhibiting serious behavioral issues and nearly half of them having a history of prior crimes against children including sexual assault and rape
• targeting victims who are female

Nearly two-thirds of all child abduction murders involve sexual assault—either before or after the child is killed.

But the problem with creating such a profile, said Dr. Robert Keppel, a criminal justice professor, veteran homicide investigator, and one of the study's lead authors, is that with these types of criminals "there is no consistency whatsoever as to what they might or might not do."

For more than three decades, Dr. Keppel has immersed himself in the world of serial killers, investigating, consulting, and reviewing more than two thousand cases, including high-profile murderers such as "Nightstalker" Richard Ramirez, "Freeway Killer" Randy Kraft, and "Green River Killer" Gary Ridgway. He also served as the primary investigator for the King County Sheriff's Department in Washington State for murders committed by the notorious Ted Bundy—and his work in that case served as an inspiration for the character Clarice Starling, an FBI trainee, in the blockbuster movie *The Silence of the Lambs*.

If there is one thing Dr. Keppel is sure about it is the serial killer's inconsistency and unpredictability: "You may have somebody who eviscerates an eight-year-old girl on his first crime and then exposes himself outside of a grocery store. Go figure that one. At times he will kill out of the blue and other times he might kidnap and sexually assault somebody and then let that person go. There is no telling."

For his crimes, Devlin appears to follow a routine: Drive into a rural area, locate and grab a slight prepubescent-appearing boy, sexually assault him, and begin the psychological brainwashing, although the exact order of abuse is unknown. In Shawn's abduction, the execution was perfect, leaving no clues and baffling investigators who, at the time, called it a "nightmare" investigation. All of which indicates Devlin may have had experience in this area.

"He's good, he's quick and it looks like he's had practice," Dr. Berrill said. "The questions I would ask are: Who did he practice with? How did he get to be so good? And are there others? Are there untold bodies buried somewhere? I don't know."

Regardless, a person who kidnaps a child is especially skewed in reality, because almost no parent gives up easily on finding a son or daughter and neither do the police, whose numbers can reach into the hundreds for one missing-kid case. The National Center for Missing and Exploited Children dispatches investigators to the scene, as do nonprofit search-and-rescue groups. Neighbors come out by the dozens, as do media. To invite such scrutiny indicates distorted judgment. Someone who would do this usually is lacking in interpersonal skills, as if they are incapable of befriending and grooming a child. That is why after their sexual needs are satisfied, the child is often discarded. What is odd about Devlin—again, how he deviates from behavioral profiles—is that he had some social skills. After all, he held down a job for more than twenty years, and he did it well. He got along with his boss. He seemed to have developed a relationship with Shawn. The question that confounds law enforcement is: Why didn't he just groom the kids at the pizza parlor? Why did he have to kidnap not one but two boys?

"A guy who repeatedly kidnaps really has a screw loose because how many times can you do it without getting caught?" said Dr. Berrill, a consultant for federal agencies such as the Department of Justice and the Centers for Disease Control and Prevention. "It's a serious offense and he can spend a lifetime in prison for it, particularly if he crosses state lines, and he's willing to risk all of this just to control a child. . . . A guy like this is so sick, it's about the impulse, the desire, living in the moment, not thinking about the future. He is psychologically very primitive, very desperate, very needy, very lonely and isolated. He can't be other than that because he can't commit this crime if he's tied too tightly into society. People would say, 'Where did you get that boy from?'"

Nobody noticed the boys in Devlin's situation. Not even his family who lived only a few miles away. According to the *Post-Dispatch,* his mother visited Devlin's apartment just once, "years ago," while his father had never stepped inside.

Sometime in 2004 or 2005, the newspaper reported that Devlin's father told Kirkwood police that he ran into Michael at a Walgreens drugstore. A dark-haired boy was with his son. He asked Michael who the teenager was. "Michael said it was a neighbor and he was babysitting," according to the article. The father said "that he did not think anything of it after that."

Family dysfunction and genetics always tend to surface as the root causes in criminal behavior, but in this case, the abductor's parents have been lauded by neighbors and the press for being a model mother and father to their biological and adopted children. Maybe this is the case—and Devlin just has an unfortunate genetic makeup, or something else horrible happened to him. Maybe Devlin suffered severe and irreparable trauma before his parents adopted him as a baby, or outside of the home during his childhood. In any case, Dr. Berrill and other experts said they find it hard to believe that his family, whom he did not appear to be estranged from, would have not known about Shawn.

"Either they know and they don't want to get involved, or they had suspicions and never wanted to play them out," Dr. Berrill said. "Or maybe miraculously, he was able to have the boy go somewhere else when they came over or say that he [Shawn] was the neighborhood kid or something. . . . I've talked to parents of murderers and they didn't have a clue, but I think part of that is denial. They didn't want to know."

For all of his crimes, Devlin succeeded in making himself an enigma, a monstrous marvel who resists conventional profiling and psychological penetration.

Dr. Berrill paused. "This is a deeper, nuttier kind of guy."

CHAPTER 11

Clinging to Hope

Shawn Hornbeck's parents had no idea what kind of monster man they were dealing with. A crazed loner? A pedophilic predator? A murderer?

Maybe all of the above, or none of the above. All that Craig and Pam Akers knew was that their happy, bright-eyed boy was missing. And still no clues had surfaced about how their son had vanished.

The holiday season was upon them. The first Thanksgiving without Shawn. The first Christmas. The first New Year's Day.

"If I had my way, we wouldn't be having any holidays," Pam told the *St. Louis Post-Dispatch*. "But I've got my other two children and my husband and other relatives to worry about. It's just really hard."

The *Post-Dispatch* published an article on that first Turkey Day without Shawn detailing how Pam and Craig planned to spend the holiday:

They'll check their e-mail instead of roasting a turkey.

They'll check in with police instead of slicing yams. . . .
. . . They'll eat, then they'll search.

Christmas proved to be an even harder emotional struggle for Shawn's family. Volunteer searchers had dwindled to a handful—on some days, nobody showed up to search for the eleven-year-old boy. On other days, inclement winter weather halted recovery efforts. And all around Pam and Craig people acted merry and bright, stringing sparkly lights on rooftops and hanging holiday ornaments on Christmas trees.

All of the mirth served as an exclamation point to the Akerses' grief, as a reminder of their son's absence. For instance, gifts wrapped in shiny paper and big bows arrived at their house for Shawn, sent by anonymous donors, but on that Christmas morning, no wide-eyed child gleefully tore off the wrappings and delighted in gifts. Instead, the presents "remained unopened, tucked under the holiday tree" at the Akerses' home, the Associated Press reported. "The most difficult part is seeing Shawn's presents still under the tree," Craig told the wire service as he recounted the family's first Christmas without Shawn. "Christmas was definitely harder than Thanksgiving, and I'm sure the next holiday will be harder than the last."

The new year, 2003, arrived with some hopeful news: a photograph of Shawn would arrive in more than seventy million mailboxes via the "Have You Seen Me?" direct-mail cards distributed by ADVO, a leading direct-mail advertising company based in Hartford, Connecticut, that collaborates with the National

Center for Missing and Exploited Children to choose children to spotlight on the cards. The "Have You Seen Me?" program began during the mid-1980s after a senior executive at the company watched the TV movie *Adam* about the Florida abduction and murder of six-year-old Adam Walsh, whose father John Walsh became an advocate for missing children and their families as well as host of the TV show *America's Most Wanted*. As of mid-2007, the cards have helped to bring home more than 140 missing children since the program's inception.

For Shawn's parents, the direct-mail campaign offered hope. Pam and Craig Akers also received continual words of encouragement and support from loved ones, who offered financial help while they took indefinite leaves from their jobs to concentrate on finding Shawn. Family and friends such as Wayne and Kim Evans, who live nearby and used to watch Shawn and their daughter jump on the trampoline in their front yard, were willing to mortgage their homes to help subsidize a monetary reward being offered to anyone with information leading to the recovery of Shawn. "I would have given anything to help bring home Shawn," Kim Evans said. "I just kept thinking, What if my child was missing?"

To cope without their son, the Akerses, with the help of relatives and friends, launched the Shawn Hornbeck Foundation in December 2002. Gleaned from the hours of experience Shawn's parents had acquired while looking for their son, the nonprofit organization helps other families in crisis in the location and recovery of missing and abducted children, according to its website, www.shawnhornbeckfoundation.com, "through a unique four-pronged approach that includes media relations and information distribution, search command center setup and operation, search and rescue team activation, and canine search teams."

The foundation also birthed the Shawn Hornbeck Search and Rescue Team, or SHSAR, a twenty-four-hour, seven-day-a-week operation, which, according to its website, www.sarteam.com, "is comprised of highly dedicated and skilled volunteers who are able to respond to both urban and wilderness emergencies in Missouri, Illinois, Arkansas, Indiana, Tennessee, Kentucky and Iowa. SHSAR team members are extensively trained in search techniques, tracking (ground and K-9), communications, wilderness search and rescue, urban search and rescue, and search management."

Like the Texas-based Laura Recovery Center, which was called in to help the Akerses coordinate search efforts for Shawn, the Shawn Hornbeck Foundation has emerged during the years following its formation as a key organization for helping missing children and their families. In return, the Akerses succeeded in channeling their grief into something positive.

Emotionally, having such a noble mission helped the Akerses survive the ordeal. Like a good therapist or psychiatric drug, engaging in altruistic acts can make people feel good, a phenomenon sometimes called "the glow of goodwill." The effect is more than just common sense but one that has been scientifically studied by academic researchers; for instance, in 2005, the *International Journal of Behavioral Medicine* published an article titled "Altruism,

Happiness and Health: It's Good to Be Good." It examines existing data on the correlation between selflessness and mental and physical health and, in essence, concludes that in most cases, those who help others experience happiness and better health.

"The greatest aspect of being a human is our capacity to give," said Dr. C. Robert Cloninger, a professor of psychology and psychiatry at Washington University in St. Louis and director of its Sansone Center for Well-Being. "When you take a tragedy and you convert it into something that helps others, then you make the whole thing meaningful. Even if you do not succeed in your case, you help someone else. . . . What Shawn's parents did was to look at things in a much more elevated way than just their own disappointment and rage. This is what the saints do in response to tragedy: They make certain sacrifices to help other people. This produces an improved biological, psychological, and spiritual state."

By contrast, wallowing in a tragedy—in the anger, the sadness, the fear—can result in poor health by fostering conditions such as stress and anxiety disorders, arthritis, heart problems, and breathing difficulties, among others. By forming a foundation to help other people, Dr. Cloninger said, Shawn's parents "converted what could have torn them up into a situation with meaning and purpose."

Even though they managed their emotions in an admirable manner, Pam and Craig Akers seemed desperate and willing to walk down any avenue that might lead them to their son. The couple consulted with several well-known psychics who they hoped would be able to provide some clues—answers that thousands of hours of searching and police investigation had failed to uncover—as to how Shawn disappeared and, most importantly, where he could be found.

One of those purported psychics was Sylvia Browne, a clairvoyant and frequent television guest on *The Montel Williams Show* and *Larry King Live* who claims to speak to the dead. On February 26, 2003, the Akerses traveled to New York City for a taping of *The Montel Williams Show*. On the show Browne offered Shawn's parents a psychic reading, in which she claimed Shawn was dead.

The *New York Daily News* reported that approximately a month after the show aired, Browne offered Shawn's parents a continuation of her psychic readings on the case for a fee—a claim that the clairvoyant has denied adamantly. "Pam was that desperate that if she had had $700 [the psychic's alleged fee] in her bank account she would have put it on the table," Wayne Evans, a family friend, told the newspaper. "We are talking about a mother who would have sold her soul to have her boy back. . . . Everybody was angry."

For her part, Browne told the *Daily News*: "I'm terribly sorry that this happened. But I think my body of work stands by itself. I've broken case after case. . . . I think it's cruel to jump on this one case in which I was wrong. I've said thousands of times I'm not God."

Shortly after Shawn disappeared, another famous psychic named James Van Praagh—who, like Browne, peddles his paranormal predictions on TV and in books—invited Craig and Pam Akers to travel to his studio in Los Angeles to appear as guests on his then-daytime talk show, *Beyond with James Van Praagh*. Like his clairvoyant competitor, Van Praagh proclaimed that Shawn was dead.

On January 21, 2007, less than two weeks after Shawn was found very much alive, Van Praagh posted a seven-paragraph mea culpa on his namesake website, an excerpt of which follows verbatim, mistakes included: "I am only human and I cannot always be accurate. I would never confess to such. If I was one hundred percent accurate. Every time one sits [to do a reading] it is indeed and experiment. I always have told every detective and family member including Shawn's parents, that I am not sure what I am getting, nor if any of this can help. I will give you my impressions and that is all I can do. There have been cases solved and others where people were brought to justice. I wish the same for this one."

Besides unnecessarily creating emotional havoc—the sting of having someone tell you that your child is dead—Sylvia Browne, James Van Praagh, and other unidentified psychics served as a distraction in Shawn's case, redirecting search efforts and draining time and resources from the police and volunteers, to say the least. A psychic is an unfortunate side effect of an already grim prognosis, said Bob Walcutt, who deals with them frequently as executive director of the Laura Recovery Center. "They're almost never right," he said. "They're a waste of time."

As if Pam and Craig Akers did not have enough on their minds.

As the first holidays without Shawn passed, and winter turned into spring and spring into summer, all with no new information about what had happened to their missing son, the family threw themselves into the Shawn Hornbeck Foundation. The Akerses hosted benefit dances and other fundraisers to defray costs incurred while searching for Shawn and launching the foundation, which offered free digital fingerprinting and photographing of children at events such as the St. Louis Boat and Sports Show at the Edward Jones Dome in downtown St. Louis.

Not wanting to lose the family's medical insurance, Pam eventually returned to work part-time at Fastrans Logistics in north St. Louis County, the *Post-Dispatch* reported; however, Craig continued his leave from Fastrans Logistics to lead the Shawn Hornbeck Foundation. "We're going to do anything and everything we can to help prevent this kind of tragedy [from] happening to someone else," Craig told the newspaper.

In July 2003, the Akerses prepared to observe Shawn's twelfth birthday without their son. The boy's family planned to spend the day, July 17, honoring Shawn with a dedication ceremony of a bench depicting a photograph of their boy as well as information describing the circumstances of his disappearance. The bench was part of a joint campaign, called "Sitting With An Angel," which was launched by the Shawn Hornbeck Foundation and Creative Placard Ads of Southern Illinois to help locate missing children.

The Shawn Hornbeck bench urges passersby: "Help Bring Me Home." Underneath the plea smiles the brown-eyed, brown-haired eleven-year-old boy, wearing a brown plaid shirt and an earring in his left ear. The bench was dedicated at a grocery store in the St. Louis suburb of Fenton, not far from Swing-A-Round Fun Town, the go-kart and bumper-boat park where Shawn had celebrated his eleventh birthday the year before.

In the months that followed, the Akerses continued to cling to hope, despite most people's belief that their son probably was dead. "There is still a lot of hope here," Craig told the *Daily Journal,* a newspaper serving parts of southeastern Missouri with a circulation of eight thousand. "Hope is what keeps us going."

Hope was all that the Akerses had. Before they knew it, nearly a year had passed and still no Shawn—and still no clues about how the boy disappeared that October Sunday. The law enforcement task force and volunteer searchers had failed to find Shawn's lime-green bicycle or even a shred of his clothing. It was one of the most baffling aspects of the case. As the one-year anniversary approached, folks kept repeating the same refrain as they did in the weeks after the boy's disappearance: it was as if Shawn had vaporized into thin air.

October 6, 2003, was a solemn day that began with a morning search of the woods by volunteers seeking evidence into the boy's disappearance. At Richwoods Elementary School, where Shawn would have been a sixth-grader, his classmates participated in a "Rally Around the Flag Pole" in his honor. A local church observed a moment of silence in Shawn's memory.

That evening, the town came together for a living memorial in honor of Shawn at the Richwoods Lions Club on Highway A, not far from where he disappeared. It was an evening of songs, of poems, and of prayers led by ministers from three local churches; an evening of tears and of tender embraces; and an evening of hope, punctuated by the planting of a maple tree in the boy's honor, just like the maple tree he liked to climb in front of his parents' house.

"Sometime when Shawn comes home, he can climb this maple tree," Craig Akers told the gathered crowd, according to the *Daily Journal*. Shawn's photograph sat beneath the tree bearing the inscription: "Remembering an Angel."

The *Daily Journal* covered the day's activities as well as the memorial ceremony of 150 people, publishing a moving account:

> Shawn's maternal grandmother, Doris Duff, often had to turn away to hide her tears during the observance. For her, the daily routine includes a morning telephone call to get instructions as to her duties for the day as part of the administrative core of the Shawn Hornbeck Search and Rescue Team.
>
> Lester Akers of Leadwood has spent most of the past year in the Richwoods area. He is Craig's father and has made the search and rescue effort the focus of his daily routine.
>
> Candles were raised high as [Pastor David] Godat sang a song based on the Bible's Book of Psalms. Tears streamed down the faces of many in the crowd, again young and old, and hugs were shared.
>
> As the observance ended, there was no rush to leave. A tragic and mysterious event had obviously bonded the people of this small community in a way not often seen.

CHAPTER 12

Becoming "Shawn Devlin"

Sometime after October 6, 2002, Shawn Hornbeck became Shawn Devlin.

Shawn had the same dark brown hair and, besides aging, otherwise looked like he did on the afternoon he disappeared from rural Richwoods. He still appeared as the brown-eyed boy on the thousands of "Have You Seen Me?" direct mailers delivered to homes throughout the St. Louis area. Like the boy grinning beneath the all-caps word "missing," which was emblazoned on hundreds of fliers distributed throughout his hometown and St. Louis metro. Like the boy in the brown plaid shirt smiling—always smiling—as he peered from a bench at a local Schnucks grocery store, imploring "Help Bring Me Home" to shoppers at the market roughly a mile from the St. Louis County apartment complex where the hostage Shawn Devlin would live for more than four years.

He was an eleven-year-old being held captive by a burly

barbarian, but no attempts were made to change Shawn's appearance to reflect his new persona as the son of Michael Devlin, a lonely pizza parlor manager, video game fanatic, and all-around loser—and, it seems, no radical attempts were made to disguise Shawn's true identity as the sweet, sometimes mischievous small-town boy whose tragic disappearance left a gaping gash in the hearts of those who had heard his story and especially those who knew him, most of all his family.

Even more curious was that Shawn lived most of his life in captivity for all to see, including law enforcement. Less than a year after his high-profile disappearance, Shawn summoned police. But he did not turn to the authorities to be rescued. Instead, Shawn called the cops to report his stolen bicycle—not the much-publicized lime-green mountain bike he was riding when he vanished but rather a 2003 Diamondback Joker BMX, according to a *St. Louis Post-Dispatch* investigation that obtained police records through a public-records request in early 2007. Based on the newspaper report, the stolen-bike incident occurred as follows:

On August 15, 2003, just ten months after Shawn's abduction, Kirkwood Police Officer Christopher Moss arrived at the run-down, redbrick apartment complex on South Holmes Avenue to check out complaints of two stolen bicycles, one of which was Shawn's BMX.

Shawn introduced himself to the police officer as Shawn Devlin. Someone had taken his new bike, he explained. He had left it outside his apartment some time around 10 p.m. the day before. When Shawn got up the next morning and went outside, at approximately 8:30 a.m., his bike was gone.

Officer Moss took notes: The BMX bike was sky-blue. It had pegs on both the front and rear tires, allowing a passenger to stand. The bike was bought the month before, in July, the month of Shawn's birthday, for $160.

"I spoke with Shawn Devlin and his father Michael Devlin," Moss wrote in the police report, which was quoted in the *Post-Dispatch*. "The Devlins had no suspect information."

Maybe there were no clues about who stole Shawn's sky-blue bike that August night.

And maybe Shawn's calm manner gave the police officer no indications that the boy was a hostage, the victim of a heinous crime.

But there were definitely clues, however veiled.

Shawn's appearance, for one. An obvious clue. The one everyone keeps coming back to: *Why didn't people recognize this boy?* The media, especially in St. Louis, had publicized photographs of the boy's face numerous times to millions of people. Shawn Hornbeck, the missing boy from nearby Washington County, was a major local crime story, and the police officer, being trained to solved crimes, presumably was aware of the case. Of all the people expected to make the connection between Shawn Devlin and Shawn Hornbeck, a police officer ranks at the top.

The name was a more subtle hint. The boy told the police officer that his name was Shawn, which was true. If there was even the slightest of notions by the officer that the kid resembled Shawn Hornbeck, the boy having the same first name might warrant further investigation—or at the very least, the name Shawn might jog a memory about the area's missing child.

Similarly, in the *Post-Dispatch* account, Shawn stated to the officer that his birth date was July 1, 1991, which is sixteen days earlier than his actual July 17 birthday, an event which was a big local story that year, in 2003: In front of the press, Shawn's parents had dedicated a missing child bench bearing their son's photograph in observance of his twelfth birthday, the first birthday since Shawn disappeared. The coverage was still fresh, almost a month to the date before the stolen-bike incident. In any case, the clues were there: Shawn Devlin was roughly the same age as Shawn Hornbeck.

Hmmm . . . the boys look alike, they are both named Shawn, and they are about the same age.

Police Officer Christopher Moss, who has subsequently left the Kirkwood Police Department to work for another law enforcement agency in St. Louis County, could not be reached for comment, so his version of the story is publicly unknown. And the Kirkwood Police Department declined comment.

To be fair to Officer Moss, he was not the only uniformed authority figure to overlook the clues, to let slip the opportunity to solve a major local crime, and, most importantly, to reunite a missing child with his family. Shawn roamed so freely during his life in captivity that he had several other encounters with police officers. In late 2006, he and Michael Devlin even smiled and waved at an off-duty Kirkwood police officer, who had recognized Devlin from the pizza parlor, according to the *Post-Dispatch*. "The officer noticed a boy with Devlin but gave it no thought." Shawn's best friend from the South Holmes Avenue apartment complex, Tony Douglas, has recounted to the media how, on at least three occasions, the cops stopped him and Shawn, once even giving the pair a ride home in a police cruiser.

The *Post-Dispatch* also reported on an additional exchange between Shawn and the police—this time, it was just before midnight on September 29, 2006, in Glendale, a sanguine suburb bordering Kirkwood: Shawn was riding his bike by himself when a police officer, who was diverting passersby away from the rubble of a house that had collapsed, stopped the boy on tree-lined Essex Avenue. Again, Shawn told the police officer that his name was Shawn Devlin. He gave his date of birth as July 7, 1991, ten days earlier than his real birthday. He said he was returning to his home in Kirkwood after visiting a friend. "He was wearing dark clothing and didn't have reflectors on his bike," Glendale Police Sergeant Bob Catlett told the *Post-Dispatch*. "The officer stopped him to find out who he was. He just appeared to be a typical fifteen-year-old kid riding his bike from a friend's house. He said he was Shawn Devlin, and we had no reason to doubt him."

Especially not when Shawn Devlin's "father" called Glendale police, thereby serving as a parental verification of sorts about the boy's identity. According to an FBI report, Michael Devlin called the officer's supervisor to complain about the cop's treatment of Shawn. He explained that "Shawn did not immediately answer the officer's questions because Shawn was out of breath from traveling up a hill on his bike." The conversation left Devlin feeling slighted. "Devlin felt that the Glendale police supervisor did not treat Devlin well. The police supervisor threatened to arrest Devlin for getting boisterous. The police supervisor also told Devlin that he did not have time for Devlin."

No one seemed to have a reason to doubt Shawn Devlin. Even if people thought he looked like Shawn Hornbeck, the boy's response to any prodding seemed to quell concerns. According to the *Post-Dispatch,* in late 2006 someone asked him directly about his identity:

> *Are you really that kidnapped boy?*
>
> *Shawn, then 15, was briefly away from his abductor. He was headed in a car with a good friend to a wrestling match. His friend's mother, Grace Milliken, drove. Her cell phone rang.*
>
> *It was her cousin, who had noticed a missing-persons poster with Shawn Hornbeck's photo outside a Kmart. The image, although nearly four years old, looked just like the boy she knew as Shawn Devlin. The nose. The shape of the mouth. The earring in one ear. Could it be?*
>
> *Milliken thought her cousin was crazy, but she turned to Shawn. "Is that your real dad or were you taken?" Milliken asked, half-joking.*

Shawn looked dumbfounded, Milliken recalls. "Why would you ask that?" he responded. "That's my real dad." And it was dropped.

Even Shawn's best friend's family joked with him about how he resembled Shawn Hornbeck. Yet Shawn's calm, unaffected response gave no indication that he was scared or sad, as most people would expect a captive child to behave. Nor did his "dad" appeared worried or distracted, as if he were hiding something, as some people would expect a kidnapper to act.

One of the few times Shawn was hidden out of sight was for a short period in June 2004, when Michael Devlin drove 1,400 miles to Prescott, Arizona, for his brother's wedding. But none of Devlin's family members or friends noticed the brown-haired teenager who had been missing for two years, according to media accounts.

Then again, Bob Collett, a family friend who attended the wedding, recalled to the *Post-Dispatch* that Devlin appeared to be the only guest from the St. Louis area who drove instead of flew. He also checked into a different hotel than the Missouri crowd. "Nobody in the wedding party saw any boy around," Collett told the newspaper. "This whole thing is so bizarre."

In October 2007, Devlin pleaded guilty in federal court to two counts of transporting a minor across state lines for sex—one for the twenty-hour road trip to the wedding in Arizona, the other for a five-day trip to Chicago in February 2004.

For the most part, however, Devlin and Shawn lived together in plain sight. The purported father and son were together all the time, coming and going, pitching a tent in the patchy grass in front of their apartment, driving Devlin's white Nissan pickup in the nearby parking lot, Shawn's face as clear as daylight. Shawn was allowed to carry a cell phone, log onto the Internet, ride his bike to a nearby Wal-Mart, and generally wander St. Louis's suburbs. Shawn had friends whose parents took him on outings and allowed him to spend the night at their homes. That Shawn Devlin could be someone else sounded like the unbelievable premise of a Hollywood movie, because common sense says that no kidnapped kid would appear so normal, and Shawn Devlin seemed as normal as could be.

So normal that when he was fifteen years old, Shawn, like other boys his age, had a girlfriend. According to the *Post-Dispatch,* the young lady lived about two miles from South Holmes Avenue, and the two held hands around the apartment complex and at West County Mall in Des Peres, a higher-end shopping center with a Nordstrom anchor in an affluent suburb that borders Kirkwood.

Shawn's girlfriend, the newspaper reported, was a freshman at Visitation Academy, or Viz as it is known locally. The all-girls college-preparatory Catholic school in wealthy west St. Louis County is highly esteemed in the community, with roots dating back to 1883 when it was founded by the Sisters of the Visitation. The school is exclusive and small, with 419 girls enrolled in the upper school that includes grades seven through twelve. During the 2006–2007 school year, the annual tuition rate for upper-grade students to attend Viz was $13,230, which includes lunch but not the required uniforms, books, and laptop computers.

In metro St. Louis, there are single-sex Catholic high schools aplenty, and natives take pride in their alma maters as they would a university. Dances, dinners, and auctions are considered huge social events. One of the most anticipated—what some of the area's well-to-do call "the social event of the season"—is the traditional winter dance for the young women from Viz and the young men from Saint Louis Priory School, an exclusive all-boys college-preparatory Catholic school in west St. Louis County.

On December 9, 2006, Shawn, who did not attend any school, and his girlfriend attended the Viz-Priory dance, held on Priory's sprawling university-like campus in Creve Coeur, a posh suburb of mostly large, elegant homes. His girlfriend had no idea that Shawn Devlin was really Shawn Hornbeck, that he was anyone other than a cute guy she liked and dated, according to the *Post-Dispatch*, which broke the story. Those who knew the Viz girl said she met Shawn at Kirkwood Park—a sprawling seventy-two acres and the city's most populated park—one afternoon when she went there with some friends from school.

That a kidnapped boy associated with a man who committed such evil acts had punctured the insulated world of Catholic school dances spooked many parents who, in part, send their daughters and sons to exclusive schools as a way to bubble-wrap them, to protect their children from societal ills by placing them in idyllic settings with peers of similar economic, ethnic, and religious backgrounds.

Once Shawn Devlin's true identity was revealed to the Viz community, it was all students and parents could talk about: *Shawn Hornbeck was at their dance!* Talk among parents and students ranged from Oh! My! God! disbelief to anger and fear over their daughters potentially becoming victims of a crime to guilt about no one recognizing the abducted child. Viz administrators brought counselors on campus to help the girls talk about their anguish.

Shawn's girlfriend apparently struggled emotionally. The last time she talked to Shawn Devlin was the night before the world discovered that he was Shawn Hornbeck. She told police that he had acted "odd all week" before he was discovered, the *Post-Dispatch* reported: During a telephone conversation, he had warned her that his dad disapproved of people just "showing up" at their apartment. He had gone to her house looking visibly upset. He told her "he would be leaving town for a wedding in Illinois over the weekend," the newspaper said.

"I know it's getting hard for her because everyone is giving her a hard time," said a Viz student who knew Shawn's girlfriend and saw the two together, as quoted in the *Post-Dispatch*. "They're saying, 'Oh, you must have known he was missing or had been abducted.' But honestly, she had no idea."

No one had a clue. That was the refrain. "We had no idea it was Shawn Hornbeck at the Viz-Priory dance," Visitation's head of school, Rosalie Henry, told the *Post-Dispatch*. "We are just in total shock about this, as any school would be."

Shocked because these sorts of things do not happen in affluent neighborhoods. Shocked because it seemed unfathomable that an abducted teenager would attend a popular and much-publicized dance between two of the area's most exclusive private schools. Shocked because Shawn was just a typical kid.

But the boy who seemed so normal also appeared to be dropping online hints—albeit subtle ones—to the world about his true identity through a bold presence on the Internet as well as cryptic postings.

In 2004 and 2005, Shawn—or Michael Devlin posing as Shawn—purportedly created at least four Internet profiles, including posted photos of Shawn Devlin on various websites. On one of the profiles—http://profiles.yahoo.com/shawn_the_pumpkin_king—the dark-haired, dour-faced boy in the photo does indeed resemble Shawn. The boy is wearing a bright-blue shirt, standing next to what appears to be the back of a chair and beneath either a framed mirror or a picture (which is odd, as all accounts of Michael Devlin's apartment described the place as messy with old and worn furnishings and no curtains, so for there to be decoration on the wall is counterintuitive). It is unclear whether Shawn created the Internet profiles, or if Devlin did, but the photos and information—which were still accessible online in the year after his rescue—seem to pertain to Shawn.

The details of the pumpkin king profile are as follows, spelling and grammar unedited:

Member Since 11/25/2005

Last Update: 02/21/2006

Basics

Yahoo! ID:

shawn_the_pumpkin_king

Real Name:

Shawn Devlin

Nickname:

Kyo

Location:

St.louis MO kirkwood

Age:

Marital Status:

No Answer

Sex:

Male

Occupation:

not jack shit

More About Me

Hobbies:

listen to music,playing games,talking to ppl on the computer,hanging out with friends,writeing poems,and some other shit

Latest News:

> if i would tell you my latest news now then when
> you look it might not be

When the other Yahoo profile—http://profiles.yahoo.com/kyo_ kmk_forlife—was created is unclear. But it is sparser, with no photograph and fewer descriptions:

Basics

Yahoo! ID:

kyo_kmk_forlife

Real Name:

shawn

Nickname:

Kyo

Location:

Kirkwood

Age:

18

Marital Status:

No Answer

Sex:

Male

The third purported profile about Shawn was on the social networking site MindViz.com, which the user joined on June 18, 2006. The profile, which was online in spring 2007 but removed by year's end, had the same picture of Shawn in the bright-blue shirt that is posted in the pumpkin-king Yahoo profile. Here is what is listed, unedited, under "Shawn's Information:"

Here for: Friends

Status: Single

Orientation: Straight

Kids? Someday

My Pet: Cat

Horoscope: Cancer

Zodiac: Ram

Body Type: Slim & Slender

Height: 5'9"

Eyes: Brown Eyes

Religion: Atheist

Ethnicity: Kirkwook

Education: High School

An avid Xbox player, Shawn also appeared in an Internet profile on GamerTagPics (www.gamertagpics.com), which dubs itself as "Xbox Live's Biggest Online Gamertag Community." Curiously, the profile appears to have been created by—or at least used by—Michael Devlin. Gamertag Radio, an online radio show "dedicated to the 'Xbox Live Community' and also to help unite all the online gamers," is credited with breaking the story linking Shawn to the Xbox site. According to its report from January 2007:

It turns out that Devlin is not only the owner of Xbox Live gamertag appropriately named "DevilDevlin," but had also registered an account on Gamertagpics.com. Gamertagpics.com is a popular social networking site for Xbox Live members. While 41 year old Michael Devlin was the owner of the profile on Gamertagpics, the profile features a picture of Shawn Hornbeck which appears to have been taken outside Devlin's apartment.

The teenager in the photo resembles Shawn—the thin, dark-haired boy is wearing an unbuttoned blue shirt over a white T-shirt and jeans. The young man is standing in front of the run-down redbrick apartment building where Michael Devlin lived until his arrest in January 2007.

Gamertag Radio's report continued: "The profile on Gamertagpics was registered in 2005 and has been inactive for 232 days. . . . The gamertag was likely shared by Michael Devlin and Shawn Hornbeck, or used by Shawn exclusively."

Another computer game fan site, Kotaku (www.kotaku. com), which claims it "provides hourly links and commentary for obsessive gamers—and explores the cultural ramifications interesting enough to attract a wider audience," analyzed stats of the gamertag DevilDevlin and reported that the account was accessed on January 12, 2007, the day of the rescue of Shawn Hornbeck and Ben Ownby, the thirteen-year-old kidnapped by Devlin four days before police found the boy.

Devlin appears to have used his home computer for more than just playing video games. In October 2007, he pleaded guilty in U.S. District Court to four counts of producing child pornography. In particular, Devlin made sexually explicit videotapes and photographs of himself with Shawn. At the court hearings that October, the Associated Press reported that "prosecutors say Devlin also made a videotape of himself torturing Shawn while the boy screamed for him to stop."

According to the website of the National Center for Missing and Exploited Children (www.missingkids.com), young victims of child pornography can face additional hurdles in their emotional recovery:

The lives of children featured in these illegal images are forever altered, not only by the molestation but by the permanent record of the exploitation. Once sexual exploitation takes place, the molester may document these encounters on film or video. This documentation can then become the "ammunition" needed to blackmail the child into further submission, which is necessary to continue the relationship and maintain its secrecy. In addition these documented images allow molesters to "relive" their sexual fantasies with children long after the exploitation has stopped.

A greater number of child molesters are now using computer technology to organize and maintain their collections of these illegal images. In addition they are also using the Internet to increase the size of these collections. Person-ally manufactured illegal images of children are especially valuable on the Internet, which provide the molester with a respected status among fellow exploiters and traders of this material. Once this status is achieved, molesters will often begin to trade images of their own sexual exploits with children among themselves.

When these images reach cyberspace, they are irretriev-able and can continue to circulate forever. Thus the child is revictimized as the images are viewed again and again.

While in captivity Shawn turned to the computer to send a cryptic message that he hoped his parents would decipher. On December 1, 2005, at 1:59 a.m., the website for the Shawn Horn-beck Foundation received an eerie posting from a Shawn Devlin of Kirkwood: "how long are you planing [sic] to look for you son?"

Later that day, at 2:56 p.m., Shawn Devlin of Kirkwood posted a follow-up message (included here exactly as it was written): "hey sorry about that last thing i put on there,i write poems and i was wounding if it would be ok to write a poem for the hornbeck fam. and they son 'shawn Hornbeck' it would be cool if i could but if you dont want me to i can understan why i guess but i was wounding if i could write a poem in his horner (sorry i dont know how to spell that last word)."

About two years after Shawn posted that message, after he had been reunited with his family, he acknowledged to TV host Oprah Winfrey that he wrote the message "hoping it might give some kind of hint."

Shawn's stepfather, Craig Akers, told Oprah he recalled the message and, at the time, thought "this is someone trying to yank my chain" because the answer to the question—how long were he and his wife, Pam, going to look for their son?—was an obvious one. "We knew that the world knew the answer to that because we had been saying all along that we will never stop looking for our son," Akers said on *Oprah*. "So I kind of found it strange. And you get so many of these messages, I mean, on a daily basis. You get so many weird, out-there messages that . . ."

> **Oprah Winfrey:** Yeah. But were you struck by this one in any way?
> **Craig Akers:** No. Unfortunately, I wasn't.
> **Winfrey:** You were not?
> **Akers:** I wish I had been.

Shawn's family. The police. The public. Everyone, it seemed, missed Shawn's clues.

The missing boy who, for years, carried a cell phone, surfed the Internet, talked with police officers, and cultivated friendships did, in fact, transmit help signals—just not the obvious ones people would have expected.

CHAPTER 13
Invisible Chains

On a frigid January day in 2007, Dr. C. Robert Cloninger sat at his big wooden desk snug in his St. Louis office, nestled among rows of filing cabinets and floor-to-ceiling bookcases overflowing with academic journals, medical encyclopedias, and hundreds of books, including eight that he wrote. As an internationally noted scientist in psychiatry and psychology, Dr. Cloninger is often asked to provide expert testimony in criminal court hearings—and on this gray day, inside Washington University's medical complex, the professor was evaluating a hostage crisis that had occurred the year before in Phoenix, Arizona.

The case involved forty-two-year-old George L. Curran, who held nine people captive at gunpoint inside a hearing room of the National Labor Relations Board. Armed with two guns and a knife, Curran was reportedly disgruntled because he had previously filed a complaint with the agency and it had been dismissed. During the seven-hour standoff, the victims—intelligent people such as a judge and an attorney—were protective of the man who could end their lives with one shot from his pistol. They urged the FBI not to hurt their captor. After the ordeal that ended with the hostages' safe release, one of the victims told the Associated Press: "I feel sorry for George. He's a troubled person. He seemed to have some psychological problems."

Stockholm Syndrome, thought Dr. Cloninger.

That afternoon, his phone rang. It was a local journalist wanting to talk with him about Shawn Hornbeck, the kidnapped boy who had been discovered alive after four years. The reporter wanted analysis about this bizarre case: Shawn had access to a cell phone and the Internet, so why wouldn't he have sought help? Shawn lived in plain sight and had friends with whom he roamed about town, so why wouldn't he have tried to escape? Shawn's parents lived only an hour away, so why wouldn't he have bolted? Could Shawn have liked his life in captivity? Why didn't he leave?

Dr. Cloninger found himself explaining the mechanisms of Stockholm Syndrome, a complex condition that, in its simplest definition, is a mental state in which people threatened and held against their will become loyal to their captor. One of the most widely cited examples of Stockholm Syndrome involves newspaper heiress Patty Hearst, who was kidnapped by the Symbionese Liberation Army in 1974. After her abduction, she publicly aligned with her captors and joined them in an armed bank robbery.

All around the country, psychologists and psychiatrists were receiving similar media calls. They, too, explained Stockholm Syndrome as a possible reason for Shawn's behavior. Thereafter, the condition seemed to become a household term, bandied about in the press, used casually as if describing an everyday ailment like the flu. As in, "Oh, he had Stockholm Syndrome. He's better now." It seemed the pat answer, perfect for a society full of people with short attention spans who like immediate resolutions and black-and-white answers.

But as Dr. Cloninger or most any other expert will attest, Shawn's behavior during his captivity is anything but simple. Shawn seemed to have exhibited symptoms of Stockholm Syndrome, but whether he had the condition per se is difficult to diagnose without professional assessment, according to Dr. Cloninger and approximately a dozen experts who are uninvolved with the case but familiar with it. Even if Shawn had Stockholm Syndrome, other psychological and biological forces were likely at play, which will be explored.

But first, let us tour Stockholm Syndrome. To understand the complexities of the condition, one must plunge into the deep recesses of the psyche, below conscious thought and into the primitive. Guiding the expedition is Dr. Frank Ochberg, who is credited internationally with helping to define the term Stockholm Syndrome. The name stems from an armed robbery that occurred at Sveriges Kreditbank in central Stockholm, Sweden, in August 1973. There, two men held four bank employees hostage in an eleven-by-forty-seven-foot vault for five days. During this time, one hostage formed an emotional attachment to one of the assailants and continued to defend the gunman after his release. She even fell in love with him, calling off her prior wedding plans to become engaged to a man who had threatened her life.

At the time, Dr. Ochberg held a high-ranking position at the National Institute of Mental Health. The Harvard-educated psychiatrist also served as a member of the U.S. Department of Justice's National Task Force on Disorders and Terrorism, in which Dr. Ochberg helped to oversee the publication of a 661-page report on law enforcement and hostage negotiations. The term Stockholm Syndrome had not entered the professional vernacular but law enforcement and behavioral scientists had for years acknowledged among themselves the phenomenon, which on the surface seemed so odd.

For law enforcement and mental health experts, the mid-1970s was an exciting time marked by the merging of the two disciplines. In 1974, for instance, the FBI established its Behavioral Science Unit in Quantico, Virginia, which develops criminal profiling techniques. The National Task Force's report on hostage negotiations also typified this confluence of specialties. By 1976, Dr. Ochberg accepted a prestigious fellowship in forensic psychiatry at the University of London and began consulting for the FBI and London Metropolitan Police (Scotland Yard). In those capacities, he continued to study the curious condition now known as Stockholm Syndrome. His research entailed interviewing dozens of people who had been held hostage both in the United States and abroad, including American embassy officials, a senior magistrate in Rome, and a top editor for one of Holland's largest newspapers. He debriefed former hostages, both male and female, who were of diverse ages, ethnicities, and economic backgrounds but similar in that they had formed an emotional bond with their captors.

"What were they all telling me?" Dr. Ochberg asked. "They said, 'I didn't expect to have this feeling. It surprised me. It was a positive feeling.'"

Based on his research, in 1977, Dr. Ochberg wrote an internal memorandum to the FBI, explaining the syndrome. "Three things must occur," he said, recapping the memo. "First, there is a set of positive feelings that are ironic and paradoxical. They flow from the hostage to one of the hostage takers. Second, the reciprocity of positive feelings from the hostage taker for the hostage, and that's very important. The third factor is that the two of them together are joined in their distrust, or even hatred, for us on the outside."

And here is where we must submerge ourselves in the murkiness of the human psyche. Dr. Ochberg has jumped in many times: "If you or I are held hostage, it's a shattering experience. You see it on television so much but it's not the same as it happening to you. It's not just that we think we are going to die, but we might reach a point where we say, 'We're as good as dead.' And it's shocking. It's out of the blue. We're not trained to handle this. We're not anticipating this, and it's stunning and terrifying."

Dr. Ochberg dives deeper: "I would postulate that in those conditions we become like an infant, like a one-year-old. We can't move without permission. We don't sleep. We can't use the toilet. I remember one woman in particular telling me how embarrassing it was to be held in captivity and have to use a bucket to defecate in front of these thugs. Psychologically, that makes you like an infant. And then, somebody gives you permission to talk, permission to use the toilet, permission to eat, and it is profound. It's like this person is your mother, and the bond is like a mother-child bond. What is that bond and how does an infant experience it? Psychoanalysts make all kinds of assumptions about what the bond is. I would say the feeling would be profound and primordial, a basic and positive feeling, undifferentiated. It is the feeling that eventually—depending on age, gender, and other factors—can be experienced as romantic love, as child-parent love, as deep friendship. All the varieties of human love come from a common fountainhead and this is the one that the hostage has returned to."

And even deeper: "There is something in the human mammal that is very important," Dr. Ochberg said. "Like other great apes, we spend a long time one-on-one with our mothers. This is not true of most members of the animal kingdom.

I've gone on observation projects with orangutans in Borneo and chimps in Liberia, and this was the case. It is something we share with our evolutionary close link. It must be something in both the mother and the infant that is a powerful, genetically determined, readily controlled part of attachment. . . . In the terror of hostage scenarios, in the opening moments of this, we are terrified and we are closely attached to the person who causes us to be in the situation but who is also our only hope for survival. And it is unconscious."

So powerful is the bond that victims can mirror their captor's beliefs and sympathize with their causes; for instance, if the hostage taker is mad at the government, often the victim becomes angry too. For instance, Michael Devlin reportedly instilled in Shawn a deep distrust of law enforcement. If the captor distrusts authority, the victim also becomes wary and, as was the case in the Stockholm bank robbery, defends the criminal to justice officials. And when the hostage is rescued—when the maternal-like bond is severed—Dr. Ochberg said a sense of loss among victims can emerge in the ensuing months, even years.

"Usually, when people talked about their feelings, after it was all over, they felt depressed," the psychiatrist said. "It's as if someone died. They've lost their mother. They've lost someone close to them. They've lost an attachment in their lives. And there it is again, this unconscious, irrational, ironic love for the person who gave them life. In their circumstances their mind denied that this is the person who could take away their life."

Stockholm Syndrome is a survival mechanism that has applied to men, women, and children in other type of hostage situations, from concentration and prisoner camps to hijackings and abductions. Some experts believe that characteristics of the condition also can be found among victims who may have the physical freedom to roam but are mentally held hostage, for example in cases of domestic violence.

With the nitty-gritty details of the Shawn Hornbeck kidnapping case shielded from the public, and without knowing the results of psychological and psychiatric examinations, it is impossible to conclude with certainty that the boy suffered from Stockholm Syndrome. But mental health professionals assessing a child who was kidnapped would look at several elements. For instance, what was the child's home life like before his abduction? The better the family situation, Dr. Ochberg said, the more likely the syndrome occurred and can explain bonding with a captor. By contrast, a child from an abusive home might form a different kind of attachment to the perpetrator because the child views the new circumstances as liberating, as warped as that might seem to the average person.

One former FBI agent said that this is sometimes the case for girls whose home life consists of sexual molestation by their fathers. An older guy comes along, befriends the girl, and lures her into his home where she stays either by choice or not. But if the girl had to make a decision between having sex with a stranger or acquaintance and having sex with her father, the father is usually the least preferable victimizer, simply because of the complex psychological and biological bonds between a parent and child.

In Shawn's case, few details have been revealed about his family life. But by all accounts, Shawn's mother and stepfather demonstrated unwavering dedication to their son in the days, months, and years after the eleven-year-old boy was kidnapped. Their love for their child beamed across the TV screens; their pain seared. And except for some criticism for allowing Shawn to appear on *The Oprah Winfrey Show* in the days after his rescue, no one has come forth denouncing Pam and Craig Akers' parenting abilities. This is somewhat amazing considering that in high-profile media cases, people often tell tall tales as they seek their fifteen minutes of fame—and any cash payout that might come with it.

The only negative public statement about Shawn's family was a *New York Post* article on the boy's biological father, the late Walter Hornbeck, "a convicted sex offender who did three years in a Missouri prison on drug and sodomy charges." The newspaper reports that Walter Hornbeck—who was sixty years old when Shawn was born in 1991—was divorced by Pam when Shawn was an infant.

The *Post* article described Walter Hornbeck being charged with rape on September 30, 1992, in Washington County, where Shawn lived with his mother and two older sisters, who were six and seven at the time. Although court records were sealed, the newspaper reported, "a court official said the reference number on Hornbeck's criminal conviction indicated the charge involved an assault on a minor. . . . Hornbeck pleaded guilty to attempted sodomy, a felony, as well as possession of a controlled substance and he was sentenced to seven years in state prison in 1994."

Shawn never had contact with his biological father after the man went to jail, the *Post* reported.

When Shawn was still a baby, Craig Akers assumed the role of father. Friends of the family said that, as a boy, Shawn idolized Craig and wanted to work with computers, like his stepfather did, when he grew up. Adoption papers were being filled out at the time of Shawn's abduction, the media reported.

Besides assessing the family in determining whether Stockholm Syndrome applies to an abducted child such as Shawn, Dr. Ochberg said, "we have to pay a lot of attention to the hours in which he was transformed from one life to another. Did that occur in a way which terrified him and victimized him and then the positive feelings happened? If the answer is yes, then the Stockholm Syndrome is a very good model for why he stayed."

Kidnapper Michael Devlin used a gun to abduct Shawn, repeatedly sexually assaulted the boy and, within the first month after his disappearance, attempted to choke the eleven-year-old to death. Based on an interview with a police investigator, the Associated Press reported that "Shawn's isolation and abuse during that first month was so intense that the then 11-year-old's identity was torn apart, the official said. Over time, Shawn began to see Devlin as his protector and surrogate parent in a pattern common to many abuse victims."

"The Stockholm Syndrome would explain the early attachment to the kidnapper," Dr. Ochberg said, "but what explains maintaining that attachment to the kidnapper for years after? At some point it is no longer the Stockholm Syndrome. At some point these dynamics grow into something else."

And here is where the mental landscape shifts. We are still swimming deep in the human psyche but now we are exploring a condition called indoctrination, and for this journey we turn to guidance from another internationally esteemed psychiatrist, Dr. Lenore Terr, who conducted groundbreaking research on a group of children in the Central California farm town of Chowchilla, where twenty-six boys and girls and an adult bus driver were kidnapped from a school bus and buried in a quarry in July 1976. The bus driver and some of the older children dug their way to freedom less than twenty-four hours later. All of the children were rescued, and no one was physically injured in the kidnap-for-ransom scheme. Dr. Terr interviewed the children shortly after their release and conducted periodic assessments of their mental state. Her research uncovered a greater understanding of childhood trauma, of how one shattering event can cause a child to suffer from long-term anxiety and disturbing recollections, of how it can cause a child to relive the terrifying incident, just like an emotionally haunted adult diagnosed with post-traumatic stress disorder.

With more than forty years' experience in child psychiatry, Dr. Terr has treated hundreds of children traumatized by kidnapping and sexual molestation, by torturous abusers and depraved living conditions. She described how the mental indoctrination typically occurs after the initial shock and surprise of the traumatic incident takes hold: "A lot of these kids are told after the first moments, told over and over again, that their parents don't want them. They're told that there is no place to go home to, that their parents are dead. I have seen children kidnapped by their own one parent who tells them that the other parent—the parent with custody—doesn't want custody, that the parent is getting married to somebody else and doesn't want the kid any more. They are told a number of things. And kids believe them."

Children believe the adults "because all kids are naughty, any normal kid is naughty," said Dr. Terr, a clinical professor of psychiatry at the UCSF School of Medicine who maintains a busy practice. "By naughty I mean the kind of stuff all kids do. They didn't wipe their rear end when they went to the bathroom, or they did something germy, or they looked at a dirty picture, or they did something at school they don't want their parents to know about. Or they cooked up some scheme to poison their neighbor, they didn't really, but they're feeling like a really bad person for thinking about it."

The guilt makes them more vulnerable to believing a child predator who, for instance, might say, "Your parents know how bad you are and they don't want you any more."

This type of technique was perfected in the case of Steven Stayner—the Northern California boy who was abducted at age seven in December 1972, lived in plain sight near his parents' home, and called his kidnapper "Dad" before escaping to police seven years later. According to a 1984 article in *Newsweek*, Kenneth Parnell succeeded in snatching little Steven when he "pretended to phone Mrs. Stayner, then said he had gotten her permission to keep Steven overnight. He [Parnell] learned that Steven had been punished by his father the day before and played on it, telling Steven later that his parents didn't want him."

Even if the abducted child's parents are on television tearfully telling the world how much they love their son or daughter and how they will never stop searching, the kidnapped child can still believe the captor's nefarious antics. He might tell the child lies along the lines of: "I just heard from your parents, and they don't want you. They're just appearing on TV so that they look good. It's all an act. They're happy that you're finally out of the house."

Such words don't just sting, they stab. This is especially true of children who come from homes where their worth is questioned, where abuse thrives. But even children whose parents make them feel loved, cherished, and valued are not protected from a predator's psychological brainwashing. "If a kid feels guilty or naughty about anything, secretive about anything, the kid gets the feeling that it has caught up with him," Dr. Terr said. "So they believe the lies. Also, kids are taught to believe adults, and they do."

And then there is the most frightening threat of all: Try and escape, the kidnapper says, and I'll kill your mom. I'll kill your dad. Your sister or brother. Your best friend. Your dog. Escape, and I'll kill you.

No one knows for sure what was said specifically to Shawn Hornbeck or Ben Ownby during their abductions. But it is known that the boys were abused psychologically, physically, and sexually. And Shawn did tell authorities he feared Devlin would "mess with my family," the *St. Louis Post-Dispatch* reported.

Dipping deeper into the mental indoctrination process, another restraining device emerges when the abductor assumes "control over the child's eating and sleeping, the child goes to the bathroom when he [the captor] says the child can go to the bathroom," said Dr. Terr, who has received dozens of professional honors, including multiple awards from the American Psychiatric Association. "That person becomes the child's only means of living. Children can't live on their own. They can't provide for themselves. There's a certain loyalty that develops to the person controlling your basic needs."

According to the Associated Press, Shawn told his grandmother that during his captivity Devlin sometimes would wake him every forty-five minutes. Sleep deprivation is a common way to break a victim's will, to coerce subordination. Shawn was only a child when he was tortured, but the technique has worked on many intelligent, strong-willed adults, including Senator John McCain, R-Arizona, when he was a prisoner of war in North Vietnam. The two-time presidential candidate has publicly spoken and written about the torture he endured at the prison camp, where guards prevented him from sleeping for extended time periods and beat him every few hours. McCain's hostage-takers employed other successful psychological tactics, as was true in the cases of Shawn and Ben. McCain succumbed to his captors' demands, and, at one point, he reported feeling hopeless and suicidal.

McCain is an example of a strong, educated military man who caved in to his captors' psychological and physical abuses. Shawn and Ben were vulnerable, impressionable, physically small children. How could they not become putty to Devlin's warped ways?

And yet people across the globe rushed to judgment in the days and months after Shawn and Ben were discovered. Not so much against Ben, missing for four and a half days. The public seemed to excuse him from scrutiny. But not Shawn, no way, not the boy who had been gone for more than four years and seemingly had every opportunity to escape. It just boggled the mind why he didn't. So people made assumptions: He liked Devlin, he hated his family. His life with Devlin was better than his life with his parents, and, gee, how bad must his parents be if their kid doesn't even want to come home?

The judgment can be found in Internet chat rooms and on blogs, as well as in articles published far and wide and, of course, on TV and radio talk shows. Most notably, Bill O'Reilly, host of Fox News' *The O'Reilly Factor*, said a few days after Hornbeck's rescue: "The situation here, for this kid, looks to me to be a lot more fun than what he had under his old parents. He didn't have to go to school, he could run around and do whatever he wanted.... And I think, when it all comes down, what's gonna happen is, there was an element here that this kid liked about his circumstances."

And now for a brief side trip into a human's ability to adapt and satiate desires—in this case for material goods— even under the worst of circumstances. It is not that Shawn might have enjoyed his identity as Shawn Devlin better than his life as Shawn Hornbeck. The iPod, the Xbox 360, the lax household rules, the no school were simply additional locks to prevent the boy from fleeing, said Dr. Charles Figley, founder and director of the esteemed Florida State University Traumatology Institute and the Psychosocial Stress Research Program in Tallahassee. Shawn's time in captivity is not about hating his prior life and loving his new one. It's about incentives and disincentives. It's about Shawn making the best of the horrible situation he was in. It's about his abductor getting Shawn to like him, sprinkling in gifts and fun among the threats and torture to create positive feelings to keep the boy afloat amidst the abuse.

An editor of an international academic journal on trauma and a researcher whose writings on trauma and stress have appeared in more than two hundred books and peer-reviewed publications, Dr. Figley offered his assessment: Shawn "seemed to thrive despite all these difficulties. He was sexually assaulted and terrorized, and his captor threatened him in all kinds of ways, not just to himself but to people that he cares about."

Shawn may have had high hopes to be rescued, as he told Oprah Winfrey. However, "it is a normal human development that you make the best of a situation," said Dr. Figley, a social work professor at FSU whose degrees are in human development. "You can fantasize about other things, but it's only a fantasy. You don't really act upon it. Probably his [Shawn's] statement about missing his family every day is true but for various reasons, he did not attempt to transform that fantasy into a reality, probably based on the perpetrator's programming."

Dr. Figley continued to wade. "The perpetrator terrorized him and convinced him that his life was in his hands," he said, "but the guillotine, the threat, was not constant enough to motivate the kid to go. So there was this amazing balance that the perpetrator used to scare the kid and to comply with what he wanted but also providing resources and incentives to convince the kid to stay. . . . My sense is he [Shawn] knew he was loved and cared for and would always be accepted at home. But at the same time, there was enough to keep him there, mostly in regard to threats, but also in the kind of resources and identity that suited his needs. Someone of his age is going through a phase in their life when they are attempting to differentiate who they are apart from other people, especially their family. So consequently, this perpetrator created an identity for him."

As Shawn Devlin, the boy allegedly committed some eyebrow-raising deeds during his time in captivity. For instance, unauthenticated photographs online show Shawn wearing a red bandanna over his mouth and nose while aiming a gun at the camera. Another picture captures him flashing what appear to be gang signs. Law enforcement officials called it a "different side" of Shawn during a broadcast on the Fox News Channel.

However, if Shawn did anything wrong, most experts agree: It was not Shawn's fault. It was Michael Devlin waging psychological warfare on Shawn.

And here we descend back into the murkiness of the human psyche. Treading among the initial terror of being abducted, the mental indoctrination, and the control of basic needs is another psychological shackle used against some kidnapped children, and that is the bottom feeder of all tactics, the sexual element. Because it is a rough trip, we have both Dr. Terr and Dr. Ochberg navigating.

Most people do not like to think of children as sexual beings, but they are—even babies whose genitals are touched can experience pleasure. Of course children are not ready developmentally for sexual activity nor, most people would argue, are teenagers. So the issue becomes charged for adults and confusing for children when a pedophile molests a child. Adults want to condemn the sexual abuser (rightly so) and believe that the molestation repulsed the child. But that is not always the case.

Constant sexual abuse can program a child to depend on the sexual acts like food or water; in a way they become like sex slaves, Dr. Terr said: "Children are blank screens upon which you can project a lot of sexuality, and you can make a child interested in that kind of sexuality by introducing it and insisting on it."

Indeed, a sexual relationship can sustain a victim's attachment to the kidnapper long after Stockholm Syndrome, Dr. Ochberg said, comparing the dynamic to the one experienced by some incest victims. "In an incest situation, the older person often is a very skilled seducer, and the younger person is not necessarily traumatized by the incest," he said. "And I've got to be careful here, because I don't want to appear to be callous in the way my words get translated. I do a lot of work to try to help people get over their trauma experience, and when I'm working with an adult, usually a woman, an adult survivor of incest, what I find is incest is not as traumatic as becoming an adult and realizing the horror that had been going on. Or lying to her mother, and regretting the loss of trust between her and her mother. There can be deep resentment of the father or father figure, the sexual abuser, but it's not as though the sexual abuse itself is the subject of nightmares, in some cases it is, but not in every case. There is a lot of self-blame, because the survivor will say, 'I did this willingly.' And I will say, 'You were a child. What does it mean to do something willingly as a child?' So we tend to reeducate the person to feel some of the legitimate anger that we feel as adults toward the perpetrator. But this sexual involvement becomes a whole other way of understanding the attachment" to the perpetrator.

And now we come up for air before we get lost in the murkiness, before we drown in the complexity and irrationality of the human psyche. We take a breather, basking in the miracle discovery of two missing boys; we look ahead to their emotional recovery, a choppy prospect that requires the help of top mental health professionals not just for Shawn and Ben, but for their mothers and fathers and sisters. For everyone was critically injured in the mind and heart.

For us, we're heading back home from our expedition into the human psyche. In this case, home is metro St. Louis, site of the boys' trauma and site of Dr. C. Robert Cloninger's cozy, bookish office at Washington University, where the psychiatrist who is also acclaimed for his works in genetics offers a simple explanation to all those who still feel fit to judge Shawn's actions while in captivity: Shawn's response to his abduction and abuse is strongly rooted in biology, and, for a mere mortal, biology is a hard force to reckon with.

Dr. Cloninger's explanation is not conjecture; rather it is based on brain imaging studies and other documented research. "There are mechanisms in the brain that basically stop people from acting in a way that is very reasonable when they are under tremendous threat," Dr. Cloninger said. "There is a part of your brain called the amygdala that gets activated whenever you are threatened. Then that threat sends a message to another part of your brain called the anterior cingulate cortex that regulates the communication between your emotional brain and your rational brain. Basically, the rational brain is hijacked or short-circuited in a state of fear. And all you've got left is to operate in a way that is going to help you deal with the threat by reducing anxiety. You're no longer thinking as a rational human being. You're operating very emotionally."

But a brain can be rewired, Dr. Cloninger said. "You have to be out of threat, reduce the anxiety and then be helped to reprocess the traumatic events in a way that isn't judgmental, so that you can face it, integrate it and deal with it rather than feeling guilty or ashamed or just blocking it out of consciousness."

A kindhearted man with bespectacled bluish-green eyes, Dr. Cloninger is ever the optimist. Not only can Shawn and Ben recover and lead healthy, happy, and fulfilled lives, but they can take pride in the positive effects of this case.

For Ben, his abduction led to Shawn's rescue. "It came at a high cost for Ben," Dr. Cloninger said, "but it's one of the greatest sacrifices he can make, and I hope he'll learn to see that as a contribution he's made to other people."

For Shawn, his kidnapping caused his parents to form a foundation that serves other families of missing children. "Because of Shawn," Dr. Cloninger said, "so many other people have been helped and will be helped during one of their greatest times of need."

It is not always easy to see, especially on the surface, good coming out of cruel crimes committed against two innocent boys. "But there is meaning," Dr. Cloninger said. "There is purpose."

But any good is hard to see when you're parents flooded with grief over your missing son.

CHAPTER 14

Life without Shawn

The thought sends shivers down the spine.

During the time that kidnapper Michael Devlin held Shawn hostage and tortured the boy physically and psychologically, Shawn's parents, on several occasions, may have driven near Devlin's run-down apartment complex, roughly an hour's drive from their home in Richwoods.

On days when Pam and Craig Akers were in metro St. Louis, likely driving on Interstate 44 near Interstate 270, they had been only minutes away from Shawn. Heading east on I-44, toward downtown St. Louis, they would have driven under a concrete highway bridge with a green-and-white sign denoting Holmes Avenue, near the highway's on- and off-ramps, which could have taken Pam and Craig toward Unit D in the run-down redbrick apartment complex where their son was living as Shawn Devlin. Had the Akerses pulled off the highway to fill up at the QuikTrip gas station and mini-mart at Big Bend Road and Holmes Avenue, they might have run into Shawn, who was known to hang out there with his friends from the apartment complex.

Shawn Hornbeck had been so close.

But Shawn's abductor was a pathological genius and a manipulative mastermind who had muzzled the boy's ability to seek help. And so years passed since their eleven-year-old son had disappeared. During that time, Pam and Craig's boy would have grown taller and stronger and more like a man. His interests would have changed from cartoon characters such as SpongeBob SquarePants to hanging out with friends at school and preparing for a driver's license. He probably would have been interested in dating.

What would their child be like now? What would their child look like now? Those are the types of questions parents of missing children think about constantly. Pam and Craig Akers were no exception. They had joined an exclusive club to which no sane mother, father, or guardian ever wants admission: Parents of Missing Children.

Membership includes no perks, besides bonding on an intense level with other parents who are experiencing the same heartbreak of not knowing where your child is or whether your child is dead or, if your child is alive, whether he or she is hurt and suffering. And knowing that whatever the situation, no matter how long or how hard you search for your child, there is often nothing you can do but hold on to hope and hang on to memories and imagine what your child's interests would be now, his favorite food, his favorite TV show, his favorite subject in school.

In fact, membership to this hideous club often bestows upon parents of a missing child a whole host of additional problems, from job loss and financial ruin to divorce and estranged relationships to substance abuse and negative addictions to a gamut of mental health ailments, including depression, anxiety, and even suicide.

The Akerses' marriage managed to stay intact throughout the ordeal, but they were not immune to other problems. After their intensive search for Shawn, they both eventually returned to the workforce, but by then the couple told the media that they had drained their savings account and borrowed against their 401(k) retirement plans. From a psychological perspective, Pam and Craig Akers told the *St. Louis Post-Dispatch* in October 2006, four years since Shawn had vanished, that they had not discussed their trauma with a professional mental health counselor; however, they acknowledged their intense emotional pain, the strain of which was taking its toll: "Pam smokes two packs of cigarettes on days such as this," the newspaper reported. "Her large blue-green eyes are sunken in her drawn, thin face."

Pam tried to describe the indescribable to the *Post-Dispatch*: "Many parents have felt the temporary panic when a child wanders off in a store. [Pam] Akers says to intensify that fear, feel the twisting in your gut, the ache of longing in your chest. And then live with it for years."

"It's been four years," Pam said in the article. "But for me, it's just been one long continuous day."

For his part, Craig was forced to return to the workforce for financial reasons, but he had spent most of the time since Shawn disappeared devoted to the Shawn Hornbeck Foundation, to finding his son as well as looking for other missing people. Anytime day or night when a local child was reported missing, Craig gathered his gear, joined in the search, and shared his firsthand experience with the distraught families.

On March 10, 2005, Craig joined in the search for a missing girl who was close in age to Shawn and also came from a small Missouri town. Shortly after 8:20 p.m., thirteen-year-old Bianca Noel Piper was reported missing from her home in Foley in Lincoln County, a rural area approximately sixty miles northwest of St. Louis. Born on December 26, 1991, Bianca was described at the time of her abduction as a brown-eyed girl with curly brown hair who weighs 185 pounds, stands at five feet, six inches tall, and has scars on her arms, legs, and abdomen. Media accounts state that she suffers from bipolar disorder as well as attention deficit hyperactivity disorder and reportedly disappeared after her mother dropped off Bianca with a flashlight on McIntosh Hill Road, about a mile from their house. Bianca and her mom had apparently had an argument over household chores, resulting in the teenage daughter becoming upset and the mother telling Bianca to walk home to cool off, a tactic that the family said a therapist had recommended.

Little did Craig know at the time that the man who kidnapped his son, who tortured Shawn on a daily basis, was likely monitoring the search efforts for Bianca, using it as "a manual for crime," according to a report aired on KSDK News Channel 5, the NBC affiliate in St. Louis.

"Did Devlin participate in volunteer searches for Bianca Piper to learn investigative techniques he would use later to elude authorities?" asked KSDK reporter Randy Jackson.

"Whether he was a part of it, in it, or in the middle, or just watching from afar, he absolutely knew what was going on," Detective Chris Bartlett of the Lincoln County Sheriff's Department told the TV news station. "I certainly believe Michael Devlin was monitoring our search and the disappearance of Bianca Piper."

For his part, Craig devoted nearly six weeks to the search for Bianca, who is still missing today. He lived out of a camper. He ignored his left leg, which throbbed in pain. The physical labor of searching for Bianca—and for all of the boys and girls before her, including Shawn—had worn down Craig, who has cardiovascular disease and circulation problems. He had to quit searching for Bianca because his foot hurt so bad, he had to go to the emergency room. The situation was so dire that doctors amputated his left leg from the knee down.

Only a medical emergency could detach Craig from an

ongoing search for a missing child. Those who know Craig and Pam Akers cite their dedication to the Shawn Hornbeck Foundation as a major source of emotional strength in the years when Shawn was missing. "They know better than anyone what it is like to have a missing child," said Kim Evans, a family friend who volunteers at the foundation. "They wanted to do everything possible to spare other people from going through what they did."

In October 2005, on the third anniversary of Shawn's disappearance, the Akerses received recognition for their work on behalf of missing children when Missouri State Rep. Belinda Harris, D-Hillsboro, honored the couple with a proclamation during a candlelight and prayer vigil commemorating Shawn at the Richwoods Lions Club, not far from where Shawn was last seen riding his lime-green bike.

At the observance, family and friends dedicated a bronze plaque in a garden where a maple tree had been planted in Shawn's honor two years before, on the first anniversary marking the boy's disappearance. The inscription read: "Missing From Our Lives . . . Forever Present In Our Hearts."

It was around this time, in late 2005, when law enforcement authorities and cybercrime sleuths began seriously to consider whether Shawn had been the victim of a serial killer and a convicted sex offender named Joseph Edward Duncan III, a wiry, pointy-nosed man who was born and raised in Tacoma, Washington, served much of his adult life in prison, and, upon his release, drifted the country and became a suspect in a long line of violent offenses.

In 1980, Duncan was only sixteen years old when he was convicted of raping a fourteen-year-old boy at gunpoint in Pierce County, Washington, and sentenced to twenty years in prison. Five years later, on July 2, 2005, Duncan bludgeoned to death a mother, her boyfriend, and her thirteen-year-old son in Coeur D'Alene, Idaho, while abducting two children: eight-year-old Shasta Groene and nine-year-old Dylan Groene. Shasta was rescued, but Dylan's remains were discovered at a campsite in western Montana.

Duncan's arrest in 2005 led law enforcement authorities to examine more than half a dozen child and adult deaths that Duncan may have committed while he was paroled between 1994 and 1997 as well as after his prison release in 2000. Additionally, authorities and Internet sleuths began looking into slain and missing children cases in at least eleven states Duncan was known to have visited. Missouri was one of them.

With no clues about how Shawn disappeared, investigators, psychologists, and other followers of the case suspected that the person who abducted Shawn—and many believed had murdered the boy, as well—represented the worst type of criminal: The kind with absolutely no conscience. The kind gifted at manipulation, outwitting, and calculated risk. The kind obsessed with fulfilling his personal physical and psychological needs at all costs, no matter how depraved.

The kind of criminal Joseph Edward Duncan III was.

While it was not Duncan, Shawn's kidnapper appears to be a brilliant criminal in his own right, for only a vile virtuoso could orchestrate such a clever con as to steal a boy in broad daylight, pass him off as his son, and, in essence, parade him around town in plain sight, past police officers, past the media, and past a nearby grocery store bench bearing a big photograph of the missing child—and even past the boy's pained parents who may have driven near the scene of the crime several times and who lived only an hour's drive away.

Michael Devlin got away with his sinister scheme for more than four years.

The ruse unraveled with the abduction of another boy.

CHAPTER 15
Beaufort

In January 2007 the monster man struck again. This time he chose to pursue his prey in Beaufort, Missouri, an unincorporated town with a population of approximately 1,680 people. It is located near the intersection of Highways 50 and 185 in Franklin County, approximately fifty miles southwest of downtown St. Louis and forty miles northwest of Richwoods, where Shawn vanished.

In addition to being old, small midwestern towns, Beaufort and Richwoods share similar characteristics: Both are surrounded by towering trees, thick brush, and rocky ridges that create natural nooks and crannies that make it easy for a person to disappear. Both are mostly Caucasian, rural areas with humble homes, modest retail and restaurant amenities, and limited employment opportunities, with some people in Beaufort working at nearby manufacturing and distribution facilities in Franklin County such as Integram St. Louis Seating, GDX Automotive, and Aerofil Technology Inc.

The City of Union sits eleven miles to the east of Beaufort and serves as the county seat of Franklin County, which has a population of 99,773 and is one of the largest counties geographically in the state. Most of Beaufort's older children ride the bus to and from schools in Union, which has a growing population of nine thousand residents and more than three hundred businesses and is home to the 3,500-student East Central College. Like Beaufort, Union was established during the first half of the 1800s; today, the city's website boasts that "Union enjoys a diverse landscape that includes new commercial developments and growing subdivisions mixed with rolling hills, farmer's fields and forest groves."

Franklin County's population has increased steadily over the years, luring residents from the St. Louis region attracted in part by the amount of land they can buy for bargain prices compared to similar acreage in highly developed St. Louis County. However, with the influx of people has come a rise in the number of violent crimes as well as in the number of residents living in poverty, according to federal government statistics that analyzed the time period between 2000 and 2005.

Compounding Franklin County's burgeoning problems is an overall lack of resources in sectors such as employment, social services, and health care, all of which help to fuel problems such as alcoholism and drug addiction. As is true in Richwoods and small towns throughout rural Missouri, methamphetamine abuse ranks as a top problem in Beaufort, which is rife with clandestine meth labs dotting the green and hilly landscape. Meth trafficking thrives along nearby Interstate 44, which crosses the county and is a ten-minute hop from Beaufort. In fact, Franklin County is a recipient of federal funding to combat the meth scourge, and it is considered one of the most meth-infested counties in the state of Missouri, which in and of itself leads the nation in meth lab busts. Statewide in 2006 "law enforcement officials responded to, seized or investigated 1,284 meth lab incidents," with Illinois, Indiana, and California coming in second, third, and fourth, respectively, according to a report by the Associated Press.

Beaufort is similar to other small towns, too, in that its people seem to possess an inherent distrust of outsiders as well as a fierce loyalty to fellow townsfolk. So when a Beaufort woman developed a brain aneurysm and needed help paying the medical bills, neighbors rallied around the cause and raised $3,000 for the ill woman—just like that. And when a sweet-faced boy named Ben Ownby went missing, just about everyone in town stopped their lives to distribute fliers, search the woods, and focus on bringing the child home—no questions asked.

Tightly knit Beaufort is not the sort of place where one expects a child to be abducted in broad daylight. Not that there is a typical town where one assumes criminals will snatch children. But after the monster man stole one of Beaufort's children, it seemed as if the townsfolk were telling each other and the media: This kind of stuff doesn't happen in Franklin County. Maybe in an urban area, but not here.

But in reality, those kinds of things did happen in Franklin County. About four months before Ben disappeared, in September 2006, a high-profile infant abduction case occurred in Lonedell, a tiny town in the county about thirty miles southeast of Beaufort. The unthinkable transpired midday on Friday, September 15, 2006, when accused kidnapper Shannon Beck knocked on the front door of Stephenie Ochsenbine's home and asked to use her telephone. Instead of making a call, Beck allegedly held the twenty-one-year-old woman at gunpoint before the two struggled, which ended when Beck stabbed Ochsenbine in the neck and arm with a fillet knife.

Ochsenbine was left for dead in the bathroom while her one-year-old son remained unharmed in the house where nobody else was home at the time.

Missing was one-week-old Abigale "Abby" Lynn Woods.

Miraculously, Ochsenbine regained consciousness twenty-five minutes after the throat gashing and managed to stagger three hundred yards to a neighbor's house at around 12:40 p.m.

"Someone stole my baby," the bleeding woman was quoted in the media as telling her neighbor, who then called 911.

The Franklin County Sheriff's Department issued an AMBER Alert, and a nationwide manhunt ensued as more than one hundred National Guard members, FBI agents, and local sheriff deputies—as well as dozens of volunteers from Lonedell, Beaufort, and other nearby towns—searched for Baby Abby, who was described as a Caucasian female with black hair and blue eyes, measuring nineteen inches long and weighing six pounds. At the time of her abduction, she wore a pink dress with a flowered collar. Baby Abby also had a strawberry-red birthmark between her eyes, a key distinguishing factor.

The story attracted national attention, not only for the gruesome stabbing of a young mother but because infant abductions are rare. Between 1983 and 2007, 248 babies in the United States have been kidnapped by nonfamily members, according to statistics cited by the National Center for Missing and Exploited Children. Of that number, approximately two-thirds took place in health care settings.

The national media were even more intrigued because Missouri claims another high-profile baby-snatching case— this one occurred on December 16, 2004, in Skidmore, a town of about three hundred people in the northwest corner of the state. The terrifying tale involved thirty-six-year-old Lisa Montgomery, who was convicted in October 2007 of murdering a young pregnant woman, Bobbi Jo Stinnett, who was near full term. Montgomery fatally strangled the woman with a rope and sliced the unborn child from the twenty-three-year-old's womb. The healthy newborn was safely recovered, and the suspect was arrested a few days later.

In both cases, Beck and Montgomery fit the FBI's profile of an infant abductor. Both women were of childbearing age, married, and familiar with the communities where the abduction occurred. Beck and Montgomery were prone to manipulation and deception—and both stated that they had recently suffered a miscarriage (Beck later told police she had lost her full-term baby on the day of Baby Abby's abduction). Both women longed for a baby.

Beck passed off Baby Abby as her own to her husband, friends, and relatives, including Beck's sister-in-law Dorothy Torrez, who visited Beck and the baby twice, the second time on Tuesday, September 19, when she accompanied the pair to a doctor's appointment at St. Anthony's Medical Center in south St. Louis County, roughly a half hour drive from Lonedell.

Torrez became suspicious when she noticed that the baby's forehead was smudged in makeup, which she rubbed away with the infant's cap while Beck was in another part of the hospital. There, between the infant's eyes, was a strawberry-red birthmark, just like the one described on the missing baby she had heard about on the news. Eerily, the thirty-six-year-old Beck also resembled the police description of the woman suspected of abducting the infant: a dark-haired Caucasian woman in her thirties, roughly five feet, eight inches tall and two hundred pounds with a "female mustache."

Flabbergasted, Torrez confronted her sister-in-law, who returned Baby Abby to law enforcement later that evening.

Police promptly arrested Beck, who received multiple charges including child kidnapping, first-degree assault, and armed criminal action. She is awaiting trial in a Franklin County jail with bond set at $1 million. She has pleaded not guilty.

Baby Abby was declared healthy by doctors at a hospital in Franklin County and returned to her mother, who was recovering from her injuries. The infant's parents appeared on national television, holding their daughter as they spoke about how ecstatic they were to have her home.

"She belongs with me," the mother told MSNBC. "We're doing great now. We're whole again and she's very content, actually."

Sitting next to mother and baby was the father, James Woods: "I just wanted to hug her."

The abduction tragedy that was never supposed to happen in bucolic Franklin County ended happily.

Everyone called it a miracle.

CHAPTER 16
A Mother's Prayer

Pam and Craig Akers had heard about the Baby Abby miracle in neighboring Franklin County. The infant's step-grandmother, Tammy Woods, lived less than a mile from their house in Richwoods; in fact, Woods used to babysit Shawn before he started kindergarten, according to an article in the *St. Louis Post-Dispatch*:

> *Woods was waiting at their house when the Akerses arrived home. She didn't say a word when she saw Pam Akers. They looked at each other and broke down in each other's arms.*
>
> *Woods took Pam Akers' advice to heart that day: "Don't give up hope. You give up hope and you're not going to have anything to hold onto." She thought about those words after her granddaughter was reunited with the family. The five days Abby was missing traumatized*

the family, and the experience can't be described in words, Woods said.

"I don't know that I could have done it for four years."

The night Abby was found, Pam Akers didn't sleep. She wondered how Abby's mother felt holding her child.

The miracle in Franklin County occurred a few weeks before October 6, 2006, the four-year anniversary of Shawn's disappearance. The Akerses had helped Baby Abby's family when the infant was abducted, coordinating volunteer search efforts, creating a website, distributing fliers, and all the missing-persons tasks they were now used to doing.

Baby Abby's safe return elated the Akerses.

But the couple also expressed to the *Post-Dispatch* their complex emotions: They wanted a happy ending, too. They wanted their son to come home, just as Baby Abby had. They wanted to hug Shawn, kiss him, and tell him that they loved him.

To soothe her emotions, Pam Akers sometimes retreated to the flower-filled garden honoring her son on the green grass near the Richwoods Lions Club. There, she could bask in the tributes to her son: the maple tree the community planted with hopes that one day, Shawn would enjoy climbing it; the bronze plaque declaring him "Forever Present In Our Hearts;" and the "Sitting With An Angel" bench that featured his smiling photo.

On the memorial bench, Shawn's family and friends had written him messages in black ink, some punctuated with lots of xxx's and ooo's.

I love you + miss you so very much . . . mom.

We count the minutes we are apart . . . waiting for your return. Dad.

Come home soon. Grandma.

Love you. Grandpa.

To me your home. . . . Just show me your smile face again. I love you. Jackie.

You will be in my heart forever. Love Aunt Shari.

Shawn we will always love you. Love Aunt Diane, Kathy, Allen, Andy, Ashley, William, Scott and Willy (Tish).

I love you. Everyone does. Come home! Luv your friend, J.C. . . .

You are a real angel. Miss you. Ryan.

See you at home.

We all miss you. Come home safe.

Always in my prayers.

Miss you lots. Miss you always.

In my heart forever.

The memorial garden beckoned, providing a place where Pam Akers could pray, ponder, and privately shed tears.

It was where she went after Baby Abby was found. First, she prayed in thanks for Baby Abby's safe return, the *Post-Dispatch* reported. "Thank you, Lord, for giving this mom the miracle she needed. Then she talked directly to Shawn Hornbeck, her son: 'We will find you one day.'"

CHAPTER 17

A Predator Hunts His Prey

Secrets deepened on January 8, 2007. On that warm Monday, the monster man decided to widen his circle, inducting into his disturbed world another victim, a bony and bespectacled boy who was exiting a school bus and running toward his house, probably looking forward to playing video games. Instead, the thirteen-year-old was plucked from the placidness of his life and thrown into a white Nissan pickup, which sped down the rural roads and whisked the child to a lascivious lair smack in the middle of suburban bliss—and only about an hour's drive from his house in Beaufort, where his family waited, worried about their son's safety.

It all seemed to happen in an instant. One minute, Ben Ownby was waving good-bye to the school bus driver and to Mitchell Hults, his older friend and neighbor. The next, Ben was gone, swiped like an afterthought, like he was some silly object a person decides to filch from a store on impulse.

But the abduction was anything but spontaneous. According to law enforcement officials, the monster man had considered stealing another boy for about three months before he took Ben. Michael Devlin even did his research, driving to small country towns around Highways 50, 30, and 141, places shrouded in trees and greens, where people cling to a pretense of innocence. He told the FBI he preferred rural areas "because the schools tended to get out a little later so he could have time to drive there after work."

The FBI report continued: "Devlin would go to schools around the time that kids were dismissed and then follow the school bus routes until he saw a boy that he liked or that was the only one to get off the bus."

Devlin seemed to prefer boys between the ages of eleven and thirteen who weighed about one hundred pounds and had brown hair.

Boys like Shawn Hornbeck, in 2002.

Boys like Ben Ownby, in 2007.

On that warm January day, Devlin may have tried to kidnap another boy but a "dog barked," the *St. Louis Post-Dispatch* reported.

In any case, Devlin zeroed in on the Beaufort boy that afternoon. "He had followed one boy who got off at his bus stop and then walked down the road by himself," an FBI report stated. "This boy turned out to be Ben Ownby. Devlin stated that he followed Ben's bus a few times to make sure that Ben was the only one that would walk down the road."

Fortunately, Devlin failed to notice that Ben got off the bus with an older boy who lived nearby. An older boy with hawk eyes, a photographic memory, and a passion for trucks. An older boy who would prove to be Devlin's undoing.

CHAPTER 18
Really Sick

People in the St. Louis area seemed to be in a good mood on January 8, 2007. The blue sky billowing with clouds and unseasonably warm weather cast a spell, a sort of enchantment that resembled the natural high folks feel on the first day of spring after the drawn and dreary chill of winter.

On that Monday, midday temperatures reached nearly fifty degrees—roughly double the average temperature for a January day in St. Louis, which is typically characterized by frigidity so bleak, spirits sink. The surprise gift of good weather—which had been felt across much of the Midwest and on the East Coast— inspired people throughout the metro area to wear turtlenecks with shorts, to eat their lunches outdoors on city benches and in park gazebos, and to exchange friendly hellos with strangers. It was as if everyone had an extra giddy-up to their steps.

Mike Prosperi basked in the brightness as he began his workday at the Imo's pizza parlor he owned and operated in downtown Kirkwood. His employees cracked jokes and laughed, enjoying each other's company as they prepared pizza pies for customers who would come in later that day.

Everybody was in a good mood except Michael Devlin.

Geez, Prosperi thought, he really looks like hell.

Sweat drenched the three-hundred-pound loner. Redness colored his face. Prosperi recalled that Devlin—or "Devo," as he was known at Imo's—seemed a bit off that day: distracted, cranky, and tired.

"Are you feeling OK?" Prosperi asked that morning.

No, he wasn't. Devo bemoaned his bad night's sleep. He thought maybe he had the flu. He just didn't feel right.

Prosperi had to smile to himself. It was just like Devo to report to work despite feeling ill. No matter how bad he felt, Prosperi knew that Devo had every intention of working his full 9 a.m. to 5 p.m. shift. That just exemplified the kind of hardworking employee that Devo was.

"Why don't you work through the lunch rush," Prosperi suggested, "and then go home and take it easy?"

Prosperi expected Devo to push back, to insist on working his full shift.

But surprisingly, Devo agreed.

Wow, Prosperi thought, Devo really must be sick.

Devo went home Monday at about 12:50 p.m.

CHAPTER 19

The Monster Man Strikes Again

Michael Devlin was sick that warm Monday in January.

But his illness had little, if anything, to do with a possible flu or fever or any other physical symptoms—and everything to do with a sick mind-set, with swirling thoughts of rampant rage fanning his pedophilic perversion and violent vices with an intensity so strong, it snapped self-restraint. For Devlin kidnapped another boy on an otherwise beautiful day, adding to his collection of captive children whom he crammed into his crappy apartment in Kirkwood where the boys endured psychological torture and sexual abuse.

Devlin's boss at Imo's pizza parlor sent him home sick just before one o'clock that Monday afternoon. FBI documents, court testimony, and media accounts provided the following details about what happened next:

On the way home, Devlin stopped at a QuikTrip near his home to buy a Diet Dr. Pepper.

He thought to himself: This is my last chance for a while to take a young boy.

He went inside the redbrick apartment to get the other kidnapped teenager, the one who had gotten too old for Devlin's sexual tastes, and insisted that he climb into the white Nissan pickup.

Also inside the truck were a 9mm Ruger P85, duct tape, and a plain gray hooded sweatshirt.

Shawn Hornbeck was livid. For months, he had known about his abductor's plan to steal and sexually abuse another boy. For years, he had heard about Devlin's disgusting desires to "do things with another kid," according to the *St. Louis Post-Dispatch*. Shawn wanted no part in the abduction. He couldn't stand to see another child endure the torture that he had suffered for the past four years and three months.

But Devlin—a looming lunatic who had once tried to kill Shawn—insisted that the teenager get inside the truck. Shawn had no choice as he sat there against his will.

The kidnapper apparently hopped onto Interstate 44 and drove approximately fifty miles southwest. The ride was an easy shot from Devlin's apartment, the westbound on-ramp about five minutes from his front door, to the rustic town of Beaufort, located near the intersection of Highways 50 and 185 in Franklin County.

Devlin dismissed Shawn's anger. The teenager—whom he later claimed to love like a son—had become resistant in recent months, especially since Devlin revealed his plans to abduct another boy. Maybe making him an accomplice in a major crime would make Shawn more compliant.

He turned to the brown-haired boy, saying, "OK buddy, now that you're in the truck with me, you're in as much trouble as I am," Shawn's lawyer later recounted to the Associated Press.

Devlin told Shawn his job was to keep the boy calm once he got inside the pickup.

Once the pair reached Beaufort, Devlin parked his white Nissan pickup by a hair salon near Ben's house. A yellow school bus affiliated with the Union R-XI School District drove by at around 3:30 p.m. Devlin waited a few minutes and then cruised down Ben's street. He waited as the bus dropped off two passengers: one a lanky boy in middle school, the other an observant high school boy.

The older boy, Mitchell Hults, a freshman at Union High School, was fifteen years old, and although he was too young to have a driver's license, he had a Chevy pickup parked on top of the hill near the bus stop for the jaunt home. As Mitchell's busmate jogged toward his home—the younger boy had a quirky habit of always running to his house, which was roughly five hundred yards from the bus stop—Mitchell got inside his vehicle.

Meanwhile, Devlin slowed his pickup near Ben. Still seated, he opened the vehicle's door, and asked Ben if he knew where a particular person lived, someone whose name he made up.

"Ben looked very nervous and Devlin thought Ben was going to run in the opposite way," according to an FBI report, based on agents' interviews with the kidnapper. "Devlin then said that the people had not been living there long. That seemed to calm Ben." The thirteen-year-old told the stranger that a new family had moved in to the first house on the right.

Devlin burst out of the truck, showed Ben his gun and ordered him into the pickup.

Ben stood frozen.

Devlin put his hand on the boy's shoulder. He shoved him into the driver's side door.

"Why?" Ben asked. "Why?"

"Just because," Devlin said. "Get into the truck."

But Ben had trouble getting into the truck because he was wearing his school backpack. He took it off, climbed into the vehicle and sat between his kidnapper and another kidnapped teenager.

Devlin told Ben to put his head down so no one would recognize the boy. He took the back roads out of town so no one would spot them.

Ben's busmate, Mitchell Hults, happened to glance in the direction of the younger boy's house when he noticed a white Nissan pickup truck in the middle of the road, in a sort of sideways position. The Nissan reversed into a ditch, drove a short distance, turned around, and zoomed out of the vicinity at a high rate of speed. The vehicle's maneuvers proved an odd sight on Beaufort's quiet and private country roads.

The teenager had never glimpsed the white Nissan pickup roaming the roads near his house—and he knows what everyone in these parts drives, not because he is nosy but because he loves anything with an engine and wheels.

Mitchell did not notice who was driving the pickup, or if there were any other passengers in the truck. Nor did he see the younger boy, William "Ben" Ownby Jr. He did not feel alarm, either, since he figured his friend already was at home.

But Mitchell observed every last detail about the mangy white vehicle:

The Nissan was an older, run-down model.

The word "Nissan" was in black lettering on the back.

The wheels lacked hubcaps.

Rust and dents blemished a rear panel on the passenger's side.

It had a camper shell with a continuous horizontal windshield instead of a bunch of smaller windows.

A ladder rack appeared to be on top of the camper shell.

Inside the white Nissan pickup, during the drive back to suburban St. Louis, "Shawn talked to Ben about the things he likes such as food and television," an FBI report stated. "Devlin never had to use the duct tape or the gray-hooded sweatshirt to restrain Ben."

As the monster man was kidnapping Ben, William "Don" Ownby Sr. was headed home from his job as a warehouse supervisor for a nearby company. Usually on weekdays, he arrives at the family's house on Wild Rose Lane about ten minutes after his namesake son gets home from school. But on that afternoon, Ben was nowhere in sight.

Don waited—and waited—at the house, a one-story with a porch and a sign welcoming visitors.

The clock struck 3:45 p.m.

Four o'clock came and went with no signs of Ben.

Five more minutes passed—and nothing.

The minutes continued to crawl: 4:06 p.m. . . . 4:07 . . . 4:08 . . . 4:09 . . .

At 4:10 p.m., Don realized his son was gone. He called the police.

At around the same time that afternoon, Doris Ownby scoured the halls of Union Middle School, searching for Ben. Anxious, she went into the campus administration office and approached Principal Nathan Bailey.

"Have you seen my son?" the principal recalled the mother asking.

Ben's mother appeared desperate. Principal Bailey wished he had better news, but he had not seen the thirteen-year-old student. He felt a growing sense of concern but remained calm. After all, it was his responsibility to provide assurance that he and everyone else at the 475-student school would do everything they could to help the Ownby family. To help find the seventh-grader.

At approximately 4:30 p.m. Principal Bailey made an announcement over the campus public address system:

"If Ben Ownby is in the building, please come to the main office. If anyone has seen Ben Ownby, please buzz or drop by the office."

Silence.

Principal Bailey stayed late that night, working the phones in an effort to locate Ben. Before he left for the day, at around 6:30 p.m., Principal Bailey made one last call to the Ownby residence. He recalled that his side of the conversation went something like this:

"Have you heard anything?"

Which was followed by: "Is there anything else you need?"

And then: "Please know that the school will do everything we can on our part."

As Principal Bailey pulled away from the campus at 503 West End Avenue and headed northwest for the thirty-minute drive home to New Haven, he tried to ease his worried mind. Maybe Ben had gone to a friend's house and forgotten to tell his parents. But he dashed his own hopes when he considered Ben's personality: responsible, cautious, and not at all absent-minded. A parent himself, he felt sad for the Ownby family, imagining the pain that they must be feeling, the agony of not knowing where their son was.

Later that evening, Principal Bailey received a call from the Franklin County Sheriff's Office requesting Ben's records.

Uh-oh, Principal Bailey thought. This is getting even more serious.

Indeed. It had become official: One of Franklin County's children was missing. Again.

County Sheriff Gary Toelke spun into crisis mode, just as he had done about four months prior when Baby Abby was abducted in Lonedell. Once again, dozens of law enforcement agents and civilian volunteers formed search teams—assisted by horses and canines—and combed the rugged terrain in and around Beaufort, looking in ditches and drainage pipes, in bushes and battered mobile homes. Humming helicopters hovered overhead. The National Center for Missing and Exploited Children was called in to provide technical assistance and to help publicize Ben's case.

The media descended on Beaufort, peppering law enforcement officials and townsfolk with all kinds of questions in their pursuit of the informational scoop. Eleven miles to the east in Union, satellite television trucks camped out in front of the boxy, reddish-concrete Franklin County Sheriff's Department at 1 Bruns Drive. Big, bulky television cameras were ready to film at a moment's notice a press conference by law enforcement officials, ready for any word on Ben or the man who abducted the bright-eyed boy.

Once again, Sheriff Toelke, a blue-eyed man with salt-and-pepper hair, would become a regular fixture on local television. During the Baby Abby case, which he led, the sheriff had attracted a group of fans, so to speak, piqued by his lulling voice, confident manner, and gentlemanly good looks, which resemble actor William H. Macy's. None of that was of con-cern to Sheriff Toelke. He expressed his disbelief to the Asso-ciated Press that his department was handling yet another missing child case, which might occur "once in the career of a small-town sheriff."

"To have it happen twice in a six-month period," Toelke told the wire service, "is quite a strain on everyone."

After Ben's father reported his son's disappearance, Toelke and other investigators grappled with whether to issue an AMBER Alert, which stands for America's Missing: Broadcast Emergency Response, an early-warning system for abducted children that originated in the Dallas–Fort Worth area in 1996 and is named after Amber Hagerman, who was nine years old when she was kidnapped in January 1996 while riding her bike in Arlington, Texas. Four days after she was reported missing, a man walking his dog discovered Amber's decaying body at the bottom of a creek bed near an apartment complex, the girl's throat slashed.

Following Amber's death, law enforcement agencies and media outlets nationwide adopted local versions of the AMBER Alert, which allows law enforcement agencies to broadcast information about a missing child age seventeen or under via television, radio, mobile phones, the Internet, and highway message boards. It was not until 2003 that the AMBER Alert became a federal program coordinated by the U.S. Department of Justice.

As of late 2007, the warning system is credited with saving the lives of more than two hundred children nationwide.

However, to deter false alarms that could waste police resources and desensitize the public to broadcast warnings about child abduction, a case must meet certain criteria before law enforcement agencies can issue an AMBER Alert—and Ben's situation, in the first sixteen hours after he vanished, did not meet the necessary conditions because authorities lacked a witness who either saw Ben disappear or who could provide a description of the abductor and his vehicle.

The circumstances put law enforcement officials in a quandary. They had concluded that a stranger had stolen Ben. Although family-related abduction is the most common type of child kidnapping, Ben's family members passed police questioning and were not under suspicion. Also, running away would have been out of character for Ben, who was a well-behaved straight-"A" student, a Boy Scout, and a member of his school's Science Olympiad team. He was a homebody who loved reading and playing computer video games in his bedroom.

Instead of the AMBER Alert, law enforcement officials issued an Endangered Person Advisory (EPA) at 8:24 p.m. Monday, the first of its kind in Missouri.

The EPA is a secondary early-warning system that had just been activated in the state the week before Ben went missing. The system arose after the 2004 case in Skidmore, Missouri, involving the woman who cut a baby out of a pregnant woman's womb and kidnapped the premature infant. Criteria constraints caused delays in declaring an AMBER Alert in the Skidmore case since authorities lacked a description of the just-born, never-before-seen baby. An EPA broadcast disseminates information to Missouri media outlets, but it gives police more flexibility than an AMBER Alert, for instance, by allowing authorities to issue a warning about a person of any age who goes missing or is in a potentially harmful situation, such as a mentally impaired elderly person who wanders off from a nursing home, a disoriented outdoorsman caught in a severe storm, or a teenager who is suspected of running away.

By Tuesday morning, however, law enforcement officials had spent hours interviewing Mitchell Hults, the missing boy's busmate, who had witnessed the white Nissan pickup speeding off near Ben's house at about the same time that the thirteen-year-old boy vanished. Mitchell's detailed description of the truck gave police all they needed to issue a federal warning.

At 8:11 a.m. Tuesday, an AMBER Alert went out about Ben.

Residents in Franklin County needed no alert system to kick into action. All around Beaufort, the townsfolk dropped everything to help bring home one of their own. Men and women trekked through the thicket searching for Ben. Volunteers distributed missing person fliers, and local business owners displayed posters of Ben on storefront windows and counters near the cash registers. An informal command center was established at the Voss Conoco Market, in the heart of

Beaufort near the intersection of Highways 50 and 185. There, volunteers worked on fliers, manned phones, and stopped to question drivers of white pickups long into the wee hours of the morning. They slept a few hours before resuming their quest to find Ben at the first sign of dawn.

"I feel sorry for the guy, if we catch him," Keith Fritzmeyer, owner of Beaufort Auto and a volunteer searcher, told the *Post-Dispatch*. "You don't mess with one of ours."

The missing person fliers featured a bespectacled, thin-faced boy with short bangs, wearing a red shirt and standing in front of a tinsel-draped Christmas tree, a photograph most likely taken during the holidays a few weeks before his abduction. Ben is grinning broadly in the picture, unabashedly bearing a nice row of perfectly straight teeth, the result of his braces having just come off a few weeks prior. And truly his smile appears as if it is a genuine expression of happiness, rather than the stilted poses so prevalent in family photo albums across America.

The fliers also included a description: Ben is a Caucasian male, 13 years old, with brown hair and blue eyes who stands at four feet, eleven inches tall and weighs approximately one hundred pounds. At the time of his abduction, the boy wore glasses, a St. Louis Rams hooded windbreaker, and blue jeans, and he carried a black backpack.

Thanks to the AMBER Alert, Ben's photograph and physical information—along with a precise description of the

Michael Devlin's yearbook photo from his junior year at Webster Groves High School, where he graduated in 1984. For unknown reasons, his senior year is not featured. **(photo courtesy of St. Louis Post-Dispatch)**

The Washington County town of Richwoods was settled during the 1770s and, in 2007, had a population of approximately 1,300 people. It is about an hour's drive from St. Louis.

(photo courtesy of Tom Geiser)

Shawn Hornbeck attended Richwoods Elementary School until the fifth grade when he disappeared. More than four years later, the school was also the site of celebrations after his rescue. **(photo courtesy of Tom Geiser)**

Cobbs Grocery is the general store in Richwoods, selling everything from cigarettes and beer to diapers and dolls to old VHS movies. Shawn Hornbeck visited the store a few hours before his abduction.

(photo courtesy of Tom Geiser)

The Richwoods Lions Club is the town's social gathering spot, and one of the last places Shawn Hornbeck was spotted riding his lime-green mountain bike before he was kidnapped. After Shawn was kidnapped, his family established a memorial garden on the nearby grassy lot. It was vandalized during the summer of 2007. **(photo courtesy of Tom Geiser)**

Michael Devlin tortured and held Shawn Hornbeck captive in Unit D in the run-down, redbrick apartment complex in the quaint, family-oriented St. Louis suburb of Kirkwood. **(photo courtesy of Tom Geiser)**

A side view of the apartment building where Michael Devlin lived with Shawn Hornbeck. Unit D is on the ground floor, facing a muddy courtyard often littered with discarded toys, bikes, and trash. **(photo courtesy of Tom Geiser)**

Imo's pizza parlor in historic downtown Kirkwood is where longtime employee Michael Devlin worked for much of his adult life. His customers often included law enforcement from the nearby Kirkwood Police Department.

(photo courtesy of Tom Geiser)

Imo's owner Mike Prosperi knew Michael Devlin for more than two decades, considering him both a friend and a valued employee. He is lauded for informing police about Devlin's suspicious vehicle, which helped to lead to the rescues of Shawn Hornbeck and Ben Ownby.

(photo courtesy of Tom Geiser)

Law enforcement arrested Michael Devlin, 41, on January 12, 2007. The burly restaurant worker, with no prior criminal record, pleaded guilty to more than 80 charges including kidnapping and sexually abusing Shawn Hornbeck and Ben Ownby. **(photo courtesy of St. Louis Post-Dispatch)**

Shortly after Shawn Hornbeck's miracle rescue, Ron Cobb, who operates Cobbs Grocery with his wife Shirley, places a "FOUND" sign over the "missing" flier of Shawn that had hung in the window of his store. **(photo courtesy of St. Louis Post-Dispatch)**

A "missing" flier of 13-year-old Ben Ownby is joyfully marked "FOUND!" four days after Michael Devlin kidnapped him in front of his family's house in Beaufort.

(photo courtesy of St. Louis Post-Dispatch)

Thirteen-year-old Ben Ownby shortly after police discovered him and Shawn Hornbeck in Michael Devlin's shabby apartment. Ben's abduction led to the safe recovery of both boys.

(photo courtesy of St. Louis Post-Dispatch)

Shawn Hornbeck, 15, and his mother, Pam Akers, exchanged hugs, kisses, and smiles after Shawn's rescue. The last time Pam saw Shawn he was 11 years old. **(photo courtesy of St. Louis Post-Dispatch)**

white Nissan pickup—became a big story, hitting the Internet and national airwaves, with major television stations such as CNN broadcasting live feeds from Beaufort.

CNN's *Headline News* personality and legal analyst Nancy Grace, whose pit-bull style softened that Tuesday during her self-titled justice talk show, led with Ben's story: "And tonight: A thirteen-year-old little boy, a model student, scrubbed in sunshine, gets off the school bus stop Monday after school and disappears. Tonight, the desperate search for a white Nissan truck with a camper on top. Will finding the truck also rescue a missing Missouri boy?"

Of course the answer is a resounding yes, but at the time, many people in town worried that the one clue might not be enough to save Ben. Then again, at least there was a clue. When Shawn Hornbeck disappeared more than four years earlier in nearby Washington County, investigators had nothing to go on. By the time Ben disappeared, most people—even the lead investigator in the Washington County case—assumed that Shawn was dead. People were desperate for Ben not to share Shawn's sad fate.

And so, they clung to the one clue they had: the white Nissan pickup. Allowing no room for error, investigators quickly corroborated Mitchell's eyewitness account, interviewing the high school student late Monday and into Tuesday, past 2 a.m. Authorities even administered a lie detector test to Mitchell to ensure that the teenager was not involved in the kidnapping or concocting stories for attention; for his part, the teenager heartily agreed to undergo a polygraph.

It is true that, at first, some law enforcement agents and media personalities wondered if Mitchell had made up some or all of his description of the truck, simply because the high school student's account was *so* detailed. For example, the teenager even recalled that the pickup's trailer hitch did not have a ball. Not many people possess the capability to absorb so much information in such a short period of time—and Mitchell spelled out everything so clearly, despite the pressure of skeptical uniformed officers probing him for information. Not to mention that his friend from the bus, a boy he has known almost all of his life, was kidnapped near both of the teenagers' homes.

Besides passing a polygraph test, Mitchell's report was confirmed by the pickup's tire tracks etched in the red clay mud, which police marked with green spray paint. Other Beaufort residents came forward as well, telling police that they had noticed the white Nissan pickup cruising the town's rural roads before Ben's school bus dropped him off. Additionally, trailing team canines from Gateway Search Dogs—a metro St. Louis nonprofit volunteer group that brings in canines certified by the National Association of Search and Rescue to missing persons cases and other emergency situations—detected correctly Ben's location during the abduction.

Law enforcement officials working on the case, which included officers from the Franklin County Sheriff's Office, the FBI, and the Missouri State Highway Patrol, felt confident that someone somewhere knew something about the white Nissan pickup and its driver. Police formed a roadblock on Highway 50 and interviewed motorists to see if they had any information about the run-down truck. Authorities also provided detailed descriptions of the suspicious vehicle to as many people as possible—a move criticized by some outside police departments that claimed Franklin County Sheriff Toelke was giving the media too much information. "They thought I never should have released the description of the white Nissan truck," Sheriff Toelke told an anchor for KSDK News Channel 5, the NBC affiliate in St. Louis.

Despite criticism from his colleagues, Sheriff Toelke proceeded with the course of action he thought best, based on his eighteen years as sheriff and the Union, Missouri, native's knowledge of Franklin County and its people, whom he knew would drop everything to find the driver of the suspicious vehicle. And so, Sheriff Toelke released the pickup's description to the St. Louis metro area and, considering the possibility that Ben's abductor could have taken the boy out of state, to the nation as a whole.

"The public is going to be very important in solving this case because somebody has seen that truck," Sheriff Toelke said in a dispatch published by a news wire service. "Somebody knows where it is."

FBI Special Agent Roland Corvington was more direct.

Speaking to the unknown offender and staring directly into the TV cameras during a packed press conference in Franklin County, he issued a stern warning to the abductor: "We're coming after you."

Since stranger abductions are so rare, authorities brought in two FBI profilers from the National Center for the Analysis of Violent Crime in Quantico, Virginia, where highly trained special agents construct criminal personality profiles of unknown suspects based on crime scene evidence and accounts by witnesses and, if applicable, victims. Criminal behavioral investigators apply this information to theories in criminology, psychology, psychiatry, and sociology as well as to their street-smart experience in law enforcement in their effort to develop an accurate portrait of a suspect.

As a criminal profile of Ben's abductor was being created, officers also pored over the list of Franklin County's 162 registered sex offenders, investigating their criminal records, current whereabouts, vehicles, and license plates. Thinking that maybe Ben somehow had known the abductor, law enforcement agents studied the thirteen-year-old's computer hard drive, as the boy was an avid video game player, especially when it came to aviation simulation. But his family said he rarely went online, and police did not immediately find anything suspicious embedded within the computer.

Those who knew Ben described him as a cautious boy and they highly doubted he would ever willingly get into a stranger's vehicle. His uncle, Loyd Bailie, who was serving as the Ownby family spokesman, told Fox TV's *On the Record with Greta Van Susteren*: "Ben and I have talked about this, and I know his parents have talked to him about this. And he's very conscious about who he talks to and definitely is . . . it would be totally out of character for him to climb into a vehicle with any stranger, even someone that he knew."

Mitchell's mom, Sheri Hults, told the *Post-Dispatch* that she had offered Ben rides home on several occasions. "He wouldn't get in the vehicle with me even when it was pouring rain," she told the newspaper. "And I'm his neighbor."

Back at the Ownbys' house, already-high stress levels continued to climb, and exhaustion had set in as Ben's parents and his older sister Amanda waited with relatives and friends for any word on the boy. With each excruciating minute that passed with Ben's whereabouts unknown, the emotional drain intensified.

"We'd like to get our son back," Ben's father told the Associated Press, while also urging the abductor to return the boy. "Drop him off somewhere where he can make a phone call."

Ben's disappearance affected all of the townsfolk in Beaufort. He was one of their own. And everybody remarked that Ben was such a good kid, the kind of boy who made you smile, delighted you in conversation, and gave you good feelings about the future. Everyone agreed that Ben came from a stable family. "The Ownbys are a loving family," said Ben's principal at Union Middle School, where teachers were prone to boasting about the boy's academic skills while admiring his happy-go-lucky personality.

During the time that Ben was missing, Principal Bailey would shake his head in disbelief recalling how Ben always roamed the campus with a smile on his face, a gleam in his eye, and a spring in his step. "That is how he is most days, just happy, optimistic, and vibrant," he said. "A model student in every way."

By Wednesday, law enforcement officials had approximately three hundred leads from all around the country—after all, a lot of people drive white pickup trucks. As far as police were concerned, the more tips, the better their chances were of finding Ben. Although authorities reiterated the truck's description to anyone who would listen, they also warned that the unknown offender could have altered the vehicle—at the very least, he probably would have washed off the suspicious red clay mud by now.

As investigators examined each morsel of information and searched the woods in the cold, volunteers also continued to look for Ben in the forests as well as on the roads, with volunteers racking up hundreds of miles on their cars as they drove around Eastern Missouri searching for the S.O.B who drove the rusted, dingy white Nissan pickup.

The race to find Ben intensified, too, because the area's mild temperatures were falling, with an ice storm predicted to pound the area by the weekend—and if it was anything like the one that hit the region six weeks prior, in late November and early December, the situation looked dire. That ice storm created a dangerous scenario, with treacherous road conditions, fallen debris, and hundreds of thousands of residents in metro St. Louis enduring days without electricity. Missouri Governor Matt Blunt declared a state of emergency in parts of the area, the National Guard was called in, and dozens of people were hospitalized for hypothermia and carbon monoxide poisoning and at least eight people died.

Ben had to be found before the ice storm hit.

But before the weather turned dangerous, an estimated two hundred people gathered Wednesday night at Union Middle School for a prayer vigil in Ben's honor. Wearing their winter wear, the crowd huddled together, holding candles lit to symbolically guide Ben home. They recited Bible passages via a megaphone, they sang "Amazing Grace," and they prayed for Ben, for his family, and even for the person who abducted him. Some cried, and all hoped that Ben would come home soon.

Many of Ben's classmates at Union Middle School attended the vigil and wanted to help find their friend. Like everyone else in Franklin County, they experienced emotional distress and physical strain with many reporting frayed nerves, sleepless nights, crying jags, and an overall sense of sadness. Some spoke to the on-site school counselors about their fears. Doing something might make them feel better, and so the teenagers distributed fliers about Ben, the boy's big smile yanking heart-strings in Beaufort, Union, and beyond, including in suburban St. Louis, where Ben's happy face stared at passersby walking the streets of downtown Kirkwood, past a bakery wafting the scent of rising dough, past a New Age–style yoga studio, and past the Imo's pizza parlor, where manager Michael Devlin would return to work after missing a few days due to sickness.

CHAPTER 20

A Funny Feeling

Mike Prosperi thought he was being the biggest dick around.

"This is so stupid," he told himself, as he left Imo's pizzeria before 9 a.m. and headed up the half block toward the Kirkwood Police Department, a chill in the air that Thursday. Later that morning, his employee Michael "Devo" Devlin was expected to return to work after being out sick.

Prosperi's guilt intensified when he chatted with Devo later that day. Devo had given his boss nothing to be suspicious about. He looked much better than he did on Monday, when he was sweaty and red-faced. He seemed fine, too, as if he had no worries. He was back to his same old self.

"This is crazy," Prosperi said, "I'm such a jerk for ratting on a friend. I'm just a big dick."

That self-deprecating refrain also had run through his head during the three-minute walk from the restaurant to the city's police station. His mind would not shut up. He even laughed out loud, shocked by what he was about to do.

He could not believe his gall. His balls.

He felt like such an ass, he had not even told his beloved wife about his plans to go to the police department.

Maybe Prosperi should just turn around and go back to Imo's.

But.

What if?

Nah.

No way.

But what if?

A TV is almost always on at Imo's, a casual eatery with booths and big tables for folks to share a square pizza and a pitcher of beer, hang out, and watch a Cardinals or Rams game or the evening news. Since Monday, the day of Ben Ownby's disappearance only an hour's drive outside of St. Louis, the abduction was the major story that all of the local stations focused on. Over and over again, viewers watched as Ben smiled at them and police pounded home the description of the suspicious white Nissan pickup.

A white Nissan pickup?

It did not take long for Prosperi's staff to notice that Devo drove a white Nissan pickup.

Of course, the guys behind the counter acted as if they thought it was hilarious. They razzed Devo about it when he returned to work. Devo's white Nissan pickup became the week's running joke. Even Prosperi laughed.

Because the idea of Devo—a big harmless oaf of a guy who disliked kids—driving down to Franklin County and kidnapping Ben was just so preposterous, it was funny.

Still.

What if?

On a lark that Tuesday, the day after Ben disappeared, after Prosperi had heard yet again the description of the white pickup broadcast via the AMBER Alert for Ben, he drove to Devo's apartment to get a closer look at the vehicle. He acted as nonchalant as ever, not believing for one second that his friend could be guilty of kidnapping. Prosperi sauntered around Devo's white Nissan pickup in the parking lot. His stomach roiled. He noticed the truck dusted in relatively fresh red-clay dirt, the kind found in Missouri's backwoods, not like the soil in suburban Kirkwood. If Devo had been sick—and he sure looked ill on the day he was sent home—why would there be dirt on his car?

But Prosperi's oh-my-God! panic proved fleeting, flittering into sigh-heaving relief as he glanced at the lettering of the word "Nissan" on the back of Devo's white pickup. It looked more grayish than black—and police had clearly stated that the Nissan lettering was in black.

Come to think of it, Prosperi reasoned, Devo very well could have driven into the country. It was not unheard-of.

Maybe he went out there the weekend before he went home sick. He liked hunting and fishing, after all. He pushed aside thoughts of Devo's white Nissan pickup. His rationale was bolstered that Thursday, when he watched Devo chat with a Kirkwood police captain about duck hunting and bowfishing in the Mississippi River, rambling about some remote island where his friend owns land. Devo had acted like his usual know-it-all self. As calm and as cool as could be. He even seemed to enjoy hearing himself talk. Devo's body language displayed nothing that would have indicated fear, as one would expect a person to feel if he was talking to a police captain and had just abducted a child a few days earlier.

No shifty eyes, no nervous twitters, no pacing. Nothing.

Prosperi's guilt grew. Here he had snitched on one of his star employees, his friend of more than two decades, all because of a funny feeling that pestered and prodded and burrowed in his head like a bothersome tick.

Ironically, Prosperi acknowledged later that he probably would not have gone to law enforcement if he would have had to drive or walk far, his reasoning being that informing the cops about Devo's truck was so asinine, it would not have been worth the effort.

But the Kirkwood police station was so damn close to Imo's. So why not?

"I'm such a jerk," he said, picking an argument with himself, a back-and-forth internal spar that went something like this: But the road dust on Devo's pickup is too weird. But this is just so ridiculous. I can't believe I'm doing this. But what if, on the very off chance, Devo did have something to do with Ben's kidnapping—and you didn't say anything to police. You're a father. Ben could be your son. Could you ever live with yourself?

No. Prosperi decided he could not.

He walked into the dimly lit Kirkwood police station, a one-story building on a tree-lined street running parallel to downtown's train tracks. Nervous, Prosperi chortled as he told Kirkwood Police Captain John Folluo about Devo's white Nissan pickup truck. He acknowledged how silly he felt telling the police captain about his funny feeling—and he emphasized that it was only a slight suspicion because he was almost certain Devo had nothing to do with Ben's kidnapping. In fact, he was probably wasting Captain Folluo's time. Devo was a good guy. A hard worker. The kind of guy who spent his weekends helping his mother paint her house, helping his father rake leaves.

"I am 99.9 percent certain that I am wrong," Prosperi told the police captain.

Prosperi described Captain Folluo's response as "nonreactive." That is until it came up in conversation that Devo loved computer video games. Then, Prosperi said, "the captain's jaw dropped."

There was that funny feeling again.

For his part, Captain Folluo declined comment through a department spokesman. However, media accounts show that Captain Folluo and his colleagues at the Kirkwood Police Department took Prosperi's tip seriously, launching an immediate investigation that included photographing Devlin's truck and notifying the FBI.

Prosperi walked back to work feeling guilty. What kind of friend was he?

"I am such a jerk," he told himself for the umpteenth time that day.

Later, Prosperi told his adult daughter what he had done.

"Dad, you're a dick."

CHAPTER 21

Missing Ben

Mike Prosperi and his employees at Imo's pizzeria were not the only ones who had zeroed in on Michael Devlin's white Nissan pickup.

Devlin's mother commented on it when she called her son, according to an FBI report.

"Are you going to be arrested?" she asked, jokingly.

Some of Devlin's neighbors at the redbrick apartment complex on South Holmes Avenue also noticed the rusty old truck parked in the uncovered lot. One guy pointed it out to his friend Thursday morning.

"Check that out."

"You don't think?"

They looked at each other and shrugged. If only they had a cell phone with them, they could call the police. But they did not, and they had other things to do that day. Maybe, the guy thought, he would call the authorities later that night.

But there was no sense of urgency. After all, what would a child kidnapper be doing here, in an apartment complex in the middle of metropolitan St. Louis?

Another resident, twenty-five-year-old Krista Jones, noticed during the week of January 8 another boy—a skinny kid with glasses—hanging out with the hulking, hot-tempered "weirdo" in Unit D, the guy who always said he was going to call the cops on neighbors, according to media accounts. The new boy was hanging out with the older dark-haired boy, Shawn, who was a fixture at the Kirkwood apartments, a nice-enough teen who played with the other kids in the weedy courtyard and, in recent months, was spotted around town, in parks and at the mall, holding hands with his girlfriend.

The new boy seemed nice, too. "Jones said she saw Shawn every day for years but figured, as nearly everyone else, that he was Devlin's son," the *St. Louis Post-Dispatch* reported. "She noticed a new boy briskly leading Shawn and Devlin, walking side by side behind him, into the apartment."

Jones did not make the connection that the skinny boy with glasses was Ben Ownby, the Franklin County boy whose sweet face was all over the media, whose big grin adorned dozens of missing person fliers posted all over Kirkwood and in surrounding communities.

In fact, look at almost any television screen on that cold Thursday and there was Ben, grinning at viewers watching from his hometown in Beaufort, from other units in the apartment complex where he was being held captive, from sofas and chairs across the country. There, too, on the TV was the boy's family—his mother, father, and older sister, huddled together in their dark winter jackets, their wan complexions belying their fortitude, their resolve to find Ben.

Their tearful plea at a news conference Thursday broke hearts everywhere.

"Our son. He's a straight-A student, a Boy Scout, he is kind of a computer nerd," said Ben's father, Don Ownby, his voice cracking at times. "He wants to go to college for programming already. He knows that. He's thirteen but he's taking his first ACT test already. He's just a perfect student and son. . . .

"To wherever Ben is, or whoever has him, we just want to get him back safely, no questions asked. We just want to get our son back home. . . .

"It's a shock to us. It doesn't seem real. Any minute it seems like we're going to see him walk out of his room or hear him playing his games, but it doesn't happen. We just need anybody who thinks or maybe even suspects they know something just to come forward with it, even—maybe it's unfounded, but it could possibly be something. It could be something that would break this thing open for us so we can get our son home safely. . . .

"As parents it's hard enough, but you just try to imagine what the kid's going through, what Ben's going through, and that's heartbreaking. . . .

"He has his whole life ahead of him still, and we just want to get him back safe. Let him finish that. Let his family have him back. We love you, and we're not going to quit looking."

Ben's mother, Doris Ownby, also appealed to the cameras for her son's safe return: "We want people to know that we just want Ben back, that we miss him, and love him, and just to get him home to us."

Inside Unit D, a drab and untidy interior with curtainless back windows and faded furniture, Ben is reported to have watched his parents on television that day. According to law enforcement: Devlin asked Shawn Hornbeck to watch Ben while he was away. On Tuesday night, the day after Ben was kidnapped, Devlin worked the overnight shift at his second job at a nearby funeral parlor. He ordered the boys pizza from Domino's. Shawn and Ben played video games that night and during the days when Devlin went into Imo's. Sometimes they watched TV.

Possibly, Ben saw Franklin County Sheriff Gary Toelke's Thursday morning news conference, replayed on local broadcasts throughout the day. "We still got a lot of work to do," he said, standing outside of the sheriff's department, wearing a dark overcoat, white collar shirt, tie, and thin-rimmed eyeglasses. "If someone gives us information we're going to check it out. I guarantee it."

Once again, Sheriff Toelke drummed home the importance of the white pickup: "The truck is very important to this investigation and getting this case solved."

Later that night, back in Kirkwood, a white Nissan pickup was about to get a lot more attention. Police Officers Gary Wagster and Chris Nelson, both with the Kirkwood Police Department, had been summoned to the apartment complex on 491 South Holmes Avenue, where the pair planned to arrest one of Michael Devlin's neighbors, a man who was not home at the time.

According to various media accounts corroborated by the Kirkwood Police Department, the following scenario unfolded: As the officers walked down the steps and headed back to their patrol car, just before 9 p.m., they noticed an old pickup parked in a spot reserved for the building's residents and near the police vehicle.

The run-down pickup was white.

The word "Nissan" appeared on the back.

It had rust, it had dirt, and it had all the criteria to fit the description of the truck linked to the kidnapping of Ben Ownby.

Officer Wagster turned to his partner. "Do you see what I see? That looks a lot like the truck on TV."

Shocked, Officer Nelson blurted an expletive.

The officers examined the white Nissan pickup in more detail.

They both knew what they needed to do next: Find the owner of the truck.

Officer Wagster went one way, Officer Nelson the other.

They knocked on neighbors' doors, they stopped passersby, asking if anyone knew anything about the owner of the white pickup. They struck up a conversation with resident Michael Devlin, who was throwing his garbage into the community dumpster.

At first, Devlin was as nice as could be. He appeared calm and friendly. The officers recognized Devlin from the Imo's pizza parlor a half a block from the Kirkwood police station. Devlin was the easygoing guy who worked at the restaurant and, like many of the city's cops, the officers often grabbed a bite to eat there.

"Is this your truck?" Officer Wagster asked Devlin, pointing to the white Nissan pickup.

Devlin said it was.

The officers continued to probe. They told Devlin that his truck matched the description of the one linked to the missing child case out in Franklin County.

Devlin seemed to understand the policemen's implication.

And that is when Devlin turned "squirrelly," an adjective the officers would reiterate in the media.

"For a guy that's laid-back, he got real defensive," Officer Wagster recalled one week later, on *The Oprah Winfrey Show*, as he described Devlin clenching his fists, darting his eyes, and acting evasive. "When I was asking him questions, it's like, I'd never seen this guy before . . . this ain't the guy who works at Imo's."

Both officers became even more suspicious. Based on their

intuition, they strongly suspected that Devlin was linked to the Ben Ownby case.

Oprah Winfrey: So it's that little hunch thing. That little . . .

Officer Gary Wagster: The gut thing.

Officer Chris Nelson: The hair on the back of your neck.

Officers Wagster and Nelson continued to talk with Devlin for as long as possible. As conversation sputtered, Devlin walked away.

By then the FBI already had been contacted and was en route. Around 9:30 p.m., FBI Agent Dion Cantu and Jeffrey Paul, a trooper with the Missouri State Highway Patrol, interrogated Devlin in the laundry room of the apartment complex, according to law enforcement and media reports. They asked to go inside the apartment, but Devlin declined entry. The pair left to pursue other suspects, believing that Devlin's tire brand did not match the one they were seeking, the *Post-Dispatch* reported.

However, surveillance of Devlin's apartment continued. As officers were watching over Unit D, they noticed a slit in the blinds of the front window, according to media accounts. Through the slip, they saw someone playing a video game at the kitchen table. Devlin had told the Kirkwood police officers that "he had a child inside but refused to tell them his name or how he was related," according to the *Post-Dispatch*. "Devlin finally told the officers the boy was his godson, but refused to let them in."

At the time, they apparently had no idea that person was Shawn Hornbeck, the boy stolen from rural Richwoods nearly four and a half years earlier, the boy everyone thought was dead, the boy who would talk with police a few hours later that night.

Investigators spoke with Shawn at the front door of Unit D, according to media reports. The teenager identified himself as Shawn Wilcox: He was the godson of Devlin, who was caring for him while his father stayed in New York on a business trip. Shawn's mother was dead.

Ben remained out of sight, hidden in the tiny apartment.

Before Shawn answered the door that night, "he and Devlin told Ben to hide behind the door of Devlin's bedroom and to remain silent," the Associated Press reported. Devlin would later tell the FBI that the police presence frightened Shawn.

Authorities said they lacked a search warrant to gain entry into Devlin's apartment, but they had spoken with Devlin on several occasions, each time asking if they could come inside his apartment.

Each time, Devlin refused.

And although police were in the process of obtaining a search warrant, at the time they did not have probable cause to force entry.

The *Post-Dispatch* cited an anonymous source close to the Devlin case: "The investigators were focused on finding Ben," the article stated, "and Shawn's disappearance was not on their radar. . . . Several law enforcement officials have questioned the move, saying investigators were lucky neither boy was harmed overnight once it was clear authorities were closing in."

The *Post-Dispatch* reported that "Devlin's mother derided investigators as early as February [2007], accusing investigators of having 'bungled' the investigation, according to police reports obtained by the newspaper under a freedom-of-information request."

The newspaper provided greater detail about the investigation, reporting that an FBI task force eliminated Devlin as a suspect that Thursday night, shortly after the Kirkwood officers notified the FBI about their suspicions. "An FBI misunderstanding about the brand of tires on Devlin's pickup subjected Ben, 13, and Shawn, [15], to an extra night of captivity" and potential sexual abuse, according to the *Post-Dispatch*. The FBI released a statement, which the newspaper quoted: The FBI "and a number of other law enforcement agencies conducted and cooperated in a very thorough, extensive, and exhaustive investigation . . . Although we cannot comment on specific investigative processes/details connected to the investigation, we are confident in the appropriateness of the investigative steps that were taken, and which ultimately led to Devlin's identification as the abductor and the recovery of the victims."

Despite the FBI's decision to focus on other leads, officers Wagster and Nelson—with the blessing of Kirkwood Police Chief Jack Plummer—continued surveillance of Devlin's apartment until their shifts ended at 2 a.m., the *Post-Dispatch* reported. At that time, other Kirkwood officers took over and continued the watch. It wasn't until early the next morning, some time after 4 a.m. on Friday, that the FBI realized "Devlin's tire brand is, in fact, a possible match," the newspaper stated.

Besides conducting surveillance at Devlin's apartment and questioning his neighbors, authorities visited his long-time place of employment earlier that night, where they interviewed the owner's adult daughter, who was serving as Imo's manager.

When police left, she called her father and told him what had happened.

Mike Prosperi laughed. "She's razzing me," he thought. "She's giving me a hard time because I was such a dick for ratting out my friend to police."

CHAPTER 22
Closing In

Michael Devlin arrived on time for his shift at Imo's pizzeria that Friday morning.

Not that he was ever late; however, on that particular morning, one might understand if he had been.

Presumably, Devlin had experienced a stressful night.

Law enforcement agents had kept his apartment under surveillance. Several times during the night, uniformed officers knocked on his front door, wanting to enter Unit D. Each time, Devlin refused their requests, not exactly winning any points with the authorities. Of course, if he had allowed them inside, police would have discovered Ben Ownby—the missing boy from Franklin County who was all over the local news—as well as Shawn Hornbeck—the missing boy from Washington County who used to be all over the news.

If Devlin was smart—and indications are that he was somewhat intelligent—he had to have known that police were closing in on him and it was only a matter of time before his purported secrets—sadistic and sinful in every which way—were revealed to the world. It is difficult to imagine Devlin getting a good night's sleep Thursday with such a burden bearing down on him.

Perhaps even more adrenaline-inducing that night was Devlin's most pressing concern: keeping two teenage boys complacent so as not to further rouse the cops hovering outside of his door. At the time, he had three guns in his apartment—a loaded Ruger pistol inside a wok on a kitchen shelf and two rifles in a living room closet, according to an FBI report. Fortunately, Devlin did not spin into a frantic fury and fire bullets at the boys, resulting in either a double homicide or a double murder-suicide.

However Devlin coped, he managed to arrive at work on time the next day. He even remembered to get to the restaurant an hour before his usual shift. Imo's boss Mike Prosperi had asked some of his staff to come in early that Friday to help with a big order: It was Pizza Day at Holy Redeemer, a Catholic school in nearby Webster Groves, and Imo's was providing the square-cut pizza pies for the elementary school students.

Still feeling guilty about going to the police, Prosperi greeted Devlin with the usual pleasantries as if nothing had happened. "Hey, how is it going?"

Devlin gave a halfhearted response. Prosperi noticed that he was not acting like himself, like the know-it-all, nice-guy

Devo everyone there had become accustomed to. He seemed distracted, agitated, and sullen. Like he had a lot on his mind. He kept to himself that morning and did not chuckle good-naturedly when the workers behind the counter joshed about his white Nissan pickup.

"Your truck still attracting a lot of attention?" one of the employees joked.

Normally, Devo was the type who would have enjoyed the ribbing. He would have laughed and probably retorted with a smart-ass comeback.

Devlin ignored any teasing that Friday morning.

Maybe he was pissed, Prosperi thought, wondering if his employee knew that he had snitched on him.

The thought was fleeting, though, because Prosperi knew police kept such matters confidential. Still, Prosperi could not stop thinking about what he had done. He felt responsible for Devlin being hounded by police, for his friend's obvious distress that morning. Prosperi, too, had experienced restlessness the night before as he contemplated his actions. His wife, who has also known Devlin for years, expressed shock that her husband had gone to the police.

"I can't believe you went to the police and never told me you were going to do it," Prosperi recalled his wife saying to him, her longtime husband.

Prosperi's adult daughter thought her dad was a big dick.

Hell, he thought of himself as a jerk.

Even though his employee was under police suspicion, Prosperi still thought Devlin was innocent. That the white Nissan pickup Devlin drove around town was just a strange coincidence, a stroke of bad luck that they would all laugh about in the months ahead. That it would all get sorted out in no time. That Devlin would act like Devo again, making wisecracks and shooting off his opinions to anyone who would listen.

And Devo, who was normally such a conscientious worker, who knew the intricacies of Imo's operations after working there for a quarter of a century, also seemed inept at his job that morning. His task was to clean the deep fryer, which entails boiling water with a solution while taking extra precaution to ensure that the hot mixture does not run over.

Not paying attention, Devlin let the deep fryer boil over. He had never done that before. Usually, he was quite fastidious about the deep fryer.

Prosperi got that funny feeling again. *Something is just not right.*

In a friendly manner, he decided to ask Devlin about the police.

"I heard you were paid a visit by the FBI last night."

"Yeah. They wanted to search my apartment. I didn't let them in."

"Why not?"

"They were too snooty."

"Wouldn't it have been easier to just let them in?"

"They didn't ask me a nice way."

OK, Prosperi thought. This was just weird. He could not follow Devlin's logic. Even if Devlin had felt badgered by the cops or was offended that they were questioning him, why wouldn't he just allow investigators inside his apartment and be done with the whole matter?

That his employee could be hiding sinister secrets just seemed too surreal to merit plausibility.

But Prosperi could not dwell on Devlin's situation. He had to go to the bank and run some other errands. He left the restaurant at about 9 a.m.

By the time Prosperi returned later that morning, about twenty-five law enforcement vehicles filled the parking lot behind the pizzeria. He walked up to a uniformed officer from the St. Louis County Police Department, who was inspecting Devlin's white Nissan pickup.

Prosperi playfully punched the police officer in the arm.

"Am I going to have to work today?"

The police officer smirked.

Inside the pizzeria, Devlin continued with the tasks at hand. He mopped the floor. He cleaned off tables. He took "breaks" to go outside and speak with authorities.

According to an FBI report: At around 12:10 p.m., Devlin agreed to an interview with FBI Special Agents M. L. Willett and Christina M. Kinney, who spoke with the pizza manager in Imo's back entrance after advising him of his rights and the reason for their questioning: his truck matched the one linked to Ben Ownby's abduction.

Was Devlin in Franklin County on Monday?

No, he was home sick with stomach problems.

Devlin also told the agents that the white Nissan pickup belonged to his brother; he was supposed to buy it but couldn't because of credit problems. Devlin owed ten to fifteen years of personal property taxes on a previous vehicle. His brother had let him use the truck for four years.

The FBI agents wanted to conduct a search of the pickup. At first Devlin balked at the inconvenience, but eventually agreed, digging the keys out of his jeans and handing them to the agents. Out in the parking lot, Devlin watched as the 1991 truck was towed to a secure and more private facility for a closer inspection.

Special Agent Kinney noticed that Devlin's left foot was in a sock and sandal. Devlin explained it was swollen, a result of his diabetes. It was raining, and she invited him to continue the questioning inside her vehicle, where he might be more comfortable. The pizza parlor worker agreed.

Devlin then provided the FBI agents with snippets of his life: How he was adopted and grew up in nearby Webster Groves. How he owned land in Washington County. How he went on vacations to the Grand Canyon and Yellowstone Park, which he described as "beautiful" and farther from the Grand Canyon than Devlin realized.

He told the agents that he graduated from Rankin Technical College with a certificate in computers. That he worked a part-time, overnight job at a nearby funeral parlor, where he answered phones, picked up corpses, and, if nothing was going on, slept. That he used to work for an alarm company and a tool company. He told agents he was fired from one job because of tardiness and quit the other "due to a difference in business opinions."

Devlin also told the agents he is "leery" of police because of several bad experiences. One involved his "godson," Shawn, who was riding his bike when he was stopped by an officer in neighboring Glendale. Shawn was not treated well, nor was Devlin when he called the police supervisor to complain.

"Devlin stated Shawn was staying with Devlin while Shawn's father was traveling on business," according to the FBI report. "Shawn stays with Devlin often. Shawn's father is an old friend of Devlin's who moved away from St. Louis and then moved back after his [the friend's] wife passed away. Shawn's father works for an electronics company. Shawn does not like Imo's pizza. Shawn is home schooled by Shawn's grandmother. Shawn and his father live in the area.

"Shawn, Shawn's father and Devlin do not own cellular telephones," the report continued. "Shawn's father does not believe in cellular telephones."

As his employee and friend was being interviewed by the FBI, Prosperi still did not believe Devlin could do anything so horrific as to kidnap a child. No way. No matter how many police converged upon his restaurant, it was all just too unbelievable.

Devo is fine, Prosperi would tell himself. It is all just a mix-up. Next week, we will all be at work laughing about this whole incident.

And then his funny feeling would return.

CHAPTER 23
The Missouri Miracle

Kim Evans also had a funny feeling. Hers tingled at the spine and knotted the stomach. It happened when she watched TV news reports about the missing thirteen-year-old boy from Franklin County.

It's him, she thought. It's the same guy who took Shawn Hornbeck.

By now, Shawn had been missing for four years and three months. The eleven-year-old boy she knew as a neighborhood kid, an occasional playmate to her children, a tireless trampoline jumper, would have been fifteen years old. The brown-eyed boy with the dark hair had changed her life. Since he vanished that October afternoon in 2002, Evans had devoted herself to the Shawn Hornbeck Foundation, the nonprofit group his parents founded in his honor. She also became close with Shawn's parents, Pam and Craig Akers. She shared in their grief over Shawn—and over any child who goes missing.

Evans saw on a daily basis how Shawn's kidnapping had affected his family: His parents seemed to have permanent drawn-in dark circles beneath their eyes. His mother was thin, with a sunken-in face and sad blue eyes. His stepfather ambled around on a prosthetic leg, after his was amputated due to poor circulation, a condition most likely strained by the physically exhausting searches in rough terrain that he participated in to find his son and other missing children. Shawn's two older sisters had suffered, too. At times, some townsfolk said, they looked lost, as if they were trying to find something important.

But no matter how weary Shawn's parents felt, they remained resolute in their belief that their son would come home. They held on to hope as if it were their only lifeline, a buoy that kept them afloat, allowing them to tread water through the mundane necessities of life until their son came home—and if they let go of hope, they let go of everything. Leaving them with nothing.

Evans admired the Akerses' ability to cling to hope. But if she was honest with herself, although she hated to think about such things, she believed Shawn was dead. Four years was a long time to be missing. She knew that his parents had done everything in their power to bring their son home, and that if he had been lost in the woods, as everyone assumed at first, the searchers committed to locating the boy would have found him by now. And through her work with the Shawn Hornbeck Foundation, Evans also was aware that stranger kidnappings are the rarest and most dangerous types of abductions. That the odds did not favor the boy being alive after all of these years.

And now, Evans's heart ached for the parents and sister of Ben Ownby, who was stolen on a rural road in Beaufort, about forty miles northwest of Richwoods, where the same thing had happened to Shawn. One boy was riding a bike, the other getting off of a school bus, but otherwise similarities were apparent:

Both boys were around the same ages when plucked from near their homes. That they were boys was curious, since girls are the majority of stranger-kidnapping victims.

Both hailed from remote locales that were within a fifty-mile radius of each other.

Both seemed to have vaporized instantaneously, indicating that the abductor executed the same opportunistic techniques with each child.

And for two local boys to be kidnapped by a complete unknown person, when only a small percentage of all abductions are done by strangers, it just seemed like more than an unfortunate coincidence.

It had to be the same guy, Evans thought, shaking her head. She had that funny feeling. She just knew it in her gut.

On that cold Friday morning as Evans and Imo's owner Mike Prosperi were having their funny feelings and as longtime Imo's employee Michael Devlin was letting the deep fryer boil over for the first time ever while taking "breaks" from his work shift to speak with police, Franklin County Sheriff Gary Toelke appeared on television. Once again he appealed to the public for help in solving the Ownby case.

Hair neatly combed and his face clean shaven, with his broad shoulders draped in a crisp dark suit and white-collared shirt, Sheriff Toelke said that the department was investigating more than five hundred leads stemming from the description of the white Nissan pickup truck provided by Mitchell Hults, the young witness. As authorities planned Friday to continue their search for Ben—especially before an impending ice storm, which meteorologists predicted would hit the area within twenty-four hours—Sheriff Toelke reiterated what he believed would be the most important factor in bringing Ben home.

"These type of cases, as we've said before, are extremely difficult to solve," Sheriff Toelke said during a press conference, his lilting voice projecting a sense of calmness, a feeling that his department had everything under control. "There's one simple thing that can solve this case. . . . Somebody other than the person who owns the truck knows about the truck. They know who it belongs to. They've seen it. And somebody is sitting there wondering: 'You know, I've seen that truck. It belongs to so and so. Could it possibly be the person they are looking for? Well he's a pretty nice person, and I just don't think it would be him.' Typically in these cases, in the past, when they find the suspect, the suspect is somebody who nobody suspected would be involved in something like this. They don't go down the road with 'I'm a child abductor' on the side of their truck. It's somebody you would not think would be responsible. When that person calls and tells us, 'You know, I didn't think it was this person but maybe it is. They've got a truck like this. Could you please check this out?' That's the person we need to call us. That's the person who is going to give us a break in the case."

As reporters flung questions at him, prying for answers where there seemed to be none, a weary expression flashed across Sheriff Toelke's face: "This is the fourth day, and time is a concern."

At the time, Sheriff Toelke did not reveal that a team of law enforcement agents had a strong lead in the case, about fifty miles to the northeast in Kirkwood, where officials continued their surveillance Friday of the apartment of Michael Devlin, owner of a white Nissan pickup with rust and dents and all of the descriptors of the truck speeding down the rural roads of Beaufort just after Ben disappeared. Investigators continued knocking on residents' doors, showing people a photograph of Ben and asking if they had seen the boy in the area. Many of Devlin's neighbors, once they had seen police snooping around the residential complex, had mentioned their concerns about the white Nissan pickup matching the suspicious vehicle being described on television. Many mentioned what they knew about Devlin: That he had a bad temper and a teenage boy—they presumed the man's son—who listened to loud banging music, played video games with the front door open, and appeared polite enough.

Authorities knew about the dark-haired teenage boy inside Unit D, as he had answered the door and spoken with uniformed officers the night before, identifying himself as Shawn Wilcox, Devlin's godson.

At a law enforcement roundtable discussion Friday morning about the Ben Ownby case, Lieutenant Kyle Marquart of the Missouri State Highway Patrol reportedly made an offhand remark about the teenage boy with the brown eyes and dark floppy hair who called himself Shawn Wilcox:

"Wouldn't it be something if that was Shawn Hornbeck?"

Shawn Hornbeck still alive after all of these years. Still alive, and so close to home.

"Wouldn't that be something," some of the agents at the roundtable are reported to have said in response to an idea that seemed too inconceivable and too idealistic to imagine.

But what if?

While he was being questioned by FBI agents at Imo's, Devlin continued to deny that he had ever kidnapped a boy. That is, until authorities asked him: "What would happen if the tire treads from his truck matched the treads found at the location of Ownby's disappearance?" an FBI report stated.

"Maybe I have common tires," Devlin responded.

The FBI agents explained that tire tracks are as unique as fingerprints.

Devlin appeared nervous. He started breathing fast.

"Shawn is not my godson. Shawn is Shawn Hornbeck. He is at the apartment."

The FBI agents asked if Ben was there, too.

"Yes."

He told the agents that Ben and Shawn were alive.

"I'm a bad person," Devlin said.

Devlin agreed to accompany the agents to his apartment, but he told them he was concerned about Shawn "freaking out."

While FBI Special Agent Christina M. Kinney got Devlin's consent to enter his apartment and rescue the boys, Devlin said "that he did not want law enforcement to 'storm' into the apartment," according to the report. "Devlin was told that the agents would not storm the apartment and that the boys would be taken care of." For his part, Devlin would tell Shawn that "none of this was his fault and if the police asked him anything just to tell the truth."

Around 3:20 p.m. Friday, the FBI escorted Devlin out of Imo's pizza parlor, leaving his coworkers staring at the spectacle with bugged eyes and gaping mouths.

For his boss, the scene was as surreal as a bad dream.

"That's not the Devo I know," Prosperi thought.

He was still in shock, in understandable denial, about his

friend and his employee whom he has known for more than two decades.

Just twenty minutes prior to police taking Devlin away, the pizza parlor received a call from Devlin's apartment. Prosperi recognized Devlin's home phone number on the caller ID. He called back, recalling that the conversation went like this:

A young boy answered.

"Hello," Prosperi said. "Who is this, please?"

"Who is this?"

"I'm Michael Devlin's boss. Who is this, please?"

"This is Shawn Wilcox. My father is a friend of Michael Devlin's."

"Can I please speak with an adult?"

"There's not an adult here."

Prosperi hung up the phone and called the police. His funny feeling skyrocketed. There should be an adult in the apartment with Shawn Wilcox, he thought. This is getting too weird. Something is not right.

Still.

He struggled to grasp that Devo—a nice guy he entrusted to count his money at the end of the day, a gabby giant whose babbles amused and annoyed, a hardworking manager who never once took home a free pizza from his employer—that a man whom he has known almost half of his life could be responsible for such a serious and soulless crime.

"No way," he said to himself. "Not Devo."

But the Devo whom Prosperi knew was gone.

About a mile to the east of Imo's that Friday afternoon, Devlin voluntarily unlocked his front door and allowed law enforcement authorities to enter Unit D. Inside, police witnessed something so unbelievable, even hardened investigators did a double take. Although Devlin had told the FBI about Shawn Hornbeck—the boy presumed dead—seeing him alive was as stunning and uplifting as watching a beautiful act of nature—a sun setting, a soaring eagle, a sweeping vista—and having your breath taken away.

And, indeed, there was the natural wonder, in the form of a brown-eyed boy sitting on a ratty old sofa in the apartment's drab living room.

Next to Shawn, sitting on the arm of a chair, was the missing thirteen-year-old.

Ben looked up at an FBI agent: "Are you going to take me home?"

An FBI agent turned to the older teenager with the shaggy dark hair. He asked the kid to identify himself.

"I am Shawn Hornbeck."

Later, investigators would describe their shock, their elation, even their tears of joy at the "miracle" of rescuing two missing boys—one gone for four days, the other for four years.

To find Ben was a glorious godsend in and of itself. But to also discover Shawn ... that was simply unbelievable. Most people assumed he was dead. Even the prosecuting attorney in Washington County, who had been working on the boy's case since the beginning, who had developed an emotional attachment to the case, had concluded by now that Shawn was no longer living.

To find Shawn, very much alive, older, heavier, taller, talking, walking, breathing, was nothing short of a miracle of momentous proportions.

"You have to face families every day, and to have something like this happen, there is no way to describe it," Franklin County Sheriff Toelke said in a quote in the *St. Louis Post-Dispatch*. "But that's nothing like what the families went through."

Later, some of the law enforcement officials would say the discovery of Shawn and Ben would be the highlight of their careers, a testament to their commitment to justice, an affirmation of hope and happy endings.

Investigators would say all of those things and more—later. Right now, they had to get Ben and Shawn home to their families.

Inside the Ownbys' house in Beaufort, Ben's parents had just sat down to do an interview for a television station when Major Mike Copeland, a chief deputy at the Franklin County Sheriff's Department, came into the room and took the family aside.

"We have him."

Ben's mother, Doris Ownby, was stunned. "I said, 'What do you mean?' I wasn't sure if we got the bad guy or Ben," she recounted to *People* magazine. "Once he said Ben, I screamed."

So did everyone else in the room. "All we were doing was crying," Connie Feth, a family friend who was with the Ownbys when the good news was delivered, said in an interview with the *Post-Dispatch*. Her son, Tyler, and Ben are best friends.

As everyone was crying and hugging and grabbing their jackets to go get the boy, Ben's father had an important mission. He ran into his son's bedroom to retrieve a pack of multi-flavor Dentyne gum, *People* reported: "It's his favorite," Don Ownby said. "I was saving it for him."

Pack of gum in hand, the family went with Major Copeland to the Franklin County Sheriff's Department in Union, the county seat approximately eleven miles to the east of Beaufort. That is where their son Ben would be waiting for his family to take him home.

During the car ride to the sheriff's department, Ben's father kept asking authorities: Are you sure it's Ben? How do you know?

"The whole time we were going there, I wanted to know it was really him," Don recalled on NBC's *Today* show. "I couldn't quite let myself go yet. When he walked in that room I finally knew he was OK. His mom got to him first, though."

"I got by everybody and I just grabbed him and just held onto him for a long time," Doris added. "I didn't say anything. I just held onto him. I didn't want to let him go. Finally, I realized I had to share him with his dad."

Meanwhile, about fifty miles to the south of Union, Washington County Prosecuting Attorney John Rupp was working that Friday afternoon in his office inside the courthouse in the county seat of Potosi when he received one of the most important calls of his career, the break in a case he had investigated for more than four years, a case that affected him emotionally.

"I'd go home and isolate myself," Rupp told *St. Louis Magazine*. "I'd go mess on my computer or sit in front of the TV and watch the History Channel like a junkie. I didn't want to talk to my wife. I didn't want to play with our two kids."

Rupp first received a call from Mark Dochterman, a sergeant with the Missouri State Highway Patrol who was one of the lead investigators when Shawn disappeared in 2002. A *St. Louis Magazine* profile of Rupp, published in April 2007, provided the following account of the initial and subsequent telephone conversations:

> *"We think we've found Shawn alive," [Dochterman] said.*
>
> *"What do you mean think?"*
>
> *"I'll have to get back to you on that one," Dochterman said.*
>
> *Rupp began his pacing. It seemed five hours passed before his phone rang again, although his clock told him that it had been only 10 minutes.*
>
> *"We're sure we've found Shawn," Dochterman said.*
>
> *"What do you mean you're sure?" asked Rupp, ever the trial lawyer.*
>
> *"Can't say, but I'll have someone else call." A minute later, Rupp's phone rang again. It was Franklin County Sheriff Gary Toelke.*
>
> *"You'd better get a hold of the parents now," the sheriff told Rupp. "He's identified himself as Shawn Hornbeck."*

Rupp scrambled to find phone numbers for Shawn's parents, Pam and Craig Akers, who were commuting the sixty or so miles from their work in north St. Louis County to their home in Richwoods. It was around 4 p.m., and the car ride was treacherous, with bleak skies and a downpour of rain that would soon turn icy. Traffic crawled along the slippery roads.

Inside the car, Pam and Craig heard their cell phones ring.

At first, Rupp got Pam's voicemail on her cell phone.

"Pam, please call me back immediately," Shawn's mother said, recalling the phone message on *The Oprah Winfrey Show.* "Of course, the first thing that popped in my mind is 'OK, Oh my God! What news does he have?' 'Cause I knew he had to have had some news to be calling me."

She wondered if it was bad news, if her son was dead.

"I definitely had thought of that," Pam told Oprah. "And then I had told myself, You can't think of that yet. We don't know."

As Pam finished listening to her message from the prosecutor, her husband, Craig, was on the phone with Rupp.

The prosecuting attorney asked Craig where he was, where Pam was.

Craig told him that they were both in the car, driving home from work.

Rupp advised them to pull over.

Pam heard her husband say it would take him a few minutes to find a safe spot to park the car. And it did. A few minutes that seemed like hours. Like forever. They braced for the information—to be instructed to pull over sounded ominous. Would they hear the news that they had feared for years? Was their son dead? Was this it?

But Rupp's news was anything but bad.

We think we found Shawn, he told Craig. We are 95 percent sure that we found Shawn and that he is alive.

Shawn is alive!

To Craig, Rupp's words were the sweetest he had ever heard—"a present from heaven," as he later described the phone call on a TV news report.

He and Pam sat in their car for a few minutes, absorbing the news, crying, trying not to get too excited. Their hopes had been dashed too many times during the past four years and three months. The couple then headed toward the Franklin County Sheriff's Department during a trip that was long for reasons other than the sleet and the ten-miles-per-hour driving conditions.

The car ride took forever because they were desperate to see their son. They had waited long enough. They needed to hug Shawn, kiss him, and tell him how much he was loved. They needed to take their boy home.

On their way to get their son, Pam and Craig wondered if they would recognize Shawn. A lot could change physically between eleven years of age and fifteen. And who knows what he had been through while in captivity. "Craig did make the comment to me, 'It has been four and a half years,'" Pam said on *Oprah*. "He says, 'Pam, how are we going to know?' And then he looked right at me and he says, 'You're gonna know.' And I said, 'Yeah, I'll know. I'll know immediately.'"

As Shawn's parents drove to the Franklin County Sheriff's Department, a caravan of law enforcement vehicles transporting Shawn and Ben also headed approximately fifty miles from Kirkwood to the department headquarters in Union, where the convoy arrived at about 4:30 p.m.

One police vehicle parked, and out stepped Ben, who was escorted by authorities hovering around him as if he were a crown jewel, rightfully protecting the child from anything and everything, with one investigator's hands on the thin boy's shoulders leading him inside the sheriff's department. The thirteen-year-old wore a long-sleeved red shirt and jeans, and he appeared relieved, looking at all of the officers and media with an inquisitive expression and a dazed look in his eyes.

Less than a minute later, another vehicle pulled up. Law enforcement agents opened the door and out walked Shawn, looking all grown up compared to the photos of him as an eleven-year-old boy. Surrounding law enforcement investigators, members of the media and bystanders stared in disbelief—in awe—at the fifteen-year-old sporting a thick mop of dark hair and ear and lip piercings, and wearing jeans and a leather jacket.

Is it really him? The Shawn Hornbeck who has been missing for more than four years, now home safe?

And it was Shawn Hornbeck, a walking miracle, the sight of him and Ben Ownby inspiring claps, cheers, and tears.

Officially, the news was announced at a 4:50 p.m. press conference outside of the Franklin County Sheriff's Department. Standing in the dark freezing rain, Sheriff Toelke—flanked by Franklin County Prosecutor Robert E. Parks, FBI Special Agent Roland Corvington, and Lieutenant Marquart of the Missouri State Highway Patrol—faced TV and digital cameras and a throng of journalists eager to scribble the latest developments in their reporters' notebooks:

"We have some good news for you this evening and probably some unbelievable news," Sheriff Toelke said. "We did locate Ben this afternoon in the city of Kirkwood and we also located Shawn Hornbeck, who was at the same residence."

Some reporters gasped. Others gaped. Brows furrowed, one journalist kept shaking his head in disbelief as he wrote as fast as he could while the rain soaked him. This story was big—front-page, above-the-fold big. The unique twists of the case, the miracle outcome—that rare news report in which there is a happy ending—catapulted the story to the national level; the bigwigs from New York would parachute in the next day, bulldozing their way across Eastern Missouri in pursuit of a scoop, ideally an exclusive interview with Shawn Hornbeck. For some local journalists, it was one of the biggest stories of their careers; their make-or-break moment. The adrenaline, the excitement, the competitive spirit—it was all palpable at the press conference.

The news kept coming, too. Robert E. Parks, the gray-haired and bespectacled county prosecutor, announced that they had a suspect in custody who had confessed to kidnapping Ben: "The Franklin County Prosecutors Office has charged one Michael J. Devlin, date of birth 11–19–65, of Kirkwood, Missouri, at this time with one count of kidnapping in the first degree and we have asked for and received $1 million bond. More charges are likely to be filed as we find out more about that. But at the present time, we've filed one charge. He is still being questioned, and we can't say any more than that."

Of course, the media began throwing questions at the law enforcement agents. One journalist asked Sheriff Toelke how he felt. "You have one of these [cases] in your career, that's quite an experience," he said, referring to the Abby Woods baby kidnapping four months earlier. "And luckily, that one had a positive ending. And then to have another one come up, this is just unbelievable."

Another celebratory factor of the case: that the description of the white Nissan pickup, which some law enforcement officials had criticized the sheriff for focusing on too much—proved to be the key to finding the boys. Ben's busmate, fifteen-year-old Mitchell Hults, became an instant hero—one of many, the sheriff emphasized, thanking the FBI and all of the investigators on the case, "the best in Missouri," as well as the public for its vigilance in reporting leads to police and the media for publicizing information about the truck.

But what everyone wanted to know about the most were the reunions: Ben and his family together again after four days; Shawn and his family after more than four years. "Obviously, they were some very happy people," said the sheriff, who only had seen the Ownbys reunited. "A lot of times, they didn't know what to say."

So little was said at first because Ben's parents and sister could not stop hugging and kissing him. When Ben first walked into the sheriff's department and greeted his family after being missing for four days, his mother ran over and hugged her son, not letting go for quite some time and then only reluctantly.

When Shawn's parents arrived at the sheriff's office a short time later, few words were spoken. At first, his parents felt a split second of shock. The last time they had seen their son, he was a boy; now he was a teenager, almost old enough to drive a car. He was approximately five inches taller and thirty pounds heavier, looking more like a man than the SpongeBob-loving child that they had known.

Then Pam and Craig Akers saw Shawn's face: his brown eyes, his dark hair, his playful grin.

Oh My God! That's my son!

Shawn's mother wrapped her arms around her son. "I love you, I miss you, and you're home," Pam is reported as having said to Shawn.

And then the family hugged. For five minutes. One big group hug. One steady stream of "I love yous" and "We're so glad you're home," the words punctuated with tears of joy, with kisses and more kisses.

The family painfully ripped apart four years ago held tightly to one another, not wanting to let go.

Ever.

CHAPTER 24

Home, Safe and Sound

Despite the freezing rain, plunging temperatures, and threats of a power-snapping ice storm, Friday night's news of the "Missouri miracle," as it was already being called, invigorated metropolitan St. Louis. All across the area, people watched the live events on television screens in restaurants and bars, in the electronics section of big-box stores, strangers clapping and high-fiving each other. The miracle was announced over a public address system in a grocery store, over companywide e-mail systems, and in a toddler play-gym, where mommies clutched their children tight and cried happy tears for the families. Cell phones rang and Blackberries beeped with messages of "Did you hear?"

All around St. Louis, people celebrated, honking horns in the street, buying rounds of drinks at bars, letting employees go home early so they could be with their families. The buzz about town, the zip, the zing, was reminiscent of a few months earlier, on October 27, 2006, when the St. Louis Cardinals beat the Detroit Tigers to win the World Series for the first time since 1982, at the city's inaugural ballpark. For a town obsessed with their Cardinals, for a town that has been nick-named "Baseball City USA," the World Series win was a collective monumental occasion—as was this, the first non-sports story in recent memory to rise to a celebratory level, the rare crime story with a happy ending.

The mood at the Franklin County Sheriff's Department remained euphoric throughout the night, as family and friends of the Ownbys braved the inclement weather to drive to the department in Union to show their support and share in the joy of having not one boy but two rescued. Along with his mother, Mitchell Hults—the young hero who provided police with the tip that unraveled Michael Devlin's crimes—went straight to the sheriff's department after he heard the news. His family had been praying for Ben's safe return. "It's crazy," Mitchell told the *St. Louis Post-Dispatch*. "I'm happy they got him and I'm glad he's OK."

In Washington County, prosecutor John Rupp rejoiced as he watched TV footage of Shawn being escorted into the sheriff's department, to safety. He turned to Don Cooksey, a former St. Louis police officer and former Potosi police chief who was one of the lead investigators on the case, and the two men shook hands, *St. Louis Magazine* reported, before heading to the local Elks Club for some beers.

Their colleague, Mark Dochterman, a sergeant with the Missouri State Highway Patrol and one of the lead investigators in the case, felt such relief. "I cried," he told *NBC News*. "I was so overwhelmed. When something comes to a conclusion like that, it's just like a dam breaking, and it was just an unbelievable feeling."

In Shawn's hometown of Richwoods, local officials opened the doors to the elementary school so residents could celebrate Shawn's rescue—which they did, hugging, jumping up and down, and screaming with excitement. So many of them had devoted hundreds of hours to searching for Shawn, putting aside their lives to save a boy some had never met. At the town's only restaurant, Bardenheier Wine Cellars, which opened while Shawn was in captivity, the marquee outside already announced: "Welcome Home Shawn."

Restaurant co-owner Kim Evans, a close confidante of Shawn's family and a worker with the Shawn Hornbeck Foundation, went to Pam and Craig Akers' house as soon as she heard that there would be some news about Shawn. She had been on her way to a Wal-Mart in a nearby town, but immediately changed her plans. Not knowing the details at first, Evans thought, "Uh-oh, this can't be good news." Happily, she was wrong. Her main role now would be to help the Akerses deal with the media, answering phones, arranging and denying interviews, and generally serving as the family spokesperson.

As celebrations continued that night throughout Eastern Missouri, Shawn and Ben and their families—by now grandparents, siblings, aunts, and uncles had joined in the reunions—headed back to St. Louis to SSM Cardinal Glennon Children's Medical Center, where the boys were examined and were both reported to be in good health. The hospital spokesman, Bob Davidson, described the scene to a local TV station:

In one room, the Ownby family sat with Ben, famished and downing chocolate cupcakes from a vending machine. "[Ben is] just sitting in a chair, grinning," Davidson said, "and while I talked to his family, his mother sat across the room and she didn't take her eyes off him the whole time."

In Shawn's room, Davidson said, "his grandmother just can't let go of his hand, and they're all talking about family memories, and things, and he [Shawn] has a chance now to make new memories."

At one point that night, the two boys' families ran into one another at the hospital. "We both congratulated each other," Ben's mother told NBC's *Today* show. "We told them how happy we were to have Shawn home too."

As people celebrated, Michael Devlin, forty-one, was being transported to the Franklin County Sheriff's Department, the TV cameras filming as investigators led the three-hundred-pound suspect, dressed in orange prison garb, to his new home, a 10-by-7-foot cell, where he was put in solitary confinement and placed under suicide watch. Handcuffed and head hung low, Devlin—a bearded, bespectacled big blob of orange—skyrocketed from an unknown pizzeria worker to one of the most hated men in America.

Devlin's boss, Mike Prosperi, could not take his eyes off the television. Is that really Devo in an orange prison suit? Is that really him being escorted to jail in handcuffs? Is that really him, a criminal? His friend Devo? His reliable employee? The guy who chummed it up at Imo's with all the law enforcement customers from the nearby Kirkwood Police Department?

Prosperi just kept shaking his head in disbelief. "That's not Devo."

At around 10 p.m. Friday night, FBI agents and Franklin County authorities received a search warrant to examine Devlin's apartment in a complex now surrounded by yellow police tape, TV cameras, a line of police vehicles, and at least three large white forensic units. Evidence technicians in surgical suits gingerly removed items from Unit D, such as a futon mattress and computer. The investigation went into the wee hours.

Shawn and Ben both got home early Saturday morning some time after one o'clock. Both boys seemed eager to resume normalcy, with Shawn asking his parents if they could stop for a McDonald's meal on the way home, with Ben requesting a snack and permission to play computer video games in his room alone.

"Don't stay up too late," Ben's mother told him.

He's Ben, she thought with relief. He's Ben.

She and her husband were able to sleep soundly that night for the first time in nearly a week. But when Ben's mother awoke later that morning, the first thing she did was to run into her son's bedroom to check on him. To make sure he was still there.

"We're just ecstatic," Doris Ownby said at a press conference later that day at the Franklin County Courthouse in Union. "We don't want to let him go out of our sight."

"You can't believe how good we're doing," Ben's father said.

Ben, his mother, his father, and his sister huddled together in front of the microphones, with a tall Don Ownby forming the apex of the family unit, his long arms draped protectively around his wife, his daughter, and his son. Throughout, Ben seemed relaxed and happy, flashing his infectious grin that the entire country—by now, the world—had come to know.

Wearing a light-brown, plaid collared shirt, Ben stood next to his older sister, Amanda, a sweet-faced girl with jet-black hair who smiled just as big as her little brother. At one point, she turned to him and beamed: "I'm just really glad to have Ben back."

Ben was not allowed to speak to the media Saturday, nor was Shawn, whose family also held a separate press conference in the gymnasium at Shawn's former school, Richwoods Elementary, where approximately seventy-five friends and family gathered to greet Shawn with hugs and kisses, with balloons and banners proclaiming "We All Missed You, Shawn" and "Miracles Do Happen."

Shawn's stepfather, Craig Akers, told the crowd that this was one of the best moments of his life—and he appeared like he was in the throes of happiness, smiling, speechless at times, occasionally teary-eyed. He looked like a man who had been to hell and had returned, triumphant, with a nothing-can-break-me spirit emanating throughout his demeanor. He had not shaved that morning, and his eyes lagged, but few could fault the guy— he and his wife had stayed up most of the night, reminiscing with the son they had not seen for four years, the son who less than twenty-four hours earlier they weren't even sure was still alive.

"It's been like a dream," Craig told the audience. "We're afraid that any moment we're going to wake up and it's all going to have been a dream. . . . This is one of those rare, rare things. To have one missing child found is just extraordinary. To have two found at the same time is one of those things— you don't even read about things like that."

Shawn's mother, Pam, choked up at one point: "Shawn is a miracle here. We're glad to have him home. I still feel like I'm in a dream, only this time it's a good dream. It's not my nightmare that I've lived for four and a half years. We've got a lot of catching up to do. He's grown up on me. That's for sure."

In fact, the Akerses said that one of the first things they needed to do was buy Shawn some new clothes, since his bureau drawer at home was still filled with shirts and pants he wore at age eleven, arranged just the way he left it before he headed out for that fateful bike ride in October 2002.

For his part, Shawn looked happy, healthy, laughing at times, holding on to his mother, burying his head in her arms in a gesture that belied his fifteen years, making him appear vulnerable, like a young child in need of a mother's comfort.

Besides going clothes shopping, Shawn told his parents he wanted to ride four-wheelers and play video games. The family planned to continue catching up, as they did the night before, as they would in the days to come. A four-year gap left a lot to talk about. For one, Shawn had a niece and nephew who were born while he was missing. His other nephew, whom he knew as a baby, would soon start kindergarten. One of his sisters had married. His stepfather had lost part of his leg.

In some ways the town Shawn disappeared from looked the same: Cobbs Grocery was still the place to buy soda and candy. The Richwoods Lions Club was still a central gathering spot for the community—in fact, it served as the site of vigils in his honor, as evidenced by the memorial garden and bench beckoning from the grassy area behind the boxy building. From the exterior, Richwoods Elementary was the same; however, the friends he knew from the fifth grade no longer roamed the halls. They were high school freshmen now, with most attending Potosi High School about twenty miles away.

The *Post-Dispatch* recounted some everyday events that Shawn missed while in captivity:

> *He didn't know that six of his former classmates had moved out of the school district. He never knew the four students who replaced them.*
>
> *He vanished before he could reach the sixth grade, when students finally get their own gray metal lockers. . . .*
>
> *He never got to play Richwoods Wildcats basketball. For young boys, Wildcats basketball looms large. "It's all we got," said eighth-grader Zach Littrell, 13.*
>
> *When Shawn was in the fourth grade, he used to stay late to watch the older kids play, recalled Carla Glatczak, a school secretary. Shawn was a couple of months from getting his shot at Wildcats basketball, on the fifth- and sixth-grade team, when he was kidnapped. He never got to see the new blue-and-white uniforms.*

Shawn had missed out on so much—and now, a few hours after his rescue, he wanted to catch up. When Shawn and his parents arrived at their Richwoods home after one o'clock in the morning Saturday, more than twenty family members were waiting there for him. After all of the hugging and kissing, the talking started, lasting for hours.

"Hey, do you remember this?"

"Do you remember when we did this?"

"Remember when we did that?"

Shawn's older sister Jackie told CBS news that she stayed up all night talking with her brother. "He's a young man now," she said, "but we picked up right where we left off."

As the night went on, Pam and Craig excused themselves into another room, where—unbeknownst to Shawn and his sisters—the parents listened to their kids reconnect after all these years.

"Every time I heard Shawn say, 'Yes, I remember. . . .' It was just like another miracle," Pam said. "I'm so thankful that he does remember his family."

What no one discussed that night, his parents said, was what Shawn went through during his life in captivity. Nor would they discuss it at the press conference. "That will come in due time," Craig said. "When Shawn's ready to discuss that, we'll discuss it. If he doesn't want to discuss it, we won't."

Understandable.

Nevertheless, people across the globe—by now, even foreign reporters were covering this story—wanted to know what exactly happened to Shawn in that crappy apartment in Kirkwood. The incongruity of the situation seemed unfathomable: Shawn lived in plain sight, with a cell phone and Internet access. He had friends and the freedom to roam about town. He talked to cops. So why didn't he escape? No matter how much mental health specialists and law enforcement officials warned the public not to judge Shawn—a child and a victim—the curious nature of the case fascinated the public.

"This is something so bizarre that the normal individual cannot grasp what this then-11-year-old boy went through," Washington County Sheriff Kevin Schroeder told the Associated Press.

Although the media were told once by the family that they would not discuss Shawn's life in captivity, journalists kept pushing—albeit gently on the day after Shawn's discovery.

"Would you ever guess that Shawn would be hidden in plain sight?" one reporter asked during the press conference.

Of course, Craig replied that he had not imagined such a thing (really, who would?).

"It's just mind-boggling that it was that easy to hide someone in plain sight," he said. "It's just hard to believe that somebody could be that brazen and—I mean, it just—it just boggles my mind that someone thinks they could get away with it. And obviously, they do. I mean, this has been going on for four years, and he's been right here under our noses the whole time."

Right under our noses. The whole time. A kidnapped child plopped amid the public for the entire world to see. And a monster man arrogant in his belief that he could get away with stealing children, which he almost did.

CHAPTER 25
Feeling Guilty

Watching the back-to-back news conferences Saturday lifted the public's spirits on an otherwise desolate day in which hundreds of thousands of Missouri residents, including the Ownbys, suffered without electricity thanks to the season's second ice storm that damaged property, roads, and lives. As people shivered in makeshift shelters and scrambled to find a warm bed to sleep in that night, and as federal officials prepared to declare a state of emergency and call in the National Guard, the heartwarming reunion of the two rescued boys and their families offered respite from the frigidity.

However, for some people, indications of a Missouri Miracle hangover were evident. Aside from the joy surrounding the safe recoveries of Shawn Hornbeck and Ben Ownby, reality had begun to set in. Imo's pizzeria owner Mike Prosperi spent much of his day Saturday talking to customers furious with him for employing a kidnapper and pedophile. Early TV news accounts Friday also inaccurately reported that Michael Devlin was a registered sex offender in Utah.

How could you employ a kidnapper?!

How dare you hire a sex offender?!

How come you didn't do a background check?!

But the truth was Prosperi had no idea that an abducted boy was living at his employee's apartment. He never did a background check on Devlin because he had hired him as a teenager, knew his parents and siblings, and never once heard about any lawbreaking behaviors. And even if Prosperi had conducted a police check on Devlin, all he would have found were some traffic tickets from the late 1980s—one for failing to register a vehicle, the other for speeding, fines paid in both cases.

Prosperi had been analyzing all of this since the news broke a day earlier. Unable to sleep that night, he tossed and turned, wondering—like everyone else who knew Devlin—if he had missed a sign, some kind of hint about his employee's secret life. But no matter how hard he racked his brain, he could not come up with one.

He went into Imo's Saturday morning and found a rock thrown through the restaurant window. Business suffered all weekend with some locals boycotting the place where the monster man made pizza. Traumatized by the notion of working side-by-side with a child abductor, some of Prosperi's employees stayed home, he said, noting that one woman who used to make the diabetic Devlin sugar-free brownies was out for three days.

Besides dealing with irate customers, Prosperi grappled with the shock, the betrayal, the "death" of his friend and employee—a strong word, death, but that is what it felt like to Prosperi. The Devo he had known for more than two decades, the reliable worker, the know-it-all jokester, the guy who hunted and played poker . . . gone forever. Just like that. One day he and Devo were laughing; the next day, no more. The Michael Devlin in the orange prison suit, the villain whose bloated-booking mug was being brandished to the world via the media, is an invidious interloper, a loathsome loser, a skilled criminal who should never walk free again.

He is not Devo.

For months after Devlin's arrest, Prosperi wondered if he could ever trust anyone other than his family. He thought he had known Devo really well, and to be deceived so badly haunted him. At night, Prosperi felt restless as he wrestled with his self-described "weird" and "crazy" thoughts, the recurrent one being:

"My wife's name is Joyce. His mother's name is Joyce. My first name is Mike. His first name is Mike. My son is about the same age as Shawn Hornbeck. My son sort of looks like Shawn. Maybe he was trying to be just like me."

Then Prosperi would think back to the Monday when Ben disappeared. If he had not allowed his sick employee to go home early that afternoon, maybe Ben and his family would have been spared the trauma of abduction and the ensuing abuse. But then again, if Ben hadn't been kidnapped, Shawn might never have been found.

Such thoughts tug and bug in the middle of the night. Prosperi sighed. "It's crazy," he said, shaking his head in disbelief. "This whole thing is crazy. Like a movie."

Prosperi's anguish is understandable. He thought he knew his employee well. And then a light is shined on Devlin's secret life, revealing deeds as dark and deep as a black hole. And it is all unimaginable and shocking. Self-doubt grips the psyche and gnaws in the back of the mind: Devlin seemed so normal—but then again, it was weird that he never mentioned a romantic interest or friends outside of work. He seemed nice enough—although, come to think of it, he once drove around a dark-haired boy in his white Nissan pickup and he didn't like the after-school kids in the pizza parlor. Should I have become suspicious? Called the police?

Since the abductor's arrest, it is probable that Prosperi and those who knew Devlin engaged in a sociological phenomenon called retrospective interpretation, in which people reinterpret and reevaluate past events and behaviors based on current knowledge and situations. It is as if they are now looking at a complete puzzle, with all the pieces neatly fitted together, with everything making perfect sense. And with this new knowledge of where each puzzle piece is supposed to go, they ask themselves why it took so long to put together the puzzle when it all seems so obvious.

And they self-flagellate: I should have known. How could I have been so stupid?

And they self-analyze: Why didn't I see the big picture before?

And they self-blame: I should have done something. I should have made it all better.

"But you didn't know because you lacked key information, the final piece of the puzzle," explained Dr. Kathryn Kuhn, an associate professor of sociology and criminal justice at Saint Louis University.

The fact that Devlin was an asexual loner seemed curious but irrelevant before his arrest. That he drove around town with a boy whom Prosperi presumed was a nephew seemed insignificant before Devlin went to jail. But now it all made sense.

"People like him [Prosperi] have no reason to feel like they did something wrong," Dr. Kuhn said. "They shouldn't beat themselves up or feel guilty. They didn't know."

But when a horrific, headline-grabbing crime detonates in a manicured suburb, it is bound to raise questions—and that is what happened in the city of Kirkwood, where residents began asking themselves if they could have saved Shawn earlier. Had they been too self-absorbed in their version of Mayberry to notice a child in need of help? Too cocooned in their safe community to imagine that such a crime could occur in their hometown?

A large photo of the boy was plastered on a bench of a popular grocery store. Why hadn't anyone noticed?

Local cops had come into contact with the missing child. Why hadn't they made the connection?

In the apartment complex on South Holmes Avenue, where Shawn apparently lived for four years, some residents noticed that Shawn Devlin looked like the Shawn Hornbeck on TV. Monserrat Urias, a fourteen-year-old who lived near Devlin, told *Newsweek* that maybe she could have saved Shawn in late 2006:

> *Sifting through the mail, she saw a flier showing a missing kid.*
>
> *"I know him, I've seen him," she told her mother.*
>
> *Urias's mother thought her daughter was being flippant about child snatching and scolded her, "This is serious."*
>
> *Urias replied: "Never mind."*

At Saturday's press conference, less than twenty-four hours after the miracle rescue, Shawn's stepfather, Craig Akers, decried a norm of noninvolvement as it pertained to his son, to the people in Devlin's apartment complex who heard suspicious screams but never called police, to the people who saw Shawn in passing and thought, "Gee, he looks like that missing boy on TV," but did nothing about it. "It's another one of those situations where in today's society, no one wants to get involved," he said at the podium. "No one wants to stick their nose in anybody else's business. They just put on blinders and go forward and 'Oh, I don't want to get involved. That's none of my business.' Well, if everybody felt that way, we wouldn't be here today."

Other people simply had no clues. Devlin's landlord, Bill Romer, who purchased the South Holmes Avenue building in 2005, barely gave Devlin a second thought, according to media reports. He had no reason to since Devlin was a model tenant who always paid the rent on time. Once he fixed a plumbing problem in Devlin's apartment and noticed a dark-haired boy sleeping, most likely the "son" Devlin had listed as the second occupant of Unit D. But a napping boy is not suspicious. Nothing in the apartment was. After news broke about his now-famous tenant, Romer became filled with introspection. He told the *Kansas City Star:* "I keep wondering, 'Could I or should I have done something differently?'"

For people like Romer, who had no inklings about Devlin and no cause for concern, the only thing they failed to do was to assume the worst. Most people do not walk through life suspecting that the people they come into contact with are perpetrators of a horrible crime—and, if they do, they should probably be in psychotherapy dealing with their paranoia and phobia issues. Even the American judicial system operates on the principle of innocence until proven guilty. For someone like Romer to engage in self-doubt illustrates the insidious nature of a crime, how one act can debase victims and their loved ones as well as the masses, albeit on a smaller scale.

Indeed, Devlin's transgressions stung people across Eastern Missouri, resulting in a systematic trauma of sorts, evinced by a collective sense of fear, disbelief, and distrust. "We delude our way into thinking that things are safe," said Dr. Charles Figley, an internationally renowned trauma expert at Florida State University in Tallahassee. When in reality, "we can go out driving and any idiot, in just one second, can run right into our car. So we all have this illusion that we're safe, and when something like this happens it penetrates the naive perception that 'It couldn't happen here.' Think of the little town in Kansas where the tornado blew away the entire town. They had twenty minutes' notice, but no one ever imagined something like this would happen, nor should they, because if they did, no one would be able to sleep at night."

In the case involving Devlin's crimes against Shawn and Ben, Dr. Figley said, "there is shock, but gradually, as time goes by, there is this tendency to return to the default that we're safer here than anywhere else—and especially if there is no harm done and the children were returned and everything is OK."

As the shock and self-examination subside, so, too, can the sounding alarms about how this case exemplifies a community's indifference toward its children. Prominent sociologist

Dr. David Finkelhor of the University of New Hampshire in Durham, said counterexamples can be found in towns big and small of people watching out for children—whether it is doing something as ordinary as stopping a neighborhood toddler from running into the street or as major as calling authorities when child abuse is suspected.

Even the Devlin case offers bright spots: Within days of the public release of the description of the white Nissan pickup linked to Ben's abduction, the Franklin County Sheriff's Department had more than five hundred leads from concerned citizens. Although Devlin's boss was filled with self-doubt about going to the cops to report Devlin's truck, Prosperi did it anyway, because he knew that if there was even a slight chance that his employee could be involved in kidnapping, it was his moral obligation to notify law enforcement. And of course, it was one teenager's eyewitness description of the pickup that ultimately led to the safe recovery of two boys.

"I don't see this case as a sign of some terrible deterioration of the bonds of social responsibility," said Dr. Finkelhor, director of the Crimes against Children Research Center and codirector of the Family Research Laboratory, both at the University of New Hampshire. "It's easy for me to imagine how this slipped under the radar without it implying that there was a tremendous lack of responsibility and community vigilance."

Besides, no matter how keen an observer one might be, it is

possible that people simply did not recognize Shawn Hornbeck as the missing child on the bench at the local supermarket. Even Franklin County Sheriff Gary Toelke—lauded by law enforcers nationwide for the safe recoveries of Baby Abby, Ben, and Shawn, whose impeccable record with missing children is applauded by the public, some of whom have urged him to run for Missouri governor—even the vigilant sheriff said he wonders if he would have identified Shawn four years after the boy's abduction.

"He looked like he'd probably grown up quite a bit," Sheriff Toelke said on the evening that Shawn was found. "He was a little taller and his hair was darker. I'm sure the parents would have recognized him, but if he'd have walked into the office, I don't know that I would have."

Even Shawn Hornbeck apparently expressed doubts about some of the age-progressed pictures of him displayed across town. "He did mention that he saw one of the benches that we put out in some of the area grocery stores," his stepfather said at the Saturday press conference. "And about the only comment that I've heard so far was that the first age-progressed photo was an insult. We agree. That was one of the ones that we didn't like, either. So we reached a consensus that the first one just really wasn't any good."

Forensic artists who render an age-progressed portrait of a missing person acknowledge that their work is not exact. Rather, it is a mixture of art and science that can involve drawing, sculpture, photo manipulation, and computer skills with the goal of achieving a person's unique likeness—perhaps a distinctive squint of the eyes, slant of the cheeks or slope of the chin—nestled within the framework of a normal aging face. Although the result may not be accurate, age-progressed pictures have helped with successful recoveries. This is particularly true when someone observes suspicious behavior surrounding a child as well as a spark of recognition from an age-progressed photo.

Whether people recognized Shawn, at this point, is less important than what the Devlin case represents: a strong reminder to notify authorities, as Prosperi did, when suspicions are raised about a child, when people get that funny feeling that something is not right.

It is a mantra repeated at the U.S. headquarters of the National Center for Missing and Exploited Children (NCMEC) in Alexandria, Virginia, where workers point to numerous success stories in which a vigilant observer notices a resemblance between a child and a photograph of a missing child and notifies police, thereby resulting in the youngster's safe rescue. At a Wal-Mart once, a shopper glanced at the missing child posters displayed on the wall and, shortly after, correctly identified to authorities a missing child who was in the store. The child was safely returned home.

Over and over again, Nancy McBride, the center's executive director, tells anyone who will listen that the public is key to bringing home missing children. "People are better witnesses than they give themselves credit for," McBride said. "Don't be afraid to tell somebody, because if you are right, how amazing is that?"

Months after Shawn and Ben were found, NCMEC staffers still buzzed about the joyous family reunions, McBride said: "We know the statistics. It's so wonderful when it happens, and the kids are okay and you think, 'Oh, this family is going to be so excited, so happy, it's going to be so wonderful.' Then you see Shawn and the length of time he'd been missing. His family probably didn't believe they were going to see him alive again. And how could you help it? How could you help not feeling that way? The leads get cold, and until you get a break in the case, it's really tough."

Until there is a miracle.

CHAPTER 26

In the Spotlight

The "Missouri Miracle" was all anyone talked about in the days and weeks following the discovery of Shawn Hornbeck and Ben Ownby, thanks in part to the media, which had stormed rural Richwoods, a town that, frankly, few cared about before Shawn.

At times it seemed as if members of the media outnumbered residents, especially if you counted the TV camera crews with their cumbersome equipment and big vans parked along Highway A, often in front of Cobbs Grocery. The store's old wooden front porch was already cluttered with stacks of cola crates, Pepsi vending machines, antique firefighting equipment, and a faded blue upholstered van seat that serves as a bench. On the wintry days following Shawn's homecoming, nosy TV journalists—men adorned in orange-tinted face powder, women with volumized hair—sometimes lingered on the porch, in front of the dusty display window that featured Civil War cannonballs and a sign advertising a twelve-pack of Milwaukee's Best Lite cans for $5.99.

Owners Ron and Shirley Cobb did not like it one bit. In and out went the media, opening and closing the squeaky screen door, not even asking permission if they could enter with their big cameras and even-bigger attitudes. Once inside, reporters snooped the narrow aisles, staring at display areas offering everything from a Confederate flag for $7.99 to a "Meat Snack Center" with six flavors of beef jerky (original, pepperoni, barbecue, teriyaki, sweet n' hot, and fat free) to more than two thousand VHS movies, each costing $2 and consisting of classics such as *Sleepless in Seattle* and *Father of the Bride* to less popular titles like *Father of the Bride Part II*, *The Butcher's Wife*, and *The Rich Man's Wife*.

And the questions some of these reporters would ask . . . don't even get the couple started.

"The media really asked stupid questions," said Ron, shaking his head in disgust, the burly shopkeeper still steamed at the spectacle nearly four months after Shawn was found. "They were just the dumbest questions."

"The dumbest questions," Shirley said with a frown, echoing her husband's repugnance.

Stupid questions, as in: Are you happy that Shawn was found?

Are you surprised that Shawn was found after four years?

Did you have any idea that Shawn was living only an hour's drive away?

As if the Cobbs would reply: No, actually, I am not happy Shawn was found.

No, I am not surprised that Shawn was found after four years. . . . I quite expected everything to happen this way.

Yes, I knew that Shawn was living nearby. . . . I just decided not to tell anyone.

Then the media—predictably, Ron would say—played into all the stereotypes about Richwoods: That it was a backwoods town straight out of the movie *Deliverance.* That it was populated by toothless barnyard bumpkins with mangy mullets and meth addictions. In fact, the media's frequent mention of meth really irked Ron. Meth had nothing to do with Shawn's situation yet the reporters kept talking about it. Besides it wasn't as if everyone in Richwoods had a drug problem.

It got so irritating that Ron had to shoo away the media, as welcome as repellent rats. He even wrote to the local newspaper decrying one journalist's "irresponsible" reporting about meth and Richwoods. He proudly hangs a cutout of the published letter on the store wall next to the front door, near a notice urging residents to help stop illegal marijuana cultivation and two signs that are meant to be funny: HELEN WAITE IS OUR CREDIT MANAGER. IF YOU WANT CREDIT GO TO HELEN WAITE and WARNING: THIS PROPERTY PROTECTED BY A PIT BULL WITH AIDS.

Just along Highway A, past an abandoned building, past parked cars with painted windows welcoming home Shawn, along a street with no sidewalks, sits a nondescript building surrounded by stacked wooden wine barrels, an old shed, and an ice machine. It is Richwoods' newest and only restaurant, Bardenheier Wine Cellars, a small, sparse eatery co-owned by Kim Evans, who served as spokesperson for Shawn's family in the days after his recovery. There, too, the media flocked, jockeying for exclusive interviews with Pam and Craig Akers and—the coup—Shawn Hornbeck.

A frail but fearless woman, Evans made it her job to corral the media, to keep them away from the Akerses' house with threats that anyone who knocked on their door would be barred from interviewing the family. She would meet reporters at dawn and at dusk to accommodate both national TV network programs that tried to bigfoot their way to a scoop as well as smaller local outlets that had covered the story since the day Shawn disappeared.

It wasn't an easy job, especially on Shawn's first night home. "I know it's a nasty, competitive business," said Evans, reflecting on the media frenzy months later. "But I didn't realize just how nasty and competitive it is. The media were fighting for interviews. Everyone wanted to be first."

At one point, Evans admonished journalists from the national networks: "Set up your cameras and play nice."

The experience left Evans with distaste for most of TV's famous personalities and their crews except for Fox News' Greta Van Susteren, one of the few big names who faithfully covered Shawn's disappearance back in 2002, and ABC News' Diane Sawyer, who, Evans said, personified professionalism.

Still, the only TV star who landed the big get—the first interview with Shawn, an exclusive by all accounts—was Oprah Winfrey, whose interview with the teenager and his parents, as well as Ben Ownby's parents, aired on January 18, 2007, less than a week after the two missing boys were found. Shawn's parents chose Oprah, Evans said, because Oprah was influential with a large audience that could deliver a message of hope to parents of other missing children.

The show was not a tell-all: Shawn did not reveal details about his time in captivity, other than he slept a lot during the day to pass time, thought about his family every day, and prayed to God for a reunion, crossing himself every night. Oprah did not push for answers from Shawn, who appeared sweet, soft-spoken, and somewhat shy, with his shaggy hair neatly trimmed for his debut on one of the world's most popular talk shows. Oprah explained to the audience that she had agreed not to ask the teenager specifics about the past four years of his life, allowing him to sort through the situation in therapy and in the privacy of his home.

Addressing viewers, Oprah said: "One of the questions the whole country wants the answer to that I did not ask on camera of Shawn because I wanted to respect those boundaries but I did ask Shawn privately: 'Why did you not call or contact your parents?' And he said to me he did not because he was too terrified to do so."

Appearing preened for their debut on *The Oprah Winfrey Show*, Shawn's parents also said that they were heeding advice from the professionals and not asking their son about his time in captivity, instead inviting him to come and talk with them when he is ready.

> **Oprah Winfrey:** I'm gonna go there and ask you: What do you think happened to him? Do you think he was sexually abused?
>
> **Craig Akers:** Yes.
>
> **Winfrey:** Do you think he . . . do you think he was tortured?
>
> **Pam Akers:** That I don't know yet.
>
> **Craig Akers:** Well, you know, there's more than one kind of torture. There's mental torture. There's physical torture. I have no doubt that mentally, that he's not the same boy that he was. Physically, we don't see any signs of anything. But that's four and a half years. It's really hard to say.

Oprah's interview generated high ratings, especially in metro St. Louis. It also sparked criticism, with commentators pontificating in media outlets the next day:

"What Were His Parents Thinking?" screamed a headline on *Newsweek*'s website.

"Shame on Boy's Folks and Oprah," read another in the *New York Post*.

In the *Post*, columnist Linda Stasi called Ben Ownby's

parents "heroes" for protecting their son's mental health by keeping him off the show. She lambasted Oprah and Shawn's parents for discussing possible sexual abuse. "At least adult women who've been raped get the respect of having their names concealed in the media. My God! This kid is 15! What in hell could his parents be getting out of this? Do you know any 15-year-old boy who'd want the allegation that he may have been sexually violated by a grown male to be broadcast around the world?"

It is true that most media outlets, by policy, do not name victims of sexual abuse, especially minors. Most only will do so in high-profile cases in which the public already knows a victim's identity. For example, in this case, the discovery of Shawn and Ben made headlines worldwide, so when police brought charges of sexual assault against alleged kidnapper Michael Devlin and referred to the victim by the initials "S. H.," most media companies publicized the full name, Shawn Hornbeck, because the majority of people already knew his identity. Plus, the families had gone public.

Regardless, some psychologists and sociologists were troubled by Shawn's appearance on *Oprah* as well as by the media naming the victims in this case. Dr. David Finkelhor, for one, is bothered by the hype that fails to protect the privacy rights of child victims, a topic he knows a lot about as director of the Crimes Against Children Research Center at the University of New Hampshire in Durham. A sociology professor, Dr.

Finkelhor is a lead researcher for the U.S. Department of Justice studies on missing children, and he has analyzed data and conducted surveys for organizations like the National Center for Missing and Exploited Children. He has written and edited approximately one hundred articles and ten books on topics such as child sexual abuse.

"It just seems to me that the public and the media should accept the notion that facts about sex crimes and other elements of victimization experiences that involve kids that we're simply not entitled to know about that and it would be better if everyone just accepted that," said Dr. Finkelhor, adding that although he holds Oprah in high regard, he questions her rationale in interviewing Shawn. "Even when a kid is well known, there is added injury that happens with each additional story and publicity that is created about this, because it does expand the number of people who know details about the situation they didn't know before. And so that the possibility of that child having people who don't know things about him that he would like people not to know is reduced. To me, this is another instance to educate people and say that this kid has suffered a terrible trauma, and we have to bend over backwards to make sure that we do not exacerbate it in any way. We have to all act as though we are his guardians."

An internationally known expert on trauma and stress, Dr. Charles Figley was more lax on Oprah and Shawn's parents. The show presented the family "an opportunity to take a photograph, if you will, of how the kid is doing at the time," said Figley, director of the Florida State University Traumatology Institute and the Psychosocial Stress Research Program in Tallahassee. "I've been on the *Oprah* show a number of years ago. They treat you like royalty, you get the red carpet, that kind of thing, so it's thrilling and fun. It's joyous to be fawned over. So that's the first thing. The second thing is that it enables him to confront what has happened and to address it."

About six months after the *Oprah* episode aired, Shawn's parents acknowledged to the St. Louis media that they regretted their family's appearance on the show, particularly the part in which their son's possible sexual abuse was discussed.

After the *Oprah* show, Pam, Craig, and Shawn stopped most media interviews and went into a months-long period of seclusion. "They're focusing on their family," Evans said. "They need the private time."

Indeed. Shawn and Ben and their families need time to recover emotionally. If they have not already, it is highly possible that both Shawn and Ben will suffer from post-traumatic stress disorder, which means they can relive the trauma psychologically and experience heightened periods of anxiety, said Dr. Lenore Terr, one of the world's leading child psychiatrists who has published groundbreaking research on childhood stress and trauma. And if Shawn and Ben do not get the proper treatment, Dr. Terr said, the boys can experience, now or later in life, "eating disturbances, disturbances in sexuality, disturbances in attachments, not being able to trust anybody, disturbances in fear-based behaviors. There are a lot of personality problems that are developed from these experiences."

At the time of a traumatic incident, a gush of neurochemicals is released that can alter brain circuits, causing people subsequently to engage in behavior that repeats the shock and surprise of the initial event, said Dr. Terr, author of several books on childhood trauma, including *Magical Moments of Change: How Psychotherapy Turns Kids Around,* released in 2007. That's why some victims of abuse—sexual, physical, mental—often partake in risky behaviors such as abusing drugs or alcohol, to satisfy their altered brain currents.

According to Dr. Terr, proper treatment for Shawn and Ben entails therapy that would allow the boys to release their emotions so they remain conscious instead of diving into the unconscious as well as therapy that helps them to see their situation in a new context, so they realize that other people have been victimized in similar ways. For instance, Shawn might benefit from learning about Steven Stayner, the abducted California boy who assumed another identity, lived in plain sight near his hometown, and returned to his family years later. Another important factor in recovery is helping Shawn and Ben to feel prepared, Dr. Terr said, "so even if they can never change what happened, having a plan for how they would react if it ever happened again makes them feel safer."

Both Shawn and Ben are reported to be under the care of trained professionals. But no matter how much the boys work toward their recovery, to reclaim their emotional strength, to absolve themselves of the shame inherent in victims of sexual abuse, another person, probably another kid, will be there ready to knock them back down, heckling them because a three-hundred-pound man forced them to have sex. As if the boys chose to do it, as if they're personally deficient because it happened, as if their masculinity is a farce. According to *Newsweek,* Steven Stayner's classmates derided him as a "faggot" when he returned to school after his ordeal, the boy's abduction and sexual abuse a widely known story in the community (as was his untimely death at age twenty-four, when he was killed in a motorcycle accident).

The jeers have already begun for Tony, Shawn's best friend from the Kirkwood apartment complex. The teenager barely had any involvement with Devlin, but that hasn't deterred Tony's peers from ruthless rants.

"Before long, Tony's classmates were taunting him," the *St. Louis Post-Dispatch* reported. "Michael Devlin, they said, must have abused him, too. They wouldn't spare Shawn either, calling him names that Tony won't repeat. 'Bad things,' is all he will say."

In Richwoods, residents said they're protective of Shawn, giving him his space but welcoming him to area events such as a motorcycle race or an informal basketball game. But even in Shawn's small hometown—where the locals said his rescue was the biggest and best thing to ever happen to Richwoods—the euphoria had begun to fade. About six months after his rescue, the *Post-Dispatch* reported:

> *At first glance, it looks as if someone had it in for Shawn Hornbeck.*
>
> *Over the weekend, vandals destroyed the memorial his parents had set up at the nearby Lions Club during the years he was missing. Someone drove over the memorial plaque, shattering the glass on the photo of a smiling eleven-year-old Shawn. They damaged the red maple tree his parents had planted. They ripped up a bench that was cemented into the ground, mangling the missing-child poster that had been the back.*

Shawn's family told the newspaper that they hoped it was a random act.

The vandalism is another act of victimization against Shawn, who will continue to be second-guessed in the years ahead, despite Michael Devlin's guilty pleas and no matter how many times professionals, even when the experts are among the world's best, explain the dynamics of Stockholm Syndrome, mental indoctrination, psychological torture, and sexual abuse victimization. To many observers of the case, it won't matter. Shawn will continue to be disparaged as the boy who refused to escape to safety when he had an open door.

And no matter how much the families of Shawn and Ben asked for privacy, the media continued to seek interviews with Shawn and his parents through Kim Evans, the family spokesperson, as well as the family attorney, Scott Sherman, whose law office is located in the affluent St. Louis suburb of Clayton. His polite response to requests is demonstrated in one of the many e-mails he has sent to journalists (this one before Devlin's guilty plea):

> *Thank you for your inquiry about Shawn and his family. However, as I am sure you can understand, until such time as the criminal cases that surround Shawn's abduction and captivity have concluded, neither they nor anyone in his family will be able to comment about his ordeal.*
>
> *Thank you again for your interest in Shawn.*
> *Sincerely,*
> *S/Scott Sherman*
> *Attorney for Shawn Hornbeck*

And after Devlin pleaded guilty, Sherman continued to decline many interviews on behalf of the family.

Hierarchically, in the media's pursuit of scoops, a sit-down with Shawn rates as *the* top get. His four years in captivity, and the freedoms he had, intrigue people. This is why some reporters—mostly from the tabloids—have ignored the family's request for privacy by going to Pam and Craig Akers' house and knocking on the door at all hours. This continued months after the rescue. "We try to settle more into a routine, but there's always something going on unpredictable," Shawn's stepfather told the *Post-Dispatch* in July 2007.

The media also pursued Ben's family. For their part, the Ownbys granted a handful of interview requests in the immediate days following the thirteen-year-old's rescue.

There was Ben beaming at NBC *Today* show cohost Meredith Vieira, one week after his abduction, talking about how he wanted to return to school: "I'm ready," he said, vigorously nodding his head. "I just need my backpack."

There he was in *People* magazine, sharing the spotlight with his five cats and a "smelly" albino ferret named Ghost, a pet Ben had saved $140 to buy. Upon hearing Ben's mother tell the magazine writer that she planned to host a party for all of the people who searched for her son, Ben grumbles. "I'll be squeezed to death by bruises," he told *People*. "Doris smiles at her son. 'He asked me how much longer I'm going to hug him,' she says. 'And I said, Forever.'"

And there was Ben, clad in his Boy Scout uniform, in an Associated Press feature on the party his mother threw, attended by family and friends who pooled their money to buy Ben a gift hidden in a blue bag with layers of red wrap. The wire service reported:

Behind his glasses, his eyes grew wide.
"Oh my God," he said.
"What is it?" someone called.
"The Wii," he said in shock, referring to the newest
Nintendo video games system.

But for the most part, the Ownby family retreated out of the media glare. As Oprah told her audience about why Ben would not appear on her show: "His parents made a mom and dad decision and said that they feel that he's had enough stress from television."

The Ownbys, too, wanted to focus on returning to normal. By the end of January, less than a month after his abduction, Ben returned to Union Middle School, where Principal Nathan Bailey said the model student was warmly welcomed back. He finished the school year with top grades and big smiles.

Still, little was normal for the families of Ben and Shawn in the months following their rescue—and it may never be again.

For Shawn in particular, normalcy may prove elusive in the years ahead. Plucked out of his home at age eleven and forced into an abusive environment where he was not required to attend school, experts said that most likely his academic and social development was arrested. "It can just stop," said Dr. Carlton Munson, a professor at the School of Social Work at the University of Maryland in Baltimore who has worked on family abduction cases. One of the problems with abducted children stunted developmentally, especially if they had any problems with language skills before their trauma, Munson said, is that in therapy "they don't have the words to tell you what happened or to describe their emotions."

Shawn received help with his studies from a private tutor in the months after his abduction and is said to have an aptitude for math, according to media reports. But his academic reentry into the world is just one obstacle. Another is closing in on the "distance" that the family referred to on *Oprah*. Gone for four years, Shawn disappeared as a child and came back a young man, almost as a stranger. Physically, he went through puberty. Developmentally, the time period between ages eleven and fifteen is marked by rapid change, too, as children transition into adolescence. And all this occurred during a time when a son and his family had no contact with each other. Whole parts of their lives were unknown to each other. They must relearn each other's personality traits and reestablish household rules, a potentially precarious balancing act: Shawn lived for four years with the freedom basically to do what he wanted; now, his parents have told the media they won't let him out of their sight.

He is always being watched.

The gifts that have poured in since Shawn's rescue—a new designer home donated by a St. Louis–area builder and local suppliers, a line of a clothing, a trip to Orlando, Florida—

can also hinder a return to normalcy. Although the gifts are well-meaning and intended to celebrate Shawn's rescue, Dr. Munson said that they can further delineate Shawn from his peers who are not receiving extravagant presents, and it can "send the message that all you have to do to let a person heal is give him objects. This is typical in our culture. We think we can make people feel better by buying them things, like a house. So you put them in a new house and after the first couple of months the euphoria goes away and you're left with other issues."

For instance, in Shawn's situation, "you're trying to return this boy to what his life was before," Dr. Munson said. "Well, if one of the first things you do is move him out of the house he grew up in and put him in a brand new house, then it's hard for him to go back and start to catch up with where the family is."

And although Devlin pleaded guilty and received multiple life sentences all but assuring he will never see the outside of a prison cell, the fear of him escaping or being released on parole—and causing additional harm to Shawn and his family—can be very real. "Even if Devlin goes to jail for a hundred years, he [Shawn] might not believe that Devlin will stay there," Dr. Munson said. "He knows how manipulating and intimidating people like Devlin can be."

Shawn, too, is watching over his shoulders.

The monster man still lurks.

CHAPTER 27

The Monster Man Caged

Hunted and captured in early January, the monster man sat confined in a 10-by-7-foot pen in the Franklin County jail. Nothing appeared outwardly villainous about Michael Devlin. His booking photo shows scraggly brown hair and a mustached beard that suggest that the middle-aged man is unkempt and unmotivated, which would be true according to those who knew him. His fat face and broad shoulders hint at his largeness—six feet, four inches, and, at the time of his arrest, approximately three hundred pounds—but to an adult, Devlin's size seems more bumbling oaf than menacing. At first glance, his eyes in the mug shot appear bluish, bored, and lonely; but upon closer inspection, his eyes look a bit sinister, irreverent, and remorseless.

Maybe it is just the imagination, how one interprets the face of a sexual predator who kidnapped and tortured two boys. Approximately two thousand pages of evidence were collected against Devlin in the months since he went to jail. During early court hearings, Devlin pleaded not guilty to his crimes, but in mid-October 2007, he decided to admit to more than eighty charges of kidnapping, sexual abuse, and attempted murder, among others, to spare Shawn Hornbeck and Ben Ownby from testifying as well as his family from a media circus, according to Devlin's attorneys. The kidnapper wanted the world to know that his family had no knowledge of his crimes and that Shawn was held against his will.

"Here's why Mike is pleading guilty—at one trial or four trials, he didn't think he could get any better of a deal," Devlin's lawyer, Michael Kielty, told the *St. Louis Post-Dispatch*. "What Mike's getting out of this is, he's not exposing his family to any more scrutiny. These are good people. They don't want to be subjugated to this media circus. And, he will not drag Shawn into court. He doesn't want to put Shawn through anything else."

But few praised Devlin's decision to confess. "He pled guilty for Michael Devlin, so you wouldn't know the full atrocities on those boys," said St. Louis County Prosecuting Attorney Robert McCulloch in the *Post-Dispatch*. "The boys are both heroes. It's a testament to how resilient they can be."

In a separate *Post-Dispatch* article, Franklin County Prosecutor Robert Parks called Devlin "evil" and said: "There is a lot more to this case than has come out—and will probably never come out—for the benefit of the boys. . . . You'll never see anybody worse than this [Devlin]."

Devlin received multiple life sentences from four judicial jurisdictions. Some people wanted him to receive the death penalty; however, in Missouri, only criminals who commit first-degree murder are eligible for execution (although inspired by the Devlin case, a state senator is trying to change the law to include child kidnappers who rape and sodomize). In Washington County, Circuit Judge Sandy Martinez told Devlin: "Any sentence this court can give you would seem unjust. It seems minimal in comparison to the long life sentence that this child (Shawn) has received. You are here because you made a choice to abduct this child. All this child was doing was being out like other kids and riding his bike."

But at least Devlin was behind bars. Both Ben and Shawn's parents expressed relief that the judicial process had concluded with the monster man in prison. "I have wished more than once that the law would allow for his execution as punishment for the crimes he committed against my son," Shawn's mother, Pam Akers, told the court in a formal victim-impact statement. "But I have come to realize that it is a far greater punishment for this predator to have to spend every hour of every day for the rest of his life knowing that he no longer has any power or control over my son or our lives. It is my hope that he will live a long life behind bars in that miserable, powerless place where he cannot touch or even see another child. . . . Today is the day that my family gets to close a chapter in our lives that we have wanted to close for five long years."

Although Devlin's attorneys said Devlin felt remorseful about committing the crimes, few people expressed any sort of compassion toward Devlin, which sometimes happens with convicted offenders, especially those who had troubled child-hoods that could help to explain why they committed crimes. Everyone from law enforcement to the public maligned Devlin as a monster, a devil, an evil being.

The universal hatred toward Devlin made him hard to defend, even without the overwhelming evidence that proved his guilt. He was represented in court by two young lawyers—Kielty and Ethan B. Corlija—who "were little-known defense attorneys" before they took on Devlin's case for an undisclosed sum, the *Post-Dispatch* reported: "They quickly became two of the most recognizable faces of the St. Louis defense bar."

A friend of Devlin's family recommended their firm, Hogan, Sokolik, Corlija, and Kielty, located in the affluent St. Louis suburb of Clayton.

For their part, Devlin's family—understandably—has avoided the glare surrounding Devlin's criminal cases, both before and after Michael's guilty pleas. On the day after his arrest, the family released the following statement via the law office:

> *The family of Michael Devlin wishes to express their gratitude to the City of Kirkwood Municipal Police Department, the Franklin County Sheriff's Department, the Federal Bureau of Investigation and all other accompanying law enforcement agencies for their professionalism in safely reuniting Ben*

Ownby and Shawn Hornbeck with their families.

As parents, the Devlin Family along with all compassionate people have prayed for the safe return of these young men to their loved ones—and yesterday those prayers were answered.

Speaking on behalf of the Devlin Family, these past few days have been incredibly difficult.

This is not to diminish the anguish that Craig and Pam Akers have felt over the previous 4½ years—or the Ownby Family over the last 4½ days.

Just as we are relieved that both Ben and Shawn are now safe, we hope that Michael will be safe as the facts of this case are revealed.

The Devlin Family respectfully asks that their privacy be preserved and that any further queries regarding specifics of this accusation be submitted to the Law Firm of Hogan, Sokolik, Corlija, and Kielty.

> *Thank you,*
> *The Devlin Family*
> *Ethan B. Corlija, Esq.*
> *Michael K. Kielty, Esq.*

Of course the media stalked the leafy street of charming houses where Devlin's parents lived, seeking interviews with the family and prodding neighbors for information about the kidnapper and his family. Surely, someone had to know that a monster was living in their midst. But no matter how much the media snooped, people only had nice things to say about Devlin's family and his upbringing.

In the days after their son admitted in court to stealing and sexually tormenting the two boys, Devlin's parents continued their public silence, no doubt their emotional wounds still raw. "The father told police the revelation that his son was a kidnapper 'hit him like a baseball bat, he was so caught off-guard,'" the *Post-Dispatch* reported. "His mother told police 'they never even thought about the possibility that Michael was responsible for this.'"

In the days after Devlin's arrest, the media also swarmed the Franklin County jail in Union, buzzing for interviews with Devlin and hissing about the one freelance journalist who landed not one but two face-to-face, fifteen-minute conversations with the kidnapper about a week after the case broke. Susannah Cahalan, a student at Washington University in St. Louis, apparently gained access to Devlin by posing as a friend on the jail visitor's log and published their discussion in the *New York Post,* a tabloid. According to media reports, Cahalan did not record her interview with Devlin nor did she take notes during their time together; however, the *Post* printed numerous direct quotes by Devlin. While media ethicists grumbled about Cahalan's questionable reporting tactics and Devlin's lawyers (unsuccessfully) sought a gag order, media outlets far and wide published lengthy excerpts of the interview that featured Devlin bemoaning being "bored" by his solitary confinement and frustrated by loud noises coming from the nearby jailhouse booking room that kept him up at night.

During the first interview, the *Post* reported that "Devlin appeared red-faced and bleary-eyed and seemed downcast. 'I feel nothing,' he said. 'I hide my emotions from other people. I hide the way I feel.'"

Devlin told the newspaper that he was too ashamed to talk with his family: "I don't know how I'm going to explain myself to my parents. It's much easier talking to a stranger about these things than your own parents."

He recalled: "I had a normal childhood— it was happy as far back as I can remember."

For his second sit-down with Cahalan, "Devlin's demeanor changed. He greeted a reporter with a big smile. His eyes were no longer bloodshot. He seemed upbeat. He has a slightly lazy eye but appeared focused and alert. He was talkative."

Devlin spoke of his "bizarre" predicament in jail, of being placed on suicide watch, of being told by his lawyers and guards that probably he would be assaulted once he is integrated with the other inmates. "They think I'll be beat up," Devlin told the newspaper. "I'm not worried. It's inevitable. I will eventually have to deal with it. I haven't exactly done a great job of representing myself so far."

But the overarching theme of the article focused on Devlin's feeling "lonely" and "bored." How his parents and siblings had not visited him in the days after his arrest. How his "second family" at Imo's had moved on, married, and had children.

"Hanging out with friends just becomes a lower priority [for them]," Devlin said.

He told the *New York Post* he spent his lonely, boring time in jail reading a Charles Bronson novel and longing to play his favorite video game Final Fantasy XI, which he liked "because it has a network that can connect to people all over the world, from Europe to Japan."

As the months passed, Devlin appeared thinner and clean-shaven at his court appearances, including for his finale tour of Missouri courthouses during autumn 2007—almost five years to date since he abducted Shawn—that ended with him officially becoming a state inmate on October 11 at 3:30 p.m., according to the *Post-Dispatch*: "By protocol, he showered and was photographed, fingerprinted, evaluated physically and mentally and issued hygiene supplies, clothing and bedding. A DNA sample was taken."

Devlin will live in a maximum-security prison, where convicted offenders tend to view child rapists more unfavorably than other criminals.

It is unclear what kind of treatment, if any, Devlin will receive in prison. During the years that he held Shawn captive, Devlin apparently had suicidal tendencies. He said in an FBI report that "many times he thought of taking Shawn back to Shawn's home and then killing himself. Devlin stated, 'As much as I fucked up, I fucked Shawn up but I still love him.'"

Whatever the situation, it is safe to say that most people hope Devlin will never again see the outside of a jail.

CHAPTER 28

Hope

"Hope keeps you going. Hope keeps you alive. Hope gets you up in the morning. I've always thought that once you lose hope, it's over. You're done. And I promised not to lose hope, not to stop looking, and I've said all along, we will not stop until we find Shawn. Well, by God, here we are . . . Miracles do happen. Good things can happen."

—Craig Akers, the day after his son was found alive after being gone for four years and three months.

The Missouri Miracle is a story with a happy ending, but it is not necessarily happily ever after. The horrific nature of the crimes committed against Ben Ownby and Shawn Hornbeck can sear scars into the soul. The media continue to hunt the families, particularly Shawn's. The legal wrangling in the months after the case and the high-profile court hearings that revealed intimate details of the boys' sexual abuse and torture can prevent the families' return to normalcy.

"Initially, we thought this would be the easy part," Shawn's stepfather told the Associated Press about six months after the teenager's rescue. "'Readjustment,' he said, 'is difficult in its own way. There's not a handbook on how to deal with this.'"

No, there is no handbook for parents whose eleven-year-old was yanked out of their midst for 1,558 days, and presumed dead by most people. Shawn's parents never got to say good-bye to their boy who returned home a taller, broader young man harboring a life they knew nothing about. It is hoped that there never will be a need for such a handbook. That the story of Shawn is so unusual, as rare as a lightning bolt to the heart, it will not be replicated. But for those with missing children—or for anyone in a grim situation—Shawn's parents can serve as a sort of living handbook for how to cope by having hope.

Indeed, hope is at the essence of this story. Because life without hope is nothing more than a cold coffin with a lowering lid. For parents who had every reason to lose hope, Pam and Craig Akers held on to hope—not as if, but because, their lives depended on it. Hope woke them up in the morning. Hope fed them strength. And hope rewarded them on a cold January day with a fifteen-year-old miracle named Shawn Hornbeck.

ACKNOWLEDGMENTS

This book would not have been possible without the perseverance and the faith of my agent, Ted Weinstein, whose calm, concise and friendly demeanor makes him a pleasure to work with, as well as all of the talented professionals at The Globe Pequot Press. In particular, I give my greatest gratitude to associate editor Jennifer Taber, whose keen editing style elevated the manuscript and whose patience is much appreciated, as I am fully aware that I can be a bit anal-retentive during the copyediting and fact-checking stages. I'd also like to express my appreciation to Ronnie Gramazio, former executive editor, and Inger Forland, executive director of Marketing, Publicity, and Design, for their support with this project.

Additionally, I thank the dozens of people who took time out of their busy schedules to share their expertise and/or their personal stories with me. Although there are too many people to name individually, I'd like to recognize those who went the extra mile in helping me with my research: Dr. Fred Berlin, Dr. N.G. Berrill, Dr. C. Robert Cloninger, Ron and Shirley Cobb, Kim Evans, Dr. Charles Figley, Dr. David Finkelhor, Dr. Robert Keppel, Dr. Kathryn Kuhn, Kenneth V. Lanning, Nancy McBride, Dr. Carlton Munson, Dr. Frank Ochberg, Mike Prosperi, Dr. Lenore Terr, and Stephen Thompson.

Acknowledgments

Personally, I have dozens of people to thank for helping me with this book, including all of my family and friends, whose enthusiasm kept me afloat during stressful times. In particular, I thank Laura Geiser, Steve Justus, and Joy Shioshita, three of the smartest people I know, for reading my manuscript before I turned it in formally—your fine copyediting and excellent suggestions saved me from looking like a fool; Sue Wilfing for her speedy transcription of hours of taped interviews; and my husband Tom Geiser and my father-in-law, Jerry Geiser, for taking photographs for the book.

From an emotional standpoint, my friend, Tricia Gianino, offered her near-daily support and, frankly, kept me sane as I struggled to balance being a mom and working on this project. And perhaps most helpful of all was the child care I received from my mom, Mary Justus, who flew in from out of town to watch my daughter while I worked, and my mother-in-law, Nancy Geiser, who often dropped what she was doing to babysit. I cannot describe how much it meant to me to have Zoe's nana and grandma caring for her.

I also appreciate my family's support during this project: My husband, Tom, whose intelligence, humor, and enthusiasm sustained me; and my spunky, sweet-soul of a daughter, Zoe, who had to make-do without me on many weekends while I worked. My parents also deserve recognition: My mom has always thought that I'm the greatest thing ever, and that means everything to me. So, too, does the delight that my father, the late James Sauerwein, always showed in my writing since I was a pig-tailed girl scribbling stories about my stuffed raccoon.

Finally, I express my sincere admiration to Shawn Hornbeck, Ben Ownby, and their families for their strength, their character, and their ability to hold on to hope. You've inspired me, and, I'm sure, hundreds of other people.

Index

Index

stranger abductions, 42–43, 103–4
Sveriges Kreditbank, Stockholm, 159
Swing-A-Round Fun Town, 8, 137
Symbionese Liberation Army, 158

T

Terr, Dr. Lenore, 13, 119–20, 121,
167–70, 174–75, 299–300
terrorist attacks, September 11,
2001, 50
Thompson, Steven, 107
Time magazine, 73, 75
Today show, 34–36, 259, 270, 304
Toelke, Sheriff Gary
abduction of Ben Ownby, 212–13,
219, 234, 252–53
investigation of Mike Devlin's
crimes, 103
rescue of Hornbeck and Ownby,
258, 260, 264, 265, 288
Torrez, Dorothy, 192

U

U. S. Department of Justice, 97, 98,
104, 126, 160, 213, 298
U. S. Environmental Protection
Agency, 6
Union, MO, 188, 212, 259, 263, 314
Union Middle School, 210, 223–24,
305
University of New Hampshire, 287,
297
Urias, Monserrat, 284

V

Van Praagh, James, 134–35
Van Susteren, Greta, 294

Vieira, Meredith, 304
Virginia Tech massacre, 50
Visitation Academy, 146–49
Voss Conoco Market, 215–16

W

Wagster, Officer Gary, 235–37, 240
Walcutt, Bob, 36–37, 135
Waller, Karen, 75
Walsh, Adam, 131
Walsh, John, 131
Washington County, 5–6, 54
Washington County Sheriff's
Department, 24, 32, 54
Washington State Attorney General's
Office, 42
Washington University School of
Medicine, 113
Webster Groves, 69, 72–74
Webster Groves High School, 72–73,
74
White, Timmy, 119–20
Willett, Special Agent M. L.,
245–47, 254–55
Woodland Lake Estates, 18, 85
Woods, Abigale "Abby" Lynn,
190–93, 195–96, 212–13, 255
Woods, James, 193
Woods, Tammy, 195–96
World Trade Center, 50

Y

Yount, Sheriff Gary, 54